MUSINGS ON A STARRY NIGHT

THOMAS HOWARD

Musings on a Starry Night

A Constellation of Cosmic Contemplations

Compiled by
Keith Call

IGNATIUS PRESS SAN FRANCISCO

All essays have been copied from previously published text, as noted in the footnotes. Slight changes have occasionally been made, primarily for consistency.

Every reasonable effort has been made to identify the original source and copyright owners.

Cover photograph of Thomas Howard

With background art (painting):
Nocturne in Black and Gold—The Falling Rocket, 1875
James Abbot McNeill Whistler (1834–1903)
Detroit Institute of Arts, Detroit, Michigan, U.S.A.

Cover design by Pawel Cetlinski

ISBN 978-1-62164-774-4 (PB)
ISBN 978-1-64229-350-0 (eBook)
Library of Congress Control Number 2025932521
Printed in the United States of America ♾

CONTENTS

FOREWORD

“Egads!” whispered Tom Howard, who was seated at my elbow, “See here, Longenecker, think of it! You a Bob Jones boy and me a lad from Wheaton sitting at high table in this august locale! Forsooth! What are we doing here among such worthies?”

The high table at which we were seated was in a college dining hall in Oxford. The gothic chamber, with its leaded windows and ancient hammer-beam ceiling glowed with candlelight. The white-coated waiters glided silently to serve the sumptuous fare on silver platters. As the conversations hummed and the wine was sipped, the serious portraits of patrons and past Oxford luminaries looked down from the paneled walls. What would they have made of these American interlopers?

Tom Howard and I had been invited to speak at one of Stratford Caldecott’s summer conferences, and the three-day event concluded with a feast in Christ Church Hall—the various colleges offered such hospitality in the slack summer months as an added revenue stream for college coffers.

“I mean to say,” continued Tom, “should we not be somewhat embarrassed? Are we not intruding in this hallowed hall? Are we not frauds? Poseurs? Faux dons? Sunday afternoon literati? Great pretenders?”

“Good heavens,” I replied, “I’ve been faking it ever since I moved over here.”

Tom chuckled, “Really?”

“Of course. I’ve been channeling T. S. Eliot and thought it was all about three-piece suits and a somber expression.”

He laughed and concluded, "Nevertheless, it is a delight, is it not, even for one evening, to sit at this table and perhaps pretend just a little and revel with the ghosts of our heroes—Tolkien, Lewis, and the other greats?"

In many ways, we were kindred spirits—both of us had journeyed from Evangelical fundamentalism through the Anglican Church to our final home in Catholicism. For both of us, England and her great literary traditions had been the bridge to another world. We should have been better friends. Apart from some correspondence over the years, and Tom agreeing to write a foreword for one of my own books, it was the only time he and I actually spent time together. I had first heard of Tom Howard through my younger sister, who was a student of his at Gordon College, and through the years our paths would cross through various Catholic contacts. It is a great honor, therefore, to offer a few words of introduction to this collection of Tom's essays.

If you never knew Tom Howard, these essays are the perfect introduction. Tom's physical presence was hard to miss and impossible to forget. His rugged handsome features somewhat reminiscent of a movie tough guy, were animated by his eager manner, his mischievous grin, and twinkling eyes. Everything about his demeanor and conversation spoke of his childlike wonder and delight in the world around him. Here was a man who retained a boyish enthusiasm all bundled up in a tweed suit, a bow tie, an impish grin, and an eccentric penchant for using archaic, poetical vocabulary. "Forsooth! A metaphor here, I must say, that verges on the uncouth if not the explicitly vulgar!"

Tom Howard's peculiar personality bubbles through this collection of essays. Was he, as our Oxford conversation hinted, a fraud, an actor, a poseur? Not a fraud, but an actor perhaps a little. Tom was an unforgettable teacher, and every good teacher is a performer. If Tom was playing the part of the eccentric English professor, he played it to perfection.

These musings on a starry night provide us with sharp literary criticism—learned insights not only on the much-loved Inklings, but also on the writings of Walker Percy, Charles Williams, Flannery O'Connor, Beatrix Potter, and more. But here also are Tom's mental meanderings on all sorts of other topics: observations on the birds at his bird feeder, current quirks in culture, conflicts in Christianity, and in-depth discussions of philosophical and cultural debates.

In "Changing Times and Permanent Things", for example, Tom tacks away from his more lightweight and linguistically entertaining style to explore serious questions in a profound but down-to-earth style that echoes C. S. Lewis. In "What My Children Won't Learn in School", he delves into the challenges and paradoxes of the educational establishment, while in "Christ and the Psychedelic Vision", he ponders the interface of spirituality and the drug culture. Most importantly, the deep faith Tom accepted from his Evangelical upbringing shines through in its maturation in Catholicism. Like the Inklings before him, Howard evangelizes through literature.

Keith Call has done for Tom Howard what Walter Hooper did for C. S. Lewis: He has gathered the scattered writings of an original and incisive mind and preserved them for posterity. Tom Howard's vast learning, irascible wit, and modest self-regard rumble on in this collection, and in reading these essays—like countless students over the years—we can still sit at his feet, learning not only from his literary knowledge and insights, but also from his humble and humorous approach to literature, life, faith, this world, and the world to come.

—Fr. Dwight Longenecker

Of Imagination, Story, and Reality

I first met Madeleine L'Engle in 1965, when she (bravely) took me on as a sort of assistant director for a Christmas pageant at the Cathedral of Saint John the Divine in New York.

One did not have to be around Madeleine long before one was aware (electrically aware, if there is such a phrase allowable) that here was a woman of more than routine interest, to borrow The New Yorker*'s phrase. Here was an imagination that seemed to know no limits. Here was a grasp of, and a love for, the knobbly, tangy, maddening, exhilarating texture of our mortal life, perched as it is on the cusp between the seen and the unseen.*

Over the years, Madeleine and her husband, Hugh, became good friends of ours. We mourned his death with her. We also (this "we" is my family and I) owe her a debt: Her work, along with that of T. S. Eliot and Flannery O'Connor, was a (the?) mainstay of our daughter's faith during her years at Harvard. So we thank God for Madeleine L'Engle.

We find, often, a breakdown between those on the one hand whose approach to God and the world is propositionalist, syllogistic, discursive, and verbalist, and those on the other hand who find themselves reaching for the vocabulary of myth, image, and sacrament as they try to grapple with what matters about the universe. The vocabulary of

Originally published in *The Swiftly Tilting Worlds of Madeleine L'Engle: Essays in Her Honor* (Wheaton: Harold Shaw Publishers, 1998), 105–17.

the two parties differs. The philosophers sometimes suspect that the poets believe in elves.

That raises a piquant question: What about elves? The peril here is of finding that the whole discussion has got suddenly frivolous.

Such a question (whatever the question is about elves) does give immediacy and color, we might say, to the sort of thing we approach when we speak of myth and reality. It has to do with one's stance, or posture, in the world. One man, for example, if you asked him about elves, might snort, "That's rubbish. There aren't, and never have been, any such creatures." This man knows a very great deal and is quite brisk about shutting down various ontological shutters, we might say. Another man, if asked, might say, "Elves? Well—if there ever were such beings, not only do we know nothing about them, their story, if there is any such story, has nothing to do with our story, at least not yet." This man may have an entirely businesslike outlook on things and would not be caught dead joining hobbit societies, or naming his dog Frodo, or turning over cabbage leaves looking for leprechauns. The borders of his metaphysical imagination, however, are indeterminate. Mists obscure the frontiers of his world. Reality for him, eventually, reaches over the hills and far away. He may be as earthy, precise, and unsentimental when it comes to sticking to quotidian reality as, say, John Knox or Saint Joseph the Carpenter; but his world spreads out into mystery, and his awareness of mystery is not exhausted by his giving a merely ontological or theological nod in the direction of that which transcends our grasp. For him, the world really is suffused with mystery, and the leaves of reality rustle and whisper with rumor. There is fear in a handful of dust for him. Angelic and demonic footfalls really do echo along the corridors of the universe for him. He lives in a world where the morning stars have been known to sing, or to fight against Sisera, or to point astrologers to the birthplace of an incarnate deity. He is less sure of what is not going on than he is of what is going on. If the sons of god come in to the daughters of men, or gigantic Anakim stride across the landscape of Mesopotamia, or dead bodies show up in the streets of Jerusalem on the afternoon of Pontius Pilate, he will not be the one to scoff. And as for elves—well, they are certainly there, fugitive and evanescent, at least in the stories that have flickered unremittingly and immemorially along the borders of the narratives told in every tribe and culture since the expulsion from Eden.

In this connection, we may recall the story that is unfurled in the Bible. We understand that story to be true in some sense that outstrips the myths—the tales, that is, that we find being told amongst the Babylonians and Egyptians and Greeks and Norsemen. We hear the tale of Adam and Eve, for example, and we receive it as true, whereas we hear about Yggdrasil and Ginnungagap, or about Chronos and Zeus, and we demur: Such tales, while they strike haunting chords in our souls, and seem to arise from the very wellspring of things, are not "true" in the sense in which the story of Eden is true.

There are problems here. We all know about literary forms, certainly, and many ferociously orthodox Christians might wish to be allowed room to speculate when it comes to taking up a point of view as to whether Adam and Eve were one man and one woman in a garden as we know gardens. When we get to these early and misty regions in the story of our world, we tread more and more gingerly. Who knows what was going on, or how to visualize it all? We believe the story, indeed; but is the story exactly the same sort of account of things as we find in the newspaper account of an event, or the description in a history text of the battles along the Somme in World War I?

Let us for the moment lean toward the ditch on the "literal" side of the question here. That is, in thinking of the huge mystery that shrouds the story of Adam and Eve, with the Lord God taking a rib out of the man, or walking in the garden in the cool of the day—in thinking of such a scenario, may we ask whether, if cameras had been hidden in the ferns of Eden, would they have yielded footage of a magnificent naked man stretched out on the moss in a deep slumber, and of hands opening up the skin of his torso and breaking off a rib? Then presently, on camera, a naked woman coming into being right there?

But now we are all embarrassed. Come, do not speak to us of TV footage and of Eden in the same breath.

Is not our embarrassment over this clumsy juxtaposition of ancient Creation narrative and modern technology—is not this embarrassment an index of our anguished awareness that we are onlookers at events that arrive on our stage from the precincts of everlasting deity? They are events that burst the boundaries of our powers, and also of the power of words. What is human language to do when it finds itself asked to report, or at least to intimate, such events?

At the deepest levels of our being, we seem to be aware of a property of ineffability that suffuses such events and that challenges language to the utmost. We do not know quite what to do at such a juncture. We have mythic language: Shall we roll out the machinery of myth as perhaps the only equipment we have by way of mediating the ineffable to our sorely limited powers of understanding? Or will eyewitness news do the trick?

The point, of course, is simply that we do not know how to visualize Eden, and since the story tells it with such and such a texture, we will not go far wrong by sticking fairly close to that texture.

But is it not just a sort of bravado, or derring-do, that inclines us to stick close to the texture of the Genesis narrative, as over against the post-Enlightenment proclivity for fraying out, or teasing out, the dense and knotty warp and woof of that narrative into a looser skein of indeterminate stuff? In the tight fabric of the story that Genesis is pleased to give us, we have those two people pacing the stage. In the looser skein preferred by our own epoch, we have aeons of time, and gradualness, and perhaps primates passing from CroMagnon to Piltdown to Neanderthal to *Pithecanthropus Erectus*, and then some universal misstep on the part of these creatures in a calamity that we may call the Fall. And even to imagine such a calamity is, really, primarily to testify to our own unhappy conviction that something is deeply amiss in our world and in our mortal experience. Something is rotten in the state of Denmark. This cannot be right. Well, then: Let us turn to these ancient tales that arose during the earliest stages of our human self-awareness, and seize upon them, and keep them alive, and look upon them as vivid and trenchant ways of recording our own deepest hunches about things.

In the light of such a discussion we find ourselves asking what we think reality is like. The closer we can make our language approximate reality, the better off we are, we say. Is reality more like the fundamentalist Garden of Eden, with ferns and palms and murmuring brooks, or is it more like the diffuse generalities and developments summoned by talk of gradualness and evolution and scarcely perceptible aeonian movements? Did we mortals fall on some unhappy Thursday morning at about 11:45, just before lunch? Or is it that we are profoundly aware of some tragic disjuncture at the very root of our humanity that stems from—from who knows what?

Must a choice be made between the two? That is, is reality such that we have some categorical reason for disallowing the fundamentalist ferns and insisting upon a truth that is more nearly approached by the language of generality? How do we know that the ferns supply "only" a picture? What is it that we have found out about reality in our latter day that obliges us to translate that child's garden of narrative in Genesis out into the propositions and generalities commonly brought into play in such disciplines as anthropology, biblical studies, and archaeology?

From the Christian point of view, reality is not far from being synonymous with "the eternal". It is what is. But what is it like? There's the rub. And we all have to confess straight off that it is impossible to raise this topic without calling into play our imaginations, since we are such creatures as want a picture of what we are talking about.

But then we find ourselves divided: On the one hand, our imagination busily cobbles up pictures for us and offers them to our thinking; but on the other, another property in us warns us away from the pictures, whispering, "Steady now. You know that that is only a picture, and that the reality you are thinking about isn't really like that. You'll get closer to the truth if you keep those pictures where they belong, namely, penned up in a pen called 'Fancy'." One part of us inclines to caper out over picturesque hills and valleys while we think, and another part summons us to stay serious and stick with the imagery of abstraction, or the categorical, or the propositional.

I have used the word *imagery* in connection with the words *abstraction* and so forth. For of course how we think of those abstractions is itself pictorial. For most of us, the abstract is wider, and thinner, and emptier than is the imagistic, and we try to keep it as colorless as our powers will permit. We think we are being more serious, that is, closer to the truth, insofar as our mind is not depending on pictures. Pictures take us over toward the neighborhood of fancy, while abstractions place us firmly in serious discourse.

But is this axiomatic? Do we, in fact, set story aside and reach for the vocabulary of abstract proposition as we struggle to get closer to reality?

Christianity and Judaism before it do not allow us to settle for the gnostic notion that "real" reality is vacuous and that matter is to be regretted. Obviously we have to do our thinking about reality in the light of what presents itself to our powers, and what presents itself to us is blue sky and blue water and green grass and green trees and red tulips and red strawberries. Oh-ho, says our gnostic friend. You've just given me the game. Those properties you just listed are in your perceptions, not in the sky and the grass and the strawberries.

This is a nettlesome topic. But Christianity, at least, would proceed upon a set of suppositions that constitutes a sort of backdrop, or better, a pavement, for all the rest of our suppositions.

First, we have a creation that presents itself to us. All of us, gnostics and hard-core sacramentalists, would agree that what we have here is rock and water and fern and thrushes and wheat and grapes. It is all very solid. Even the so-called intangibles, like the song of the hermit thrush, are, when you come down to it, material, since it takes the bird's little throat membranes, and air waves, and your eardrum membranes to get the song. The creation presents itself to us thus.

And it presents itself, secondly, to *us*. What are we? We are not angels who, they tell us, can perceive reality directly, unfiltered through eardrums and retinas and olfactory nerves and taste buds and fingertips. The reality of creation is mediated to us via our taste buds and so forth. A corollary from the Christian point of view here would be that it is mediated in some sense faithfully and not fraudulently. Christians believe in the trustworthiness of Creation, since we attribute trustworthiness to the Creator. All the blueness and greenness and sweetness and wetness and tang and bite and solidity of it all testifies in some sense truthfully to the One who made it.

But who, or what, are we? We are creatures made for this Creation, or rather, for whom it was made: So would run the Christian account. And we share this Creation's particular sort of solidity. Our flesh and bones and viscera are at home in this blueness and wetness and sweetness. And all of these "-nesses" present themselves to us in blueberries, and in the water of Lake Maggiore, and in the feathers of the indigo bunting, or in the color of my love's eyes. I, unlike the archangel Raphael, do not live amongst blue-ness: I live under a blue sky and wear a pullover knitted with blue yarn. It is the kind of creature I am.

Myth is the sort of narrative par excellence that bespeaks most nearly my being this kind of creature. It addresses at the profoundest level the unity that binds us mortals into the integrity of body and soul that we mean when we say "man" or "woman". To speak to us as though we are a sort of paste-up job of nonmaterial and material substances is to do us a sad disservice. That toe they just had to amputate was *me*, somehow: I am lessened by the surgery. It is I who ache with this migraine. My stomach is wrenched and my tear ducts overflow over this grief that has come upon me. My muscles tighten and my forehead sweats and my adrenalin rushes when danger approaches. In all of our experience, there is very little separating out of the components that make us what we are, namely, body and soul. In death we are tragically disfranchised and sundered, and our souls yearn for the resurrection, presumably, since we were not made to be nonmaterial. The

Resurrection—that flagrantly and embarrassingly physical event—is the great triumph over all gnosticism.

And myth is the kind of narrative that approaches most nearly the kind of integrity that we believe about the Resurrection, or, more to our purpose here, about the Incarnation. In the Incarnation you have the seamless integrity of form and content. The Incarnation is not a symbol. Nor is it even a metaphor. It is That Toward Which all symbol and metaphor strain. For in symbol and metaphor, and in all of art, you have the effort to make B stand for A, or B suggest A, or B evoke A, or B make A present. The octagonal signpost at the corner of the two streets means stop. The shamrock means Ireland. The gold ring means married. The trumpets mean Here comes the king.

When you raise this to the level of art, we find ourselves drawn into a subterfuge that seems to bespeak matters of vast weight. We will all cooperate with Rembrandt in allowing oily pigments spread over canvas to "be" Aristotle Contemplating the Bust of Homer. We will be accomplices with van Eyck in agreeing that that flat surface with the tints on it "is" the Mystic Lamb of Saint John's Apocalypse.

In all of these situations, you have B (a shape; a color; oil paint) standing in for A. And it is thus with all of the arts, which are in some sense activities that touch exquisitely on the sort of creature we mortals are, since they seem to spring from the deepest levels of our being, and to reach to our origins. Certainly art is protohistoric, ubiquitous, and unremitting. You cannot stop us painting, dancing, singing, and telling stories.

Telling stories. Another activity that is protohistoric, ubiquitous, and unremitting, and seems to touch on the central mystery of our humanity. In drama, we do all sorts of pretending. We allow the amphitheatre to be Thebes, or the Globe to be Verona, and we allow John Gielgud to be Hamlet or Paul Scofield to be Lear. And not only that. By a sort of alchemy, we are pleased to see Hamlet or Lear to be us. That is, when Hamlet mutters his tortured ratiocinations, we thrill at hearing our own deepest perplexities given perfect shape. Lear is a frightening warning to us not to allow ourselves vanity and foolishness like that. His grandeur is our grandeur, and his peril our peril. In all of this it is the fiction that, paradoxically, bundles us, not away from what is serious, but toward it.

Myth is the kind of narrative that most nearly approaches this same seamlessness of form and content that our own personhood manifests. For there is no "meaning" in myth to be precipitated out like curds. Theseus' labyrinth does not "mean" complexity, for example: It is a labyrinth. Hercules does not "mean" prowess: He is a big strong hero. The Gardens of the Hesperides do not mean the fulfillment of desire: They are ultimate gardens. In this sense, myth defies interpretation, since when we interpret we winnow out of the stuff something else, namely, meaning. We do this winnowing most characteristically with Shakespeare's plays, say, and with all narratives in some sense, of course. Henry James and James Joyce positively cry out for this treatment. But with the myths, insofar as we put a Jungian or Freudian or even "literary" interpretation on them, we feel that we have in some sense put them in a Procrustean bed. Or, to change the metaphor, we have driven a wedge between form and content. In order to do justice to the fabric, we have to leave it as it is. We have to connive wholeheartedly in the fiction if we want to have the full worth of it.

If this seems too precious, we may recall the obvious here: When we mortals make our supreme attempt to raid the precincts of reality, we indulge in fictions. We play let's pretend. For in the deepest, most serious experiences that attend our mortality, namely, birth, marriage, and death, we sense that we are in precincts that resist the efforts of proposition and statement to penetrate them. So, by way, not of escaping the full force of the experiences, but rather of entering more deeply into them, we play. We pretend. When the obstetricians and clipboards and midwifery have done all they can do vis-à-vis birth, we bring out the candles and the champagne, neither of which does the slightest bit of good on the utilitarian front. Marriage: When we have signed the license and have made our solemn pledges to each other privately, then again we "play": elaborate costume, procession, public ceremony, highly wrought ritual—this is all an effort to vouchsafe the truth to us, not to escape from it. Nay, we know that the play—the ritual or the ceremony—is the only method available to our humanity by which we may enter fully into the meaning. And death: long palls, drawn hearses, nodding plumes, crepe, winding sheets, hatchments: None of it is worth a ha'penny on the rational front. But we have outstripped the solely rational and its resources in these precincts.

Ceremony and art and fiction, and most notably myth, turn out upon reflection to be indispensable. But that is too weak a word. Those phenomena bear in their very texture the texture of reality. The propositional, the discursive, the ratiocinative, the abstract—these, too, bespeak reality after their own species and to the utmost of their powers. But if we wish to descry Reality, then we are going to be aware that from the fountainhead of Reality we find rumbling at us, not just decrees from Sinai, and not only books from the prophets, but also stars and sun and moon and earth and water and rock and strawberries and the bodies of man and woman. And we will be aware of the fact that the redeeming of all of this, when it had fallen into ruin, came at us in the pelts of animals slain by the Lord God to cover our nakedness, and in the stone of altars and the blood and burned fat of goats and lambs, and in hyssop and incense and gold and purple. And in the culmination of that drama we find, not the transcending of all that Hebrew tackle and gear, but, lo, a conceiving and a gestation and a parturition and suckling; and water to wine at a wedding; and stones made bread; and a fast in the wilderness; and, finally, our salvation played out with whips and thorns and nails, and then a body out of the grave and taken into the midmost mystery of the Holy Trinity. All very solid.

Christians see in that story not mere surface events with a subsurface meaning that can be teased out of it all. The events *are* the meaning. The Incarnation is the Eternal Word at its most characteristic. Islam has a book; so far they are like us in that we also have a book. But unlike Islam, Christianity celebrates an Incarnation: The ineffable becomes solid with the particular solidity that belongs to this creation in which we belong.

The myths are the stories par excellence that never let us dissociate ourselves for one instant from the solid. We cannot fend off the texture of the myths with a cerebral or propositional barge pole. We have to stay with Ulysses as he dodges Polyphemus' boulders, and with his men as they grunt and snuffle, having been turned into pigs by Circe, and with Leda as the swan ravishes her. Humiliating as it may be to our sense of our own cerebral dignity, we find that we live in a story like that.

We live in a story in which the Lord God is to be found walking in the garden in the cool of the day. We live in a story in which men build a great tower with a top aimed at heaven. We live in a story in which a great boat saves the remnant of animals and men, and a bush burns with the presence of the deity whose name is I Am, and a great horn blows so loudly from the mountain that the people cry out to Moses to intercede for them, and the King of Heaven is found in a stall, and the whole of mankind is redeemed by the torture endured in the flesh of one man, and the dead rise. It is a mythic narrative, surely?

Yes, but with this slight difference. Christians believe that in this last set of events, that which all the other myths strained toward, the god made himself known to us, actually stepped through the scrim that hangs between the seen and the unseen, out into the light of real, historical, geographical day. Myth became Fact.

And the events in this enormous drama are such that we find that sheer proposition will not quite do the trick, much as our rational selves would be gratified to discover that it would. And we also find that in the presence of these events, we mortals must do what we always do with the ineffable: We must enter into them by means of ceremony. We must eat actual bread and drink real wine, and go down into real water. Our whole flesh cries out to be allowed to do obeisance, and to hear the organ and sweet voices, and to smell the incense. Our piety yearns to fasten upon the Story, since it is a true story, on the one hand, and, on the other hand, since the truth can only be got at, finally, by means of story.

Waking Up Is Hard to Do

Walker Percy's novels and essays tackle what C.S. Lewis called "the great platitudes" and T.S. Eliot called "the permanent things". That is to say, they concern themselves with far more than manners, psychology, or social issues.

This locates Percy in an odd spot, if we are trying to place him in the ordinary tradition of the English-language novel. This tradition characteristically concerns itself with manners and psychology (I am thinking of Jane Austen, Anthony Trollope, George Eliot, and Henry James) or with social issues (Dickens and Hardy).

Unlike Dostoevsky, Tolstoy, Kafka, Mann, or Camus, English writers have, as often as not, seemed to avoid the immensities that arch over our mortal existence. It cannot be urged that English-language writers are superficial. Their art exhibits, in its own mode, a very high level of perfection.

But when you get a writer who carries his tale into a realm where sin is a real category, or divine grace, you realize that you have crossed a certain threshold. Flannery O'Connor, who is frequently mentioned in the same breath with Percy, maintained that she never wrote about anything but grace. Take little Tarwater in her novella *The Violent Bear It Away*.

The oddities of behavior that this boy displays are, of course, partly a result of his peculiar birth and upbringing, but at the end of the day we are obliged to agree with

Originally published in *Touchstone* (October 2006). Reprinted with permission.

O'Connor that he is morally and spiritually responsible for his choices, young though he may be, which must be expiated before God. There is no question of his getting comfortable with his feelings or "giving himself permission" to follow his own preferences. Obedience to the divine will seems to be the touchstone, and it is grace that has pursued him all through the story, like the Hound of Heaven.

What Henry James, D. H. Lawrence, or Virginia Woolf would make of this, I have no idea. Your average reader of *The New Yorker* will titter knowingly when he comes across Old Tarwater, the archetypal redneck, sweating and preaching doom from his shanty in Powderhead.

Or again—Evelyn Waugh: As amusing, scintillating, and urbane as *Brideshead Revisited* is, we find that all the disorders that bedevil the Flyte family eventually reveal themselves, not as dysfunctionalities, but as sin. Confession and repentance seem to be the touchstone here. Lord Marchmain must repent of his adultery, and Julia of hers. Charles Ryder, the agnostic narrator, must get on his knees in front of the Blessed Sacrament before he is truly free, and it is grace that has crowded him along the way.

Each member of the beleaguered Flyte family, who are all deeply flawed Catholics (except for Cordelia, perhaps), is discovered as having failed in one way or another in the sanctity sweepstakes—even the devout Lady Marchmain, who is something of a dragon, and her oldest son, Lord Brideshead, who in the interest of the Faith tends to tramp on everyone's insteps.

Or we may mention Graham Greene in this connection. In his so-called "Catholic novels", we find that the protagonist is not merely confused or neurotic, which would be acceptable categories for your *New Yorker* reader. We find him hag-ridden with guilt (think of the priest in *The Power and the Glory*) or trying to deny it (think of the adulterer in *The End of the Affair*). And he is very far from suffering your post-Freudian guilt feelings.

No. The trouble is that the man is actually and objectively guilty before the Divine Tribunal and that there is nothing for it but that he repent, more often than not of his sexual excursions. Otherwise his immortal soul is in real danger of eternal damnation, understood, not as a psychological metaphor, but as the doom preached by our Lord.

It may be apposite here to put forward a difficulty that all of these writers, and hence Walker Percy, encountered in their effort to write stories that will be heard by their modern audience.

Whereas Homer, Virgil, Dante, and Shakespeare, not to mention Austen, Eliot, and Dickens, all told their stories to audiences that shared altogether the moral and metaphysical point of view from which they wrote, you have no such luxury in the twentieth century.

Nowadays the Christian writer of fiction finds that he must cobble up some trick to circumvent this disjuncture between his own assumptions and his readers' Darwinian, Freudian, and postmodern assumptions.

How, in other words, do you go about drawing your blasé secular readers into this peculiar world where disordered behavior must eventually be confessed as sin? How do you get your twentieth-century sophisticate willingly to suspend his disbelief and recognize your story as being serious and not merely quaint? (For this reason, among others, the operation of grace on their protagonists is always implicit. You don't get anything about the person having a conscious, momentary, explicit "conversion experience".)

The tricks Percy and company reach for vary. O'Connor, for example, beats us about the ears with the grotesque. Awful things happen in her stories, and her characters are often virtual gargoyles or trolls. Many readers turn away from her fiction with a sigh: I don't want to read about all this squalor. But if we allow her fiction to percolate through our shallow imaginations, desiccated as they are by modernism, then we will find that she knows exactly what she is doing.

Her characters really are answerable before the Divine Tribunal. Any merely psychological mollifying of things in the case of little Tarwater, or of the boy in "The Enduring Chill" who comes home from New York to his mother in Georgia to die, would be frivolous. That water stain on his ceiling really is the Holy Ghost descending on our sick laddie. Old Tarwater really is a prophet of God, who, like many true prophets, is taken for a lunatic.

O'Connor takes this stuff seriously and has to lure her readers into these Christian precincts with all sorts of bizarre tricks. She says at one point, "I have heard it said that belief in Christian dogma is a hindrance to the writer, but I myself have found nothing farther from the truth. Actually, it frees the storyteller to observe. It is not a set of rules that fixes what he sees in the world. It affects his writing primarily by guaranteeing his respect for mystery."

Or this, from her marvelous collection of essays *Mystery and Manners*: "My own feeling is that writers who see by the light of their Christian faith will have ... the sharpest eye for the grotesque, for the perverse, and for the unacceptable.... The reason for this attention to the perverse is the difference between their beliefs and [those of] their audience." The Christian novelist, she continued,

> will find in modern life distortions that are repugnant to him, and his problem will be to make these appear as distortions to an audience that is used to seeing them as natural; and he may be forced to take ever more violent means to get his vision across to this hostile audience. When you

> can assume that your audience holds the same beliefs as you do, you can relax a little ... [but] when you have to assume that it does not, then you have to make your vision apparent by shock—to the hard of hearing you shout, and for the almost-blind you draw large and startling figures.

Of the Christian novel she says, "Its center of meaning will be Christ; its center of destruction will be the devil." Well, you can't write about the Devil and expect your *New Yorker* readers, or your graduate departments of English, to take you seriously. It is a problem. Or again: "The Christian novelist is distinguished from his pagan colleagues by recognizing sin as sin ... not a sickness or an accident of environment, but as a responsible choice of offense against God that involves his eternal future." Find me the place in Henry James where any of his heroines are endangering their eternal souls.

Like O'Connor, Percy speaks of the novelist "who has explicit and ultimate concern with the nature of man and the nature of reality", and hence, says Percy, it "is fitting that he should shock and warn his readers by speaking of last things." He poses this question: "Is it too much to say that the novelist, unlike the new theologian, is one of the few remaining witnesses to the doctrine of original sin? ... Either this novelist is crazy or ... in his confused Orphic way [he] is trying to tell us something we would do well to listen to."

He goes on to ask, "What is the task of the Christian novelist?" And he gives us his own answer: The Christian novelist "calls on every ounce of cunning, craft, and guile he can muster.... The fictional use of violence, shock, comedy, insult, the bizarre, are the everyday tools of his trade."

In other words, Percy and the rest of these novelists are stuck with having to smuggle into their tales notions that are quaint, archaic, or outrageous to modern readers. He has worked up a special, even idiosyncratic, vocabulary for his tactics, which comes into play in all of his novels, I think, and certainly in *The Moviegoer*.

His stories reach beyond the psychological realm and always record some assault that turns out to have been launched by divine grace on the protagonist's normal dim state of awareness. It calls into question the hero's whole being and bundles him along toward an awakening to his true state, that is, of his state before God. In *The Moviegoer*, his hero, Binx Bolling, finds himself thus assaulted. The assault comes in very odd forms.

For one thing, Binx stumbles into what Percy calls "certification". Binx and his cousin Kate are at a movie. A scene in the movie shows the neighborhood of the theatre, and in the street afterward Kate looks around and says, "Yes, it is certified now." Binx, who is the narrator, tells us this: She refers to a phenomenon of movie-going which I have called certification. Nowadays when a person lives somewhere, in a neighborhood, the place is not certified for him. More than likely he will live there sadly and the emptiness which is inside him will expand until it evacuates the entire neighborhood. But if he sees a movie that shows his very neighborhood, it becomes possible for him to live, for a time at least, as a person who is Somewhere and not Anywhere.

There we have "certification". By seeing our own street in a movie, suddenly we are awakened to the curious actuality of the very place in which we have dawdled for years without ever seeing it. Suddenly here on the screen is William Holden walking along my own street. Hey: I live in this place, and this place is Somewhere, and not just Anywhere. Percy capitalizes Somewhere and Anywhere, by the way. To live Anywhere is to be lost in despair, since it adumbrates hell's own stupor.

For Percy, despair is not merely a state of extreme despondency. It is far more dangerous, since our eternal souls are at stake, and no psychiatrist can get anywhere near my eternal soul. In his usage, the word despair refers to the dim torpor in which almost every one of us passes his life. The saints have been awakened from this lethal miasma, but the rest of us most of the time shuffle along in the murk of unawareness.

Percy owes this notion to Kierkegaard. If you are in this dim state, of course you do not know it. You are just going along in the torpor that settles upon our mortal state, or, perhaps worse, you are what Eliot called "distracted from distraction by distraction." Both Eliot and Percy would understand this state of semi-consciousness as a final danger. Since we are all moving toward the Last Judgment, we had better wake up and look to our knitting.

But what will wake us up? Well, various things pluck at Binx' sleeve. This movie, for instance.

To be "Anywhere", for Percy, means just that: I am living in just any old where. Nothing plucks me by the sleeve. Nothing jolts, startles, ravishes, or alarms me. If I go on this way, I will eventually need a priest or prophet to help me. No psychiatrist can come near these precincts where Everything is at stake. His "expertise" is myopic. He can't see doom but only dysfunction, and that is not how the Christian vision understands our mortal situation.

So again and again in Percy's novels we find this somewhat frightening distinction between Anywhere and Somewhere. If I am never hailed by the sharp individuality of a place—the crunching of camphor berries underfoot as I walk to school, say, or the smell of a privet hedge—then I am veering toward Kierkegaard's despair, which is to say damnation.

In this connection we may notice the names Percy gives to his minor characters. There are no Joneses, Smiths, or

Browns here. Binx' landlady, who is, socially speaking, a person of no importance at all, is Mrs. Schexnaydre forsooth. The name flags us all down. She is Somebody, not just Anybody. You can't vanish in the throng if you are called Schexnaydre.

Or we have Mr. Sartalamaccia, who wants to buy a piece of Binx' land. Or Mr. Kinsella, who really is nobody: He runs a cracked and peeling outdoor cinema in the boondocks where Binx likes to go to see B-movies.

But we find that Binx is intensely interested in these people. They are Somebody, and not Anybody. He wants to get to know them. He even likes to talk to the ticket taker in the booth at the cinema, who for most of us would most certainly be of no account whatever. But Binx has been awakened from the despair that lives Anywhere amongst Anybodies.

Besides this certification, we find what Percy calls "rotation". Rotation occurs when, as Binx puts it, we stumble into "the experience of the new beyond the expectation of the experiencing of the new".

For example, if you go (as Binx does) to the Grand Canyon having never been there before, you expect a new experience. But everybody is a tourist; everybody goes there; you have seen it all in travel brochures. But if you get lost on the way, you have stumbled into "rotation". Now you are keenly and uncomfortably aware of terrain that was not at all a part of your expectations. The whole thing has taken on a certain sharpness. You have been awakened.

Most of the time we all live in what Percy calls "Everydayness", which is virtually synonymous with despair. But think of Noah, who found that a flood was coming, or Abraham, who was told to pull up his tent pegs, or Joseph, who found himself in a pit, or Jonah, who was told to go preach doom to Nineveh, or Saint Paul, who was struck down en route to Damascus when his expectation was merely to savage some Christians. These would all be instances of rotation.

Percy's assumption is that unless or until we are jolted awake by something, we may be in grave danger of Everydayness, which may in its turn land us in hell. (We will come presently to the big rotation that awakens Binx forever from despair. But I must squeak in another of Percy's tricks before we get to that.)

This time it is "repetition". "What is a repetition? A repetition is the re-enactment of past experience toward the end of isolating the time segment which has lapsed in order that it, the lapsed time, can be savored of itself and without the usual adulteration of events that clog time like peanuts in brittle."

Percy has our friend Binx tell us here about his experience of going into a theatre to see *The Oxbow Incident* fourteen years after he had first been there to see it. On the first visit, he had emerged from the theatre and smelled the smell of privet, and found camphor berries popping under his feet on the sidewalk. The same thing happens now. The latter visit vividly conjures the former.

But what about the intervening fourteen years? What has happened in them? What, for example, about the split plywood seats in the theatre, enduring nevertheless as if they had waited to see what I had done with my fourteen years. [There is a very strong hint here of Judgment, surely?] There was this also: a secret sense of wonder about the enduring, about all the nights, the rainy summer nights at twelve and one and two o'clock when the seats endured alone in the empty theatre. The enduring is something that must be accounted for. One cannot simply shrug it off.

Clearly something has happened to free Binx of Everydayness. His routine hometown streets; a routine trip to the Grand Canyon; and two routine visits to a theatre. It almost seems like a curse: Binx can no longer merely pass through routines. He must notice everything.

(This is exactly what happens in the Sacrament of Confession, where I must rake up everything. I must give an account of every thought, word, and act. Heaven have mercy on my soul if at the Last Judgment I am hailed with a mountain of items for which I must give an accounting and which I have habitually allowed to drain off into Everydayness.)

Now we come to Binx' original awakening: In the Korean War, he was shot in the shoulder. Listen to how Percy has Binx tell us about it: "I came to myself under a chindolea bush.... My shoulder didn't hurt, but it was pressed hard against the ground as if somebody sat on me. Six inches from my nose a dung beetle was scratching around under the leaves. As I watched, there awoke in me an immense curiosity. I was onto something. I vowed that if I ever got out of this fix, I would pursue the search."

My own hunch is that it is not only the wound, which has certainly jolted him awake, but also the sight of the dung beetle that seems to be busy digging a hole around him. If you are vouchsafed a glance at your own gravediggers at their work, you may find, as Dr. Johnson put it in his usual lapidary way, that your mind is wonderfully concentrated. (I think Dr. Johnson said that it was the prospect of being hanged, but never mind.)

So. Binx is "onto something". He has embarked on a "search". (These are key words in Percy's writing.) Mere "Everydayness" has been interrupted for him. We find out as the story progresses that he has made himself a sort of ascetic, for exactly the same reasons that drove the desert hermits and the Cistercians to renounce everything.

The reader will find himself wondering why Binx lives in such a nothing neighborhood and reads such inconsequential newspapers and pursues such a boring life. The truth is that he has divested himself, quite sedulously, of every single one of the gratifying distractions that distract his family and all of his friends. Family pedigree, membership in the right clubs, travel, beer-drinking, self-congratulatory aestheticism, the socially correct neighborhood, charming houses—it is all so much wood, hay, and stubble for Binx, since he has got "onto something" and has embarked on the Search. Like those hermits, he forswears everything in order to find the Pearl of Great Price.

Binx lives in a Somewhere, not an Anywhere. He sees himself and everyone else whom he encounters as Someone, not Anyone. All of this, of course, makes sense to Christian readers, but Percy is luring his *New Yorker* readers into a region where one's immortal soul is at stake.

There is nothing in heaven or earth that does not matter, most of all one's own self before God Most High. The final torpor is to be found in hell, where everything is reduced to a grey murk. Paradise is the place where every created thing and creature, and hence one's own self, dances out in all of the glory with which it was invested at the Creation.

From now on Binx is blessed, or cursed, with this attentiveness. Every routine place, person, object, or event presents him with the chance to wake up. You can see this in the punctilio with which he speaks of things. In Korea, for example, he awakens not merely under a bush but under a chindolea bush. There is a bird singing, but it is not just a bird: It is an oriental finch. The bug near his nose is not just a bug: It is a dung beetle.

When he drives his little MG along the Gulf Coast, the enormous cumulus clouds are always "booming up over the horizon", as though we all carry on here under the turbulent threat of something titanic that arches over our mortal affairs. Binx sees a wading bird at one point, but it is not merely any old bird. Here is how he records it for us: "The egret pumps himself up into the air and rows by so close I can hear the gristle creak in his wings."

I won't tell you Binx' whole story. (Percy, as you may know, was an adult convert.) I don't want to give away the punch line. But let me, in closing, touch upon what strikes me as being the most significant event in the whole book.

Binx is a lapsed Catholic. Most of Percy's heroes are. But they are not comfortably lapsed Catholics who have packed in on the Faith and find themselves exhilarated by the freedom that follows upon one's having left behind the nettlesome restraints of faith. Percy's characters all seem to be bugged by Something. It is, of course, the Hound of Heaven—the Holy Ghost.

Anyway, Binx visits the fishing camp where his mother, her second husband (she has been widowed), and their seven children live. They are perfunctory but scrupulous Catholics, off to Mass regularly, believing everything, but, unlike Protestant Evangelicals, never chatting about the Faith. No earnest conversations about the Faith and no "sharing" ever occur in Percy's work, or in that of any of the Catholic novelists I've mentioned.

One of Binx' half-brothers is called Lonnie. He is crippled. He and Binx have a special devotion to each other. When Binx arrives at the fishing camp, we have this:

> Lonnie has gone into a fit of excitement in his wheelchair. His hand curls upon itself. I kiss him first and his smile starts his head turning away in a long trembling torticollis ... his face is handsome and pure when it is not contorted. He is my favorite, to tell the truth.... We are good

> friends because he knows I do not feel sorry for him. For one thing, he has the gift of believing that he can offer his sufferings in reparation for men's indifference to the pierced heart of Jesus Christ. For another thing, I would not mind so much trading places with him. His life is a serene business.

Well. There we have it. Lonnie's suffering, purity, and devotion to Jesus Christ pluck Binx by his lapsed-Catholic sleeve. He knows it is all true, even though he has long since ceased practicing the Faith.

We never see Binx falling to his knees in an act of repentance and renewed faith. And our *New Yorker* readers are never put on the spot. We simply pick up Binx' sharpening awareness of what it is that his "search" implies. We hear very little about anything religious going on in him. But in the very last scene of the book, we see him offering his own life, as it were, in behalf of his poor neurotic cousin Kate, whom he has now married.

Nothing in the scene tells us "This is religious." It is a very small scene, and a very small act on his part—actually, he just promises to be thinking about Kate as she ventures out to the shops. But his promise sets her at least momentarily free from the fears that paralyze her.

The scene is not symbolic. Rather, it presents a case in point of what occurred also at Golgotha, namely, the offering of oneself for another. In the one case we have a life—the life—offered in behalf of the whole world. For Binx, it is only a matter of offering a little bit of his time and attention (more, presumably, than he'd give otherwise) for the relief of Kate. And indeed we are meant, I think, to see his marriage as such an act. Charles Williams calls this whole business "co-inherence", or "substitution and exchange".

So: In *The Moviegoer* we see sin and grace illustrated for the *New Yorker* reader, who might learn in this way something of the divine life he would not learn (would not let himself learn, perhaps) from writing that wore its religion on its sleeve. Percy, like O'Connor and Waugh and the others, has found a way to speak to the hard of hearing.

Percy takes us much, much farther into the region of the self than any psychological novel or novel of manners ever attempts to do. Here you have the human self at stake—but (whether you know it or not) that self is an immortal soul who eventually must give an accounting before the Divine Tribunal of every word and act.

Real and Imagined Stories

That watercolor picture in *Peter Rabbit* of Old Mrs. Rabbit coming along a sandy path in the woods with her red kerchief and market basket may have stuck in the memory of readers. Certainly it has in mine. The Beatrix Potter books drew my young imagination into a world that seemed to cast a warm and sunlit radiance back into the common, light-of-day world that I inhabited—the world, that is, of breakfast, the playroom, my yellow tricycle, my playmates, and my parents and family. Tom Kitten, Mr. Jeremy Fisher, Mrs. Tittlemouse, Jemima Puddle-Duck, Mrs. Tiggy-Winkle, and the rest of them: My reveries were shot through with the soft light that illumined the fields, woods, farmyards, and grassy hills of the Potter books.

Of course, it was all merely an imaginary world. One had to set it aside presently and come to terms with the plain business of life. But two words there might bear scrutiny: "merely" and "imaginary".

Merely, for a start: This word carries with it the suggestion that a thing is of little or no significance and must sooner or later be supervened by the call of sober responsibilities. You can't have a schoolboy forever retreating into the domain of Winnie-the-Pooh, say, when he should be doing his Latin or his household chores. And *imaginary*: Ordinarily, this word suggests a domain that stands over against the real world to which we mortals must address

Reprinted with permission by CatholiCity, July 5, 2010.

ourselves. A man may make mountains out of mere molehills in his daily exchanges or seek escape from his responsibilities in the mirage of his imagination—we say that such a man is in great trouble. The mere and the imaginary must bow to the call of the real when the two conflict.

But then, Mrs. Rabbit and Pooh turn up in a world that has other inhabitants: Zeus, Hyacinth, Arthur, Lear, Jean Valjean, David Copperfield, and the rest. Surely this is all the mere world of the imaginary?

Well, yes, mostly. But when that impressive cast appears on stage, we begin to wonder whether "mere" quite does justice to the thing. And even the word "imaginary" starts to take on a weight that we hadn't counted on when we were talking about rabbits.

What is this weight that seems to attach itself to that merely imaginary world? Distinctions could be drawn between lightweight and heavyweight, to be sure: One would stop on the hither side of juxtaposing Mrs. Rabbit, much as we like her, with King Lear. On the other hand, this insubstantial world of the imagination has for millennia imbrued our "real" world of affairs. The pharaohs, the caesars, J.S. Bach, Bismarck, John D. Rockefeller, Winston Churchill, you and I—here is the real world. But from the beginning, men have told tales. Whatever saber-toothed tigers prowled about, whatever Huns were at the gates, bubonic plagues raged, or famine brooded, the odd thing is that *story* seems somehow to be in the cards. Not only will we not cease telling tales in such calamitous times; the tales seem to have suffused the world and have driven us by their strange power to mull over the sheer depth, immensity, luminescence, and gravity of our situation as mortals. Hoeing turnips, driving back the Huns, inventing the internal combustion engine and computers, and raising our families—the details of these enterprises exist front and center, so to speak. But what is the backdrop against which all of these affairs proceed?

Surely it is that world evoked and embodied in the great figures of the imagination? Courage, hardiness, nobility, suffering, intrepidity, grace, sweetness, self-donation, heroism—these qualities are at work in the real world of our mortality and are incarnate and vivified and heralded in the stories and figures that the human imagination has created. Somehow, story is always in the cards, and the call for us mortals not merely to *live through* all that life asks of us, but to pause and *set forth* our experience—in story and painting and statuary and dance and song—that call will not leave us alone somehow.

That last list is what constitutes the world of art—of the works of imagination, that is. To tally, explain, and analyze human experience is one thing, and that is the work of the sciences and various intellectual disciplines. But from Cro-Magnon man on down through the Greeks, the Romans, the Middle Ages, the Renaissance, and even under the lethal hand of the Enlightenment and Modernism, we seem to have been obliged not merely to *live* but to *create.*

From the Christian point of view, two or three points would seem to arise in this connection.

For one thing, we are all aware of living in a tale that is just that—a tale. It opens, "In the beginning", and a story unfolds. It is hemmed in by no boundaries whatever. Angels and archangels, Adam, Enoch and Moses and the Virgin, not to mention the incarnate God, inhabit the story—and this story is the true one, played out on the real stage of our history. Light years shrink to mere milliseconds as the size of the whole scene opens out. Joy pierces things, and wickedness, and terrible sorrows. The plot thickens on the first page with the arrival of evil. And we men, as opposed to the elephants and the titmice and the gnats, find ourselves burdened with *awareness.* We wonder, what is going on?

What does it all *mean*? (Your gnat doesn't ask.) And how shall we find a way to bespeak the immensity and bliss and tragedy at work in the story?

"Once upon a time", we try, by way of giving resonance to our effort to grasp the whole. And in trying that phrase, we find that we have, in fact, stumbled into a dimension that does not always present itself in the clutter of immediacy that marks our common pursuits and responsibilities. Our efforts in this connection spring from imagination, to be sure. But imagination, after all, is *image*-ination: It is the image-making faculty in us that reflects the image of God, which, we are told, crowns us mortals and distinguishes us from the beasts. We alone are made in the image of the Maker. It is not said of the angels.

And in making images—of Arthur and Jean Valjean and Mrs. Rabbit—we answer the call that comes from the abyss wherein lies the mystery of Man and God. And, we are told, Jesus Christ is "the image of the invisible God". The Incarnation: the making solid and visible and proximate that which lies, otherwise, entirely beyond any powers that we ourselves have to grasp.

And the sacraments: These all have their existence in the solid world of flesh and blood. They stand at the pinnacle of all dogma, doctrine, theology, and discourse. (It is worth noting here that Protestantism has, in effect, evacuated the sacraments as they have been understood by the Church from her apostolic birth.) The sacraments all do their work via the physical world. Water, bread, wine, oil, yes—but even Confession. You can't text your confession or e-mail it in. There has to be a human eardrum right there, and your larynx. And Holy Orders? There must be your head and the hands of a bishop. There are no disembodied sacraments.

So. The Story—our story, and all of the stories that we mortals have told ourselves. What does it all hint at? Indeed—what?

A Photo in Transylvania

A sumptuous travel magazine—to which, I need scarcely add, we do not subscribe—arrived in our letter box the other day. Things are so beautifully laid-out these days that one cannot always tell whether a given item is actually just a piece of advertising.

In any case, the cover shows a Romanian Orthodox priest in gold vestments blessing a plowed field. Two small acolytes stand by, as well as a layman with a banner and some villagers. Low wooded hills lie in the background. All seems idyllic. The main article inside carries the theme along. A harried Westerner is invited to think, "Ah. Tranquility. The simple life. I must book a ticket."

The scene turns out to be Transylvania, which readers at all familiar with Balkan history will know has not at all been a tranquil region, if we are thinking of Hungarian and Romanian questions.

But the photos started a train of thought in my mind. The people in the farming village whom the photographer had picked out tended to be immemorially old. Wrinkled, toothless crones in babushkas, old men in flat cloth hats. One supposes that most of them have not dashed very often to spas in Brazil, Indonesia, or the Caribbean.

What has happened in their lives? Well—birth, work, childbearing, work, eating and drinking, work, family life, work, the Divine Liturgy, festivals, work, death, and so forth.

Reprinted with permission by CatholiCity, January 7, 2008.

But various things probably have not happened. Most of them have never been featured in an article or been "known"—even locally—for anything particular, or tried a fancy restaurant, or leafed through a hefty highbrow Sunday paper or one of the startling magazines of fantasy, or sent any e-mails. There are doubtless very few "names" that any of them can drop.

Here, then, must be a recipe for the despondency that follows on the heels of sheer ennui? I mean, what have they got to ginger things up for them? There's no *spice* in their lives! No distractions. How on earth do they carry *on*?

It is a set of questions that might burst, quite understandably, from someone whirling around on the calliope of the West. But there is another possible reaction to such a set of photographs. It is, of course, the very one that the magazine sought, except here it would be carried through from mere tourism to a sort of pious fantasy. The tranquility that, it is supposed, reigns in the farming villages of Transylvania must also reign in the hearts of these old folks. Good old saints, all of them, surely, with their liturgy and icons and festivals?

Well, heaven grant it. It might well be the case—or, shall we say, it most certainly is the case for any of them, as for any of us, whose lives are hidden with Christ in God, as Saint Paul puts the matter. The photographer may place me in a plowed field with low wooded hills for his picture, or in a mall, or a gridlock at 57th Street and Madison Avenue, or an airport security line in my stocking feet. The setting won't really change things, or so Paul (and the saints) would urge.

Here is one of the old themes of Catholic spiritual life: The region that my soul inhabits is interior. Great blocklike words bespeak that region: hiddenness. Obscurity. Anonymity. Detachment. Withdrawal. Oblivion. Silence. Poverty. Stillness. Renunciation.

We all know that list, heaven knows. But what a thunderous abyss opens when we utter even one of them. And how they have all fled before the roar, speed, distractions, and strobe lights of Instant Everything.

On the surface of things, it would appear that the fields and wooded hills might be the easier region in which one may pursue holiness (which, after all, is the only point of all those block-like words). But it is too easy to romanticize those fields and hills. The sheer tedium of plowing and chopping and carrying on, decade after bone-wearying decade, often under terrible governments, leaches away the romance.

In the old Requiem they sang *Ad te omnis caro veniet*—To Thee shall all flesh come. That is the Day on which I must give my accounting. If I find myself caught short, the gridlock won't count for very much when it comes to making my excuses.

The Other Inkling

We all know about the Inklings, that astounding coterie of men who met twice weekly for some years in the 1940s and 1950s at Oxford to drink beer and talk about everything. J.R.R. Tolkien and C.S. Lewis are, of course, by far the best known of the group. But there was another regular, namely, their friend Charles Williams.

Williams was an editor at the Oxford University Press, which had moved its offices to Oxford when the blitz began hitting London. He was a self-educated and omnivorous reader, and he seems to have been a sort of animating spirit in the group's meetings at The Eagle and Child ("Bird and Baby") pub or in Lewis' rooms at Magdalen College. Lewis and Tolkien managed to secure a lectureship for him at the University. T.S. Eliot describes Williams lecturing—hopping about, perching on the desk, jingling coins in his pockets, and pouring out a torrent of coruscating prose. In one place, Eliot remarks that he looked somewhat like a monkey.

Williams also poured out books: poetry, literary criticism, theology, drama, and novels. It was his novels that gained him a modest measure of fame.

They are hardly novels in the ordinary sense. Eliot tried the category "metaphysical thrillers" to refer to them, and that is perhaps the closest anyone can come to describing

Reprinted with permission by CatholiCity, September 6, 2010.

them. The thing is, it turns out in each of his seven novels that heaven and hell lie under every bush.

This would seem to be a wild overstatement, of course. There may be grass or twigs or insects under the shrubbery: but heaven and hell?

Well, yes. The story will open, for example, at the rehearsal for a summer drama being put on by the local players' group. There is the usual bustle. The playwright, Peter Stanhope, is present, as it happens, and it very quickly becomes clear that he is an unusual man. There is none of the officiousness or self-importance that we might reasonably expect of such a key figure. He has been happy to oblige the group with a pastoral drama, if that is what they want (not perhaps his own preference); and he obliges them all, most especially the outspoken, opinionated, and self-assured producer, one Mrs. Parry, when it comes to the thousand potentially sticky details attending upon such a production. It turns out, as the action proceeds, that this modest and self-effacing pliability, far from suggesting anything flaccid or weak in Peter, arises from the tremendous well of Charity, that fountainhead of all virtues, in the depths of his being. It has been won at great cost to him, as the saints all testify.

Another character, the aged Margaret Anstruther, exhibits this same strong tranquility, and both she and Stanhope are called upon presently to come to the aid of the young and appealing Pauline Anstruther, who, it turns out, is being pursued by a *doppelganger*.

Obviously, the arrival of such a spectre on stage opens the whole scene out onto unmanageability, we might say. What happens in the ordinary, light-of-day foreground is occurring, clearly, against a mighty backdrop that reaches finally to heaven and hell—which, come to think of it, is the bald truth about our ordinary, light-of-day, mortal existence.

Christians know this, of course. The smallest detail—the lift of an eyebrow, say, by way of disparaging somebody—stands at the near end of a road that, if followed all the way, leads to hell, since hell is the place where the inhabitants all disparage each other. Quarrelling and disdain and wrath and treachery and fisticuffs and finally murder lie along that road. The other road, the way of Charity, leads finally to everlasting Joy, and the milestones along that road are courtesy and self-forgetfulness and generosity and self-giving and eventually crucifixion.

We all know this. But we don't always think about it. And certainly the novels we read for our relaxation don't ordinarily punch through the scrim that lies between the commonplace exchanges of life and the domain where those exchanges loom in their true and final color. Envy, for example, often enough a merely passing mood, if habitually indulged, leads on to a parsimonious state of soul where self-forgetting delight is impossible. Or sloth: Just harmless little procrastinations and dawdlings whose final end, if indulged habitually, is a torpor of soul that finds itself unable to arise and respond to any call of duty; that way lies inanity, which is one of the properties of damnation.

Very ferocious stuff when one comes to ponder it all. But it lies about us hourly. The main character in this tale is one Wentworth. He is a respectable and aging historian. But he has gradually allowed jealousy of other scholars' work to supplant his original interest in history. He has become defensive, and thence surly, and thence misanthropical altogether. Anyone *else*—anybody at all—is a bore and a threat to him, except for one person, a young woman named Adele, who has awakened a fugitive flicker of romantic interest in him. Here is the offer of an *other*—someone besides himself, who *might* become the occasion for his escaping this self-wrought cell of his. But no. So fiercely has he barred all other selves from his life that even the real selfhood of Adele turns sour for him, especially when it turns out that she has now become interested in a nice young fellow named Hugh. Wentworth has lost her. But now, instead of making the admittedly difficult effort of wishing them well, or of *trying* to wish them well, he retreats into sullenness and malice, and presently finds that he prefers an imaginary, undemanding Adele—a ghost who whispers sweet nothings to him—to the flesh-and-blood Adele. He refuses offer after offer of kindness from others, and finally opts for bitter solitude—that is to say, hell. (The title of the novel is *Descent into Hell.*)

In all seven of his novels, Williams raises the stakes in this unnerving way. Surely it's all unpardonably far-fetched—until one pauses and reflects. Is it perhaps cold realism? Either there are everlasting consequences that follow upon everything I think and say and do, or there are not. Sacred Scripture and the Church would seem to suggest that there are.

Williams' Use of Arthurian Materials

The danger that arises when people get to talking together about the work of Charles Williams is that, unless everyone watches out, the tone will soon enough slip into gobbledygook. A special vocabulary, used by the insiders with the other insiders. The cognoscenti talking to the illuminati.

This is an understandable enough danger, but nonetheless a danger. How on earth are we to *avoid* sounding like a lot of peeping, twittering initiati, when the very terms of our discourse force us to trot out a whole bundle of phrases and nouns like "coinherence", "This also is Thou ... neither is This Thou", The Incarnacy, the Golden Ambiguity, the two-natured Deivirilis, Byzantium, Logres, the porphyry stair, largesse, the Acts of Identity, the Hallows, and so forth. There, if there ever was one, is the argot of a mystery cult.

But no. The way out of this bog is right there in front of us. If we suppose that Williams is primarily interested in arcana, the occult, and the Eleusinian, we mistake him wholly. He is not the high priest of a mystery cult. He is, always and everywhere, a man of the plain, light-of-day, meat-and-potatoes, workaday world.

It is not for nothing that so many of his important characters (Peter Stanhope, Sybil Coningsby, the Archdeacon, Anthony, Jonathan, and Dinadan), for all their sanctity (no other word will quite serve), for all their sanctity, have,

Originally published in *Mythlore* (May 1978): 6–10. Reprinted with permission.

nonetheless, a certain wry, dry, slightly amused, self-deprecating "nonreligiousness" about them. You don't find yourself all entangled in tortuous spells and dark mumbo-jumbo when you follow these people: You find yourself bang out in the plain light of day, where people chuckle and light cigarettes and stretch their long legs luxuriously out in lawn chairs and so forth. The only Sibyl in Williams spends her time baking cakes and taking hot baths and reading by the fire in her brother's house.

For Williams, all this peculiar matter he lays hold of is, always and only, to point us back to the plain path that any ordinary good people are plodding along anyway. It is not adeptness in the use of the Tarot pack that he nudges us toward, but adeptness in plain goodness. Even in his book entitled *Witchcraft*, he never once rouses in us any interest in the dark arts for themselves.

But then the obvious question arises, Why, then, does Williams write about peculiar stuff? Why does he reach into these odd corners for his materials?

The answer to this is to be found, it seems to me, by our looking to see what the task was that he had set himself in his poetry and fiction and drama.

There is one sense in which he set himself the same task that any poet or novelist or dramatist sets himself, namely, the rendering, as Joseph Conrad put it, of the highest possible justice to the visible stuff of experience (I haven't quoted it correctly, but that is the gist of what Conrad said). Any poet has got, when the chips are down, to take his materials from the world of our experience; and one way or another, he has got to give that world of experience back to us in forms that make us sit up and take notice, perhaps for the first time in our lives. A case can be made out to show that Williams shares with James and Conrad and Lawrence and Joyce and any other modern novelist the effort to render a faithful accounting of ordinary human experience. That a novel is difficult or bizarre (say *Finnegan's Wake*, or *Mrs. Dalloway*) is no indication that it concerns difficult or bizarre *subjects*. Both of those novels, if we may call them that, are about very ordinary experience. The bizarre quality that we find in them is part of the novelist's technique to boost us, all sunk as we are in torpor and cliché, toward a fresh grasp on experience.

It is thus with Williams' novels—and his drama and poetry. Every line that he wrote, we might argue, had the end in view of putting our ordinary experience in some sort of clear light. A faithful rendering of human experience.

But Williams tackled a particularly difficult part of the whole task—a part that very few poets (and we may call him a poet from now on, I should think, both in the broad sense of a *maker* of imaginative literature, and in the narrower sense of a writer of verse, since it is his verse that we are thinking about mainly here)—a part that very few poets tackle. He undertook to give some sort of perceptible shape to sheer charity, or, put another way, to the motions of grace in human experience. That is the next thing to impossible for a poet to do. Auden has spoken of the difficulty of this task, and Eliot has. Eliot commented in his introduction to one of the editions of *All Hallows Eve* that the task Williams had set himself would not yield itself easily to the novelist's art, and perhaps not to any conceivable mode of art (again, my quote is not exact, but it is close enough). We have only to look at the annals of poetry to see how difficult this task is: Dante perhaps came as close to bringing it off as anyone, but how successful, actually, is his picture of the final bliss? Nobody has ever gotten any closer than Dante to giving poetic utterance to the state of grace, or bliss as that state eventually becomes;

but there is something about that state of affairs that eludes the poet's office, just as it eludes the theologians' office, or even the evangelist's office (Saint John the Divine had to try every conceivable image in order to come at what he was writing about, and even then found himself mute and on his face). Milton had a bash at it, in his pictures of the bliss that the Son and the Father knew before the rebellion in heaven, and in his pictures of Eden. (I realize that neither of these two scenes is, theologically, to be called the state of grace, but the category is the same. The state of grace is the state in which we fallen men begin to encounter again those vast and terrible blisses.) We applaud Milton, but I suppose all of us who read *Paradise Lost* are *least* satisfied with precisely these scenes.

The difficulty that poets have in finding ways of articulating these high reaches of human experience raises a piquant question: What *is* the office of the poet? It is clearly not synonymous with the offices of either priest or prophet. Poetry is not a sacrament, and it is not quite prophecy, either, although poetry like *Four Quartets* (and, I should think we might ever so shyly suggest, Taliessin) certainly sails close to the prophetic wind. But no poet can, without overweening pride, preface his word to us with a naked "Thus saith the Lord." Taliessin himself knew that the office of the poet was, precisely, superfluous.

But we must come to the topic. What use did Williams make of the Arthurian materials in his poetry? Or, just before we ask that one, we are asking *why* Williams used the Arthurian materials.

He used them, for a start, because he *liked* them. He liked Malory. And that whole world of high courtesy, of vision, of sacrament, and of ceremony, appealed enormously to him, and that is a good enough warrant for any poet when he is looking about for materials.

But that isn't the whole story. He liked all this because, among other things, the Matter of Britain held rich possibilities for Williams' whole vision of things. Nay, that is putting it far too mildly. It isn't as though Williams came along and said "Here, let me pull this out, and this, and this, and see what I can do with these rich stuffs." Rather, it is as though he, like Taliessin, came upon a shell into which the stone fit perfectly. Or again, we might say his invention (in the old sense) of the Arthurian materials was an Act of Identity—a case in point, that is, of the happy union of form and matter that we find in a thousand images all through his poetry: geometry and passion; the Empire and Broceliande; Gaul and Logres; all caught into the figure of the Graal itself. That is, the events in the Arthurian narratives, and the figures who move in those events, *were* the enfleshing of the vision that Williams saw.

But, we object here, that's not quite true. Gildas, and Nennius, and old Geoffrey of Monmouth, to say nothing of Chretien de Troyes, Robert de Borron, and Mallory himself, or even Tennyson and Swinburne—these gentlemen never for a moment dreamed of anything like the construction that the twentieth-century poet Williams was going to give to these materials. Surely this is a wholly private, and peculiar, not to say unwarranted, handling of all these events? Mount Badon, and the Round Table, and Lancelot and Guinevere, and Camelot and Caerleon and Carbonek—where is the warrant for the extraordinary use to which Williams put these things?

I think Williams would have replied (and I think he would have had the backing of Lewis, his most successful commentator) that, so far from doing violence to the Matter of Britain, this latest working of the Arthuriad brings the Matter along one more step in the way it is already going. Or, to change the figure here, Williams imposes nothing *on* the Matter from outside: Rather, he arrays the Matter in such a pattern that hitherto unsuspected significances emerge. In virtually every case, it seems to me that Williams submits himself to what is *there*. He works, we might say, in obedience to his masters in the school of the poets.

But this question of *why* Williams uses these materials still has one thread dangling. The obvious objection to a twentieth-century poet's choosing to work with the Matter of Britain, and particularly to involve that Matter with Byzantium, is that nobody has a clue about all of that any more. The charge of mere obscurantism and nostalgia might be levelled at the Williams Arthuriad.

But, to catch up this thread, it seems to me we need only point out that, as Henry James insisted, we must grant the poet his *donnée*. The problem comes, not with *what* he chooses for his matter, but with his handling of the stuff, and also with our capacity to respond. For example, Flannery O' Connor tried to write about things that precious few contemporary writers of fiction know anything about (she wrote about grace, too, let's face it). So she chooses rural Georgia and populates her landscape with freaks and misfits. All very grotesque. But she brings it off. The world she evokes for us is 100 percent unimportant and irrelevant to the rest of us as it were, but alas it turns out to be the whole world caught in a span, albeit a very odd span. Again, Tolkien drops into the middle of the whole twentieth century literary scene with an outrageously atavistic scenario: *elves*, forsooth! and *dwarfs!* What would Henry James say, for heaven's sake? Or F. R. Leavis? But old Tolkien just went on spinning his tale, and we're all jolly well going to have to take this stuff into account when we get down to giving an overview of twentieth-century literary history. And Lewis: He cooks up an unabashed child's garden of fantasy and serves it up to us from his rooms at Magdelene. What is the man doing?

They are doing exactly what any serious teller of tales does: They are telling us stories that are true. They want their tale to be *dulce et utile*, sweet and useful. And, if the materials that lie close by won't serve, then they reach out to find some materials that *will* serve. If the story they want to tell us is going to involve majesty, and they can't get any majesty out of the imagery of chairpersons and ad hoc committees of the whole, then they are going to have to have kings with golden crowns on in their stories. If valor is of the essence of their tale, and they can't wring the idea of valor out of the imagery of denim and pot and beads, then they are going to have to reach away for knights in armor, or hobbits in mithril, or Ransom interposing himself physically between the Green Lady and the Un-man. Or, if they need virginity in there and can't find it in the imagery of liberated swingers, they may have to introduce the figure of an elven princess named Arwen Pvenstar, about whose virginal femininity no question can be asked. The tellers of tales may, in other words, have to reach away with a long reach in order to find materials adequate to the story they have in their heads.

There was something that Williams wanted to say; and there was the Matter of Britain; the latter embodied with almost perfect success the vision that Williams had. Hence he reached for that Matter. He astonished us, we might say, by hailing us with the banners of Logres, when we were almost blinded by the banners of contemporaneity. He sang sweetly to us with his lyre, piercing ears well-nigh deafened by internal combustion engines and jazz.

I think that this is *why* he chose Arthuriana.

But what about what he did with it?

In the first place, he had a sure warrant from tradition for what he did. As of Geoffrey of Monmouth, the Matter of Britain became, as it were, the poet's domain, as the Matter of Greece and the Matter of Rome and the Matter of France had done before. It is not, however, as though everyone suddenly had carte blanche to do whatever he pleased with the materials. It is, rather, as though there was asked a twofold warrant for permission to come at them: First, one had to be a poet; and second, one had to swear fealty to the sovereignty of the materials themselves. That is, one had no warrant to come in with scissors and paste and pull everything to bits and rearrange everything into one's own Arthurian scrapbook. Just as the stories of Achilles or of Aeneas possessed an integrity that is not to be pillaged, so the story of Arthur. You have, as it were, to submit yourself to the sovereignty of the tale itself if you propose to try your hand at telling it once more. Williams did this, I think.

Perhaps the easiest way for us to come at the question of what Williams did with these materials is to itemize a few of the major images, or themes, that appear in his Arthuriad. The best way, of course, would be for me to put this paper away and pull out the two little volumes, and get somebody here—some bard—to read to us. That is always the best way with poetry. That's what it's for. Papers about poetry are a second-rate affair at best. But nonetheless, here we go.

For a start, the mere *geography* matters infinitely, in Williams' handling of the tale. The earlier poets had, of course, had the events happening somewhere—but that is about all it was: somewhere. There were forests and cities and chapels. But the map wasn't all that exact, we might say. Not so with Williams. All of a sudden, it is necessary to have a wholly exact picture of just where everything is. It is not enough to say that Merlin or Percivale headed into the woods. You have got to know that they headed *west*, into *this* wood, that lies between Logres and the sea, and that beyond *a certain part* of the wood lies Carbonek, and farther than that lie Sarras and also the Antipodean Sea. Again, you can't just have Taliessin coming down the road. He is headed south on this road, and on his *right* is the wood again, and on his *left* is a place called Britain. And so it goes, all the way through. The location of Gaul, and of Rome, and of Caucasia, and of Jerusalem, matter, not just because they are where cartographers put them on maps, but because they exhibit, by their exact placement and relation to each other, the pattern of the whole vision.

The key place is, of course, Byzantium. Byzantium is, on one level, an element that Williams introduced *de novo* into the tale. But it fits, historically, geographically, and poetically. Byzantium was, in fact, *there*. And an idea of sacred majesty, and of ritual exactitude, that no one who reads two lines about Byzantium can miss, is there and nourishes, as it were, the very thing that the Round Table and the Grail were about (even before Williams came along). That is, the center point of the whole Byzantine phenomenon was the sacred liturgy, and the thing that is enacted and exhibited in that liturgy is an idea of coinherence—of substitution and exchange. We may owe this particular vocabulary to Williams: But nobody can argue that he *made up* the idea. If the divine liturgy is not about that, it is about nothing. So Byzantium. But then there is the Round Table. Here, even before Williams came along, as I say, there was an idea of substitution and exchange: The knights were to pledge themselves—in a bond of acknowledged coinherence, if you like—to good works—works done for the sake of the Kingdom. (More than the Voice is the Vision, the Kingdom than the King—or than the Knight.) And, without stretching history too much, we may say that the Britain of Arthur, if it knew its international politics well enough, did owe its eventual fealty to Byzantium. The sacred liturgy celebrated in Hagia Sophia *did* nourish the exchanges of the Round Table.

And the particular idea of ritual exactitude. From Williams we find the new vocabulary of logothetes, and themes of empire, and of the porphyry stair. But again, these items are, in fact, historical (I'm not 100 percent sure that the steps to the throne of the Sacred Emperor were *porphyry*, but I bet they were); and this vision of the Empire, all humming and speeding in obedience to the Will of the Sacred Emperor—what is Byzantium about if not that? What empire has there ever been in whose politics and diplomacy we can see more precisely and splendidly exhibited the pattern of the Glory that almost settled on Logres? To have Taliessin travel down to Byzantium is entirely permissible: After all, palmers went all the way to Jerusalem.

But it is not merely a terrestrial geography at work. Everything that rises must converge; and the diagram of Empire here in Europe rises to the sphere of Venus, the Region of the Summer Stars. There we find, coming to a hard and brilliant mathematical point, all the tracks along which the manifold images move. The City, the Empire, the Grail, the Round Table, Logres, Broceliande, Camelot, Caerleon, Carbonek, hazel, the golden and rose-creamed flesh, Iseult's forearm, the spine of the servant girl cranking water up from the well, the spear, Virgil's hexameters, and Taliessin's verse—they all speed along their tracks, calling antiphonally to each other; for they all move toward the one point, the Union, the Identity.

Broceliande is to my mind one of the most interesting places in Williams' Arthuriad. Anyone who has ever read *That Hideous Strength* will know something about Broceliande, although I can't remember that Lewis uses the word anywhere in that book. Bragdon Wood in Edgestow does not equal Broceliande, but the Merlin who emerges from

Bragdon and the Merlin coming out of Broceliande, are the same wizard. I recently glanced at one of the endless commentaries on Lewis and Williams, and the author of this one was suggesting that Broceliande is a sort of nexus between flesh and spirit, or between the seen and the unseen world. That is wrong. It is no such thing. Williams would start up from his coffin with cries of "gnosticism!" and "Manichaeanism!" if he heard us burbling on with that idea. The great division in Williams (and in Lewis) is not between matter and spirit at all: It is between the City and the denial of the City; or between heaven and hell; or between caritas and cupiditas; or between coinherence and the denial of coinherence. There are a hundred ways of phrasing it, but matter vs. spirit is not one of them. Both realms entail the whole of nature and archnature; that is to say, all of us, good and bad, Galahad and Mordred, Saint Michael the Archangel and Beelzebub, move in a universe that exists under the modalities of matter and spirit, and we have all got to come to terms with things one way or another. If we make a grab and press the possibilities of both flesh and spirit to our own ends of knowledge, ecstasy, and power, then we serve the headless emperor. We short-circuit the pattern. We rip the web. We deny the coinherence. Thus Nigel Considine, Giles Tumulty, Simon the Clerk, Wentworth, Mordred, and the rest of us insofar as we manage to fend off, in effect, Baptism. For that is what it is. We must die, not in a moment of gnostic illumination, but in the cold, wet element water. We must be sprinkled with the asperges of the Coinherence, as it were, if we will be saved.

Broceliande must be sprinkled. In that dark sea-wood lie all the potentialities of power—all the conjurations of nature; all biddings of ents and spirits and wights; all familiarity with the virtues of roots and herbs and leaves; all spells and mutterings. Power is there, certainly. The question is, who is calling it up? And for what end?

Is it Gandalf or Sarumen? Is it Bombadil or Old Man Willow? Is it Mr. Fisher-King or Wither? Is it the Archdeacon or Giles Tumulty? That is the part that matters. It is obedience to the whole rubric rather than the manipulation of part of the rubric. It is dancing clockwise rather than revolving anticlockwise. It is the Mass rather than the Black Mass.

The point is, Broceliande *will* yield up its secrets without asking who is knocking. Sarumen can conjure things up as well as Gandalf, Weston wields power as well as Ransom. Nay, there is the difference: Weston *wields* it: Ransom puts himself at the disposal of the Mercy, we might say, who alone has the warrant to wield the power. For we cannot even say that *mere* submission is quite right, since the whole trouble with nearly everyone but Antony in *The Place of the Lion* was that they had abandoned their adamic office, namely, the office of *ruling* Nature. Antony is the one who rides Pegasus. It is as bad to be the slave of Nature as to be the evil sorcerer of Nature. Neither relationship to Broceliande will do. Broceliande is there, the ancient seawood, misty, silent, and dark. But beyond a *part* of it lies Carbonek. You can *start* toward Carbonek that way, but it is perilous in the extreme, and your chances of getting there rather than floundering into the Antipodean Sea are slender. And nobody comes out unaffected.

But, just as Saint Anne's needs Merlin in the fight against Belbury, so Logres needs Merlin in the fight against chaos. The chaos comes from Broceliande (but then so did Merlin come from Broceliande); or it may come from the king's table itself; or even, alas, from the king's bed. Mordred; Lancelot and Guinevere; Lancelot and Elayne: What are we to say of these chaotic couplings? What account does Williams give of these unhappy events?

Williams is obedient enough to his materials not to try to deny anything that happened. It would be pure schmaltz, for example, if he decided to fumigate everything and turn the passion of Lancelot and Guinevere into intellectual nuptials. Lancelot was no Dante. He was no Taliessin. He went to *bed* with Guinevere. And, as if that weren't enough adultery, he then violated his pledge to Guinevere and bedded Elayne. And not only that, but he begat a son of Elayne, Chaos. Perfidy. Concupiscence. The tearing of the fabric.

But Williams believes in redemption. He believes, we might say, in transubstantiation—that gracious and salvific action by the Mercy in which, not only the plain stuff of our poor lives—our bread and wine, as it were—but also the messes we have made of things (the bread that we have burnt, say, and the sour wine) can be changed into the Body of Glory. *All* exchange stands on the hither side of Gomorrah. *Any* coupling, therefore, has at least some rag of acknowledgment of the *other.* (Wentworth finally slid down the rope alone, remember: I do not think even his succubus accompanied him there.) There is some poor, dim flake of fire in the ash of our very concupiscence (in Lancelot's then) that can be raked out and blown upon by the Mercy and the agent of our purging. So Lancelot and Guinevere. Their passion is, precisely, passion, and hence holds within itself the potentiality of salvation as well of damnation. Luckily (Williams believed in holy luck), these two lovers are saved: Guinevere ends up in the convent, and Lancelot becomes a priest: Nay, the last we see of him, he is saying Mass: How so?

If anything in the whole Arthuriad was ever true, and if anything in Williams' vision (let us say, the catholic vision) is true, then we may expect to find these lovers saved. Ah, to be sure, the loss is real. There is no question of just smuggling scandal into a corner. The price is paid. Logres is riven. Arthur is dead. Myth drains into history. Alas, alas, and well-a-day: But Guinevere and Lancelot are saved from the ruin—and who of us hopes to be saved from any other state of affairs?

But then there is Lancelot's tryst with *Elayne*. What about that? Here we have, added to the smudgy situation of a double adultery, the further and intractable datum of *issue*. The lady has *conceived*, damn it all. Now we have a child to cope with (abortion on demand had not got through the moot in Camelot yet). So Galahad, How can we have the virginal High Prince come from this sordid stew?

Well, there are two things to be said. First, there is an analogy lying not far away. The High Prince, the Golden Ambiguity, the Incarnacy, Messias himself, came from a distinctly smudgy lineage (the Bible goes to some pains to make sure we've got it clear that *Rahab* is in there). Or again, to take another angle of the same analogy: The flesh that the Incarnacy took on himself was, precisely, *fallen* flesh—the flesh of the Adam. Shall we make the High Prince of Logres more immaculately conceived than the Prince of Glory?

And secondly, the thing that "saves" the situation, as it were, is an act of substitution. By a spell, Lancelot is made to believe that he has Guinevere in his arms. But it is Elayne who has been "substituted" for the queen. From this act of substitution and exchange, there issues the prince who achieved the Grail via the affirmative way of virginity.

But, we object, this is jiggery-pokery. Williams is being a wag here. There's no way we can accept this "cleaning up of the act", as it were. Well, then, Williams might say to us, you're going hell-for-leather toward Gomorrah, because if you don't accept a much bigger cleaning up of the act than this, you're refusing the whole Web of the Glory. You are denying the Acts of Identity. What else is in the cards *but* a cleaning up of the act by bizarre acts of exchange? *My* story is no more outrageous than *the* Story.

We do not see any such happy issue coming from Arthur's dark union with his sister, the sinister Morgause of Orkney. Here we have Mordred. Perfidy. Defeat. The wreck of Logres. And, we must admit, a terrible price *is* exacted. The uttermost farthing, we might say. But here again, two things may be observed in the tale. First, the last we see of Arthur, he is being taken graciously to Avalon, for the healing of his wounds, both the wounds, we might believe, received in his last battle with Mordred and the wounds on his inner being from his sin with Morgause. But secondly, Logres isn't completely wrecked. It is not the end of the tale. To be sure, the Glory draws away into Sarras once more, and history closes in on Logres so that you and I have only Britain in our schoolbooks. Even if we go to Glastonbury itself now, there are only tombs and tumbled foundations. *But*—has Logres been decimated? No. The glory is to be seen, now, in the household of Taliessin the poet. There we may see the lovely and courteous exchanges that were, so briefly, begun and enacted in the kingdom of Logres. There we may see the fellowship of holy men and women eating and drinking together, as the knights were to have eaten and drunk in fellowship around the Round Table. There we may see majesty, cloaked, to be sure, in the demure garb of the ordinary, but majesty nonetheless. And there we may see grace, decked now in the mien of a wife or a sister, walking without the panoply of trumpets and pearls. And there we may see coinherence, in all the plain rhythms of a house well-ordered.

But even the household is not to last as such. The permitted lieutenancy, borne for a while under the Mercy by Taliessin, is withdrawn, at least in any visible sense. Now the company will be simply the company of any and all holy souls who walk in the way of Caritas; they will recognize each other always and greet each other nobly. But passersby will no longer see the house, nor will travelers pass across any discernible borders into the kingdom. The kingdom is abroad now, in the hearts of the company.

Is Williams being fanciful? Surely he has a threefold warrant for this denouement? For one thing, the tale itself furnishes such a warrant. After the withdrawal of the principal characters into Sarras, what are we to say of the events? Shall we close the book and drop a nineteenth-century tear, moved to luxurious wistfulness by the remoteness and splendor of it all? We may do that. It has been done. But if we press the tale to its end, will we not find the *track* of the events left on history, no matter how faintly? Remember, Aeneas came to Rome, and the Brut came to Britain. Those old stories did feed out into history.

But secondly, Williams has once more a gold-plated *analogy*, and once more it is found, not just in some tale of Oz, but in *the* Story. A kingdom was announced, and it seemed to come very close, briefly, with angels and Magi attending it. But then perfidy and wreck intervened, and it all apparently disappeared, leaving us stabbed with wistfulness, staring at the golden blur it left behind. Except that there was a small company who met at table and who, we discover, wore the mantles of that kingdom. The household was in some unlikely place like Bethany probably, or maybe Jerusalem. But then even that company scattered, and now where is the story? Well, the *analogy* ends there, but we may at least not say that Williams had no warrant in the annals of narrative for pressing the events through, beyond what may have seemed the final curtain.

But his third warrant, surely, would be plain human life itself? And now we are back at the original point I was urging: Williams is always writing very plain, very workaday stuff. He is not a writer of fancy, or of escape, or of the occult. I had a dangerous quarrel on this point with a man, an enormously famous scholar, during my defense of my dissertation at New York University. I say it was dangerous because of course he held all the trumps, at least the trumps that would decide whether N.Y.U. was going to give me my degree or not. But I had the greater trumps, I think. His point was that I ought to have linked Williams in with Arthur Machen and A. E. Waite, and Edgar Cayce, in my dissertation. He said I hadn't done my homework. But my point was that these were the gentlemen whom I most emphatically did not want to link Williams in with. I wanted to link him in with the serious writers of fiction in the twentieth century, not, of course, because Williams' novels *looked* like James' and Conrad's and Virginia Woolf's; but rather because both he and they were passionately interested in doing justice to the texture of plain, daily life. None of them invites us *away* from ordinary life. It is superficial in the extreme to talk of Williams as a writer of the occult.

Which brings me back to this third warrant I was talking about—the warrant that Williams had for pursuing the tale beyond the withdrawal of vision, out into the light of our plain life in history. Williams avoided three traps that he might easily have fallen into at the end. He might have left it at mere vision and the withdrawal thereof, which would have been sentimental; or he might have had the whole thing fall apart in merely sordid disintegration, which would have been modern; or he might have wrapped it all up tidily and reflected on it, which would have been moralistic.

But he did none of these, because none of these is true. Williams always has plain human life for his touchstone. How *does* life work? How *shall* we speak truly about our existence? If there is a worthy syllable in the whole of the Arthuriad, then we shall find that this final picture of Logres as being offered, as it were, to whomever will care to be one of the company, is very much of the essence. It is of the essence of plain life, and of Williams' handling of the materials, since all the images, splendid or small, rise to that point among the summer stars which so far from being remote from us, is, alas, the point where we must find ourselves or else choose Gomorrah. These images—Bors, Percivale, and Galahad; Camelot, Caerleon, and Carbonek; Arthur, Lancelot, and Merlin; hazel, roses, and gold-creamed flesh: Is there a single one of them that is not in our laps right now, so to speak? Is there one of them that is otiose? One of them that beckons us *away* from the life we find in our offices and kitchens and along the freeways of California? If Logres is not to decide our attitude in a traffic jam, then of course Gomorrah will, and we will join the angry, honking imbroglio. If the Grail does not nourish us, then the bitter drink of P'o-l'u will, and we will find ourselves cutting into ticket lines and grabbing seats on subways and generally demanding our rights with a shrill and testy voice.

The final piquance about Williams' Arthuriad is, of course, that he would, with a wry twist at the corner of his mouth and a merry glint in his eye, tell us that the whole work is superfluous. The divine largesse didn't *have* to have Williams to tell us this story, any more than Arthur had to have Taliessin to command that charge at Mount Badon. Another would have served. But what a lovely thing it is that, in the plenitude of that largesse, Williams *was*, in fact, chosen to sing us these songs. We will miss that largesse wholly if we suppose that these songs are anything more than songs about Something Other and even more splendid than themselves.

Granting Charles Williams His *Donnée*

In his introduction to Charles Williams' last novel, T. S. Eliot says this:

> What he had to say was beyond his resources, and probably the resources of language, to say once for all through one medium of expression.... What it is, essentially, that he had to say comes near to defying definition. It was not simply a philosophy, a theology or a set of ideas: it was primarily something imaginative.[1]

Williams is a peculiar figure in English letters. His poetry is altogether incomprehensible without a mastery of his odd handling of the Byzantine Empire and Logres as images of order, and his novels evoke a world on the frontier between the pedestrian and the preternatural that is unsettling to readers accustomed to the tradition of the English novel. John Heath-Stubbs places Williams in the tradition of Christian transcendentalism along with Spenser, Vaughan, Coleridge, and Patmore.[2]

Nearly every commentator on Williams finds that he must come to terms with the difficulty of Williams' work.

Originally published in *Mythlore* 28 (Summer 1981): 13–14. Reprinted with permission.

[1] T. S. Eliot, "Introduction", in Charles Williams, *All Hallows Eve* (London, 1945), pp. xi, xiii.

[2] John Heath-Stubbs, Charles Williams, no. 63 in *Writers and Their Work*, ed. Bonamy Dobree (London, 1955), pp. 8, 15.

Eliot, Auden, C.S. Lewis, Anne Ridler—they all confess this. The problem arises over placing Williams in any category that is useful to criticism and that does not exist for Williams alone.

Auden remarks,

> To begin with, (Williams) is interested, like Blake, in states of being, rather than individuals, and fiction is not an ideal medium for describing such. Secondly, it is virtually impossible to describe the state of grace artistically, because to this state, the capacity of the individual soul for expression is irrelevant.... In describing the state of damnation this problem does not arise, and I know of no other writer, living or dead, who has given us so convincing and terrifying portraits of damned souls as Charles Williams.[3]

If anyone ever saw the fear in a handful of dust, it was Williams. There was nothing—no epiglottis or ventricle, no chance remark, no natural phenomenon, no social convention—that did not signal everything to him. And this briskly energetic vision of his determined his literary technique. It issued, for one thing, in an astonishing, even jolting, juxtaposition of situations, characters, and images, so that in one novel we find a chase for the Holy Grail carried on over the fields of Hertfordshire, and in another a blizzard roused by the Tarot cards, and in another archetypal lions and butterflies appearing in Oxford. There are satanists and doppelgangers and succubi and wizards consorting with dons and clerks and housewives. The imagery may switch with no warning from the curve of a girl's arm resting on a table to the Byzantine Empire, the assumption being that, in the end, they come to the same thing.

[3] W. H. Auden, "Introduction", in Charles Williams, *The Descent of the Dove* (New York, 1956), pp. vii, viii.

In all of Williams' work, we find order (that is to say, fact, bliss, and liberty) fighting whatever tends toward disorder (that is to say, illusion, horror, and bondage). This conflict may be read on the psychological, the social, the moral, or the metaphysical level. What is true of one realm is true of all, on Williams' view. He himself, of course, understood this order to have been supremely unveiled and enacted on the stage of our own history in the events of the Christian Gospel. But one does not have to believe in a geographical hell, so to speak, to see as trenchant Williams' picture of hell as the realm marked by ennui, irritation, myopia, incoherence, obscenity, fragmentation, cupidity, and aimlessness; or to agree that Williams' exploration of the attitudes and actions that lead toward this realm is frightening in its accuracy.

The focus is on states of being, as Auden has suggested, and this is not really what one thinks of as the province of the modern novel. One has only to read a Williams novel to see immediately that he has here something not quite at home in the tradition of Fielding, Jane Austen, George Eliot, and Henry James. It would be hard to find points, other than the general category "English prose narrative", at which Williams and these novelists could be discussed together.

At several points, Williams' novels depart obviously from the tradition of the English novel. To begin with, the English novel has ordinarily pursued its course by following the movement toward self-awareness of a central figure (Clarissa, Becky, Emma, Dorothea, Pip, Jude, Isabel). It is only in his last two novels that Williams achieves anything at all like this.

Again, the tradition is a mundane one. That is, its purlieu has commonly been this plain world, as opposed to Paradise, Helicon, or Xanadu. Williams' novels do not fit here.

In his stories, shutters blow open in the flimsy wall between our light-of-day ordinariness and the abyss. Elemental conflicts are aroused, as they were in *Macbeth*, by someone's or something's suddenly peering over the windowsill or rattling onto the floor (a talisman with the Tetragrammaton in it, say). Whereas a tightly woven pattern of believable events conspires to nudge Isabel Archer to a more sober view of what personal freedom may mean, Williams' Damaris Tighe is bundled along toward a similar sobriety by archetypal lions and pterodactyls.

Then there is the question of sheer subject matter: These states of being that Auden speaks of; can we accept them as worthy or credible topics for the modern novel? That is, how can a world whose intellectual climate is a doctrinaire post-Enlightenment and post-Freudian one read this sort of thing and find it at all compelling? It is one thing to read Dante or Langland and accept their frame of reference. After all, they were writing of their own world, and we may grant their point of view. But surely there is something disingenuous about a writer who turns to ancient categories and asks us to accept them as credible indices of contemporary life.

We no longer, for example, find the notion of blasphemy to be a very useful one, since the idea of the sacred has disappeared from our world officially, and where there is no sacred mystery, there can be no blasphemy. How, then, can we follow with any interest a character who is guilty of blasphemy? The question is, of course, at least answered for us by the analogy of the Greek myths; we do not suppose that Zeus will be found on Olympus, or that Odin is in Asgard. But we find the stories about them perennially true. Or again, most of the world would not now accept Milton's angelology, but his figure of Satan will last as long as the English language lasts, if not because Satan exists in hell, then at least because he exists in Milton's poem.

So that, if we complain of Williams' work that it evokes a world that disappeared with the Enlightenment, we must ask whether he can show us that what occurs in that world is as true as what occurred on Mount Purgatory or in Eden. If he cannot, then that is his failure as an artist, not as a believer.

Henry James' conditions for the novel may serve to help place Williams in some relation to the tradition of English fiction. James says, "The only reason for the existence of a novel is that it does attempt to represent life." He insists that the novelist is "occupied in looking for the truth."[4] Here, of course, Williams may be given full marks, for it was his whole artistic effort to get a distance and an angle from which we may be given the clearest possible picture of human action. All of Williams' manipulation of time and the preternatural was with the one idea in mind of gaining this distance and angle so that the truth of experience as he saw it might be thrown into stark relief.

James goes on: "The only obligation to which in advance we may hold a novel, without incurring the accusation of being arbitrary, is that it be interesting." Now this would seem at first to open the door indiscriminately to every kind of thing, as do James' further comments: "The execution belongs to the author alone.... The advantage, the luxury, as well as the torment and responsibility of the novelist, is that there is no limit to what he may attempt as an executant—no limit to his possible experiments, efforts, discoveries, successes.... We must grant the artist his subject, his idea, his *donnée*...."[5]

In this connection we may include Wellek and Warren's commentary:

[4] Henry James, "The Art of Fiction", in Henry James, *The Future of the Novel*, ed. Leon Edel (New York, 1956), p. 5.

[5] Ibid., pp. 10, 17.

> The reality of a work of fiction ... is not necessarily or primarily a reality of circumstance or detail or commonplace routine. By all of these standards, writers like Howells or Gottfried Keller put to shame the writers of *Oedipus Rex*, *Hamlet*, and *Moby Dick*. Verisimilitude in detail is a means to illusion, but often is used, as in *Gulliver's Travels*, as a decoy to entice the reader into some improbable or incredible situation which has "truth to reality" in some deeper than circumstantial sense.[6]

David Daiches has an interesting observation about a peculiar problem for twentieth-century practitioners of prose fiction, and we may see Williams in this light. Daiches has been speaking of the English novelists as selecting their materials from a pool of publicly shared principles as to what human life is all about. "The modern novelist is born when that publicly shared principle of selection and significance is no longer felt to exist, and can no longer be depended upon."[7] He goes on to canvass the efforts of Virginia Woolf, Joyce, Conrad, and Lawrence to overcome this collapse of this public edifice of suppositions about life. "The great surge of experimentation fiction which went on in the 1920's and 1930's was in large measure caused by the novelists' search for devices that would enable them to solve the problem of the breakdown of a public sense of significance each in his own way. All the novelists mentioned brought some of the techniques of poetry into prose fiction."[8]

Both Arnold Kettle and F.R. Leavis give some space to what they both call the "moral fable". Leavis includes *Hard Times* and *The Europeans* in this category, and Kettle

[6] Rene Wellek and Austin Warren, *Theory of Literature* (New York, 1956), p. 202.

[7] David Daiches, *The Novel and the Modern World* (Chicago, 1960), p. 5.

[8] Ibid., pp. 5–6.

includes *Gulliver's Travels* and *Jonathan Wild*. Kettle says this: "... in the moral fable the central discovery seems to have been made by the author prior to his conception of the book. In other words, the fable-writer starts off with his vision, his moral 'truth,' and, so to speak, tries to blow life into it.... The danger is that it will be limited in an unfortunate way by having to illustrate something else rather than develop freely by its own laws of growth."[9]

This is exactly what Williams was up against in the task he set himself, and in the course of his seven novels there is manifest his movement from mere "illustration" to something that could stand in its own right because it developed freely by its own laws of growth.

Leavis says this: "I need say no more by way of defining the moral fable than that in it the intention is peculiarly insistent, so that the representative significance of everything in the fable—character, episode, are so immediately apparent as we read."[10]

It was with this intention that Williams struggled. If the place of Charles Williams in the annals of English language fiction is ever to be determined along disinterested lines (and this means that neither his fans nor those who would dismiss him as a writer of the occult may be permitted a merely *prima facie* case), then an early task of Williams criticism will be to establish firmly that his subject, his *donnée*, in no way excludes him from serious discussion. We must grant him his Logres, his Tarot pack, and his Grail, on exactly the same grounds that we grant Shakespeare his ghost or Melville his whale or Keats his *belle dame sans merci*.

After that, of course, comes the hard question: How well did he do?

[9] Arnold Kettle, *An Introduction to the English Novel*, vol. 1 (New York, 1960), pp. 17–18.

[10] F. R. Leavis, *The Great Tradition* (New York, 1967), p. 227.

The Barber Shop

Our local barber shop is run by a cheery woman named Pearl who knows everyone in town. She waves at them all as they walk past the big window where you sit to have your hair cut.

Pearl's assistant is Ethel. Some months ago, I noticed a Bible in an open cupboard at her end of the working shelf in front of the barber chairs. When the chance presented itself, I asked, "Are you interested in the Bible?"

That opened the sluices—a great fountain of delighted incredulity that a local duffer should pick up on a topic that does not commonly form the coinage of chat in the shop. Oh, yes! The Bible is the most interesting thing in the world! There's so much *in it*!

What had particularly flagged down her attention was all the business in Genesis about the Nephilim—sometimes translated "giants". Who were these "sons of God" who "came in to" the daughters of men?

Certainly we have all been titillated by that exiguous reference. Ethel had on hand several further books that picked up on this strange tale and pursued it on to what used to be called "British Israelism". The idea here is that the Anglo-Saxons are the Ten Lost Tribes. Ethel was very excited about it all. Perhaps *we* are among that lost Chosen! (I have only the sketchiest picture as to how widely this "Saxon"

Reprinted with permission by CatholiCity, May 4, 2009.

net is to be cast. Does it encompass all Teutons? Nordics? Aryans? Who?)

Presently she registered a certain diffidence, indicating with rolling eyes and bobbing head that she was not entirely comfortable with our going on about the topic in the shop.

The next time I was in the shop, there were only the two of us. When she discovered that I am a believing Catholic, the fountain opened again. Talk ranged from the Nephilim to the Lost Tribes to the apocalypse and the antichrist. She was agog that I seemed to know all about everything that she brought up.

Intermittently I'd ease in a hint about how the real point of the whole drama is the Incarnation of the Savior. I am not much of a Christian "witness", however. I find refuge in C. S. Lewis' remark, made in a letter to one of his correspondents who had asked him about this sort of effort: "Concerning putting one's Christian point of view to doctors and other unpromising people ...", he began. I took the remark for my own ensign.

Ethel is always glad when I turn up, even though it is Pearl who cuts my hair. The note struck is very much that here we are—fellow Christian believers.

The whole business has set me to thinking about faith and its endless variations. Only God knows what constitutes faith. Curiosity about the Nephilim: Surely it's a start? Not everyone has sat at the feet of Bonaventure, Saint Francis de Sales, or Pope Benedict XVI. Who knows what, finally, constitutes the faith that is asked of us mortals? A biblical scholar at Tubingen in the nineteenth century, for example, who knows his Hebrew and Greek, and whose busy task is to purge Sacred Scripture of any taint of the miraculous: Is his faith—what is left of it—received by the Most High as salvific? For him, the stories of creation, Red Sea, incarnation, and resurrection are fairy tales.

When is faith *not* faith? What, exactly, is the faith of your toothless, mumbling Balkan crone in a black babushka? I have a friend who has left the Protestant Fundamentalism of his youth, with all of its exultation in the great drama of Incarnation, Passion, and Resurrection, to the view that the whole thing comes to nothing at all but (in his words) "spreading Shalom". The Paschal Mystery is to be given a wide berth. Scriptural documents are untrustworthy anyway. He now wonders if there is a God at all.

Only God can assess this sort of thing. What interior struggles with honest doubt lie in a man, and what tincture of any culpable decision to jettison the Faith—such matters are reserved to the Divine Mercy to decide upon.

And what of good people clapping and sweating in dingy Sunday night chapels, innocent of the things that would appear essential to a Catholic visitor? Or, for that matter, what of Catholics who line up in a hangdog way for Communion and who, if you asked them about the Faith, would say, "What?" Or the happy-Jack-squirrel folks who can quote volleys of Scripture but who seem never to have paused long enough to ask, "Who art Thou, Lord?" Or the centuries of those lonely Japanese who kept a lambent flame alive after the Portuguese missionaries were all slaughtered and who seemed to have only the dimmest inklings as to what their residual set of observances meant?

Or what about oneself? Is there a rag of integrity in one's profession?

That, alas, is the only question that will be asked of one at the Last Tribunal. It gives one pause.

Augustine's Pears

I am reading Saint Augustine's *Confessions* these days, for the second or third time. The whole thing is a great antidote for all that is confused and squalid about our own epoch, but more particularly for the sloth and folly that marks one's own inner being.

The book itself is an astonishing thing. You find this out in the first line. It is an autobiography, to be sure, and there are thousands of them. But this one astonishes us because the whole thing is addressed *to God*. It is a prayer. When you come to think of it, though, what possible other audience should an autobiography have? How can I possibly give an account of my life that has any rag of integrity in it if I am not laying it out before the "Thou" who made me, who knows every thought of mine before I think it, who is not allured by the whole muddy palette of self-display that marks the thing, and who alone can rescue me from my own fatuity? In the light of such a book as this, the ordinary enterprise of autobiography is thrown into odd relief.

Besides all of this, a reader finds himself agog at Augustine's fierce candor. Has there ever been such remorseless self-scrutiny? Oh, to be sure, Samuel Pepys and Rousseau, and Harold Nicolson in his diaries, most certainly have gazed at themselves with great wit and intelligence. But it is always difficult to disentangle candor from exhibitionism

Reprinted with permission by CatholiCity, September 2, 2009.

when we mortals get to telling our own story. (I myself attempted such a piece when I was far too young, and I would expunge a great deal of it now if I could.) The note struck in Augustine's account is modesty in the service of a giant intelligence and a remorseless pursuit of the truth. He rejects the tactics that most of us might trot out in our own defense. Having chosen to spread the whole account before God, what else can he do?

The most famous anecdote in the account is the matter of the pear trees. If people know nothing of Augustine's pilgrimage and conversion, they know about the pears. And ordinarily, the incident is retailed with a certain amount of patronizing raillery: "Stealing *pears*, forsooth? When he was a mere boy? It was a prank, for heaven's sake! Why all the breast-beating?"

Anyone who gives more than a moment's heed to this response hasn't read the account. For what we have in the *Confessions* is an anatomy of sin. An anatomy: The word was current in the seventeenth century at least (Robert Burton's *Anatomy of Melancholy*) and referred to a systematic and narrow scrutiny of the topic in question. Burton, for example, wrings melancholia dry, so to speak, exhausting the varieties by which it afflicts us mortals. It is thus with Augustine. You totter away from each section of his work thunderstruck both at the brilliance with which he dissects the real nature of sin and at his fierce refusal to marshal the least scrap of self-defense ("Oh—we were just high-spirited boys!").

When it comes to the pears, Augustine lays bare (anatomizes) the true nature of the act:

> Yet I was willing to steal, and steal I did, although I was not compelled by any lack, unless it were the lack of a sense of justice or a distaste for what was right and a greedy love of doing wrong. For of what I stole I already had plenty,

> and much better at that, and I had no wish to enjoy the things I coveted by stealing, but only to enjoy the theft itself and the sin.... And now, O Lord my God, now that I ask what pleasure I had in that theft, I find that it had no beauty to attract me.... It did not even have the shadowy, deceptive beauty which makes vice attractive....

He goes on to canvass pride, ambition, cruelty, lust, inquisitiveness, stupidity, sloth, extravagance, covetousness, envy, anger, fear, and grief as possible excuses for committing some act of sin. He can find nothing at all to invoke in his own defense. "What was it, then, that pleased me in that act of theft? ... What an abomination! What a parody of life! What abysmal death! Could I enjoy doing wrong for no other reason than that it was wrong?"

Finally he gets to the miserable nub. He was craven. He went along with his pals: "To do it by myself would have been no fun.... For the sake of a laugh, a little sport, I was glad to do harm and anxious to damage another.... And all because we are ashamed to hold back when others say, 'Come on! Let's do it!'"

Where does this cold and implacable scrutiny leave my own confessions? How one rummages around for some contemptible "reason" for what one did or said or thought. I was taken off guard. I wasn't thinking. It was an impulse. I didn't really *mean* it. Surely one shouldn't magnify such a tiny item? Let's not get morbid here.

Well. The matter is worth pondering—not in the murky light of efforts, widespread now, designed to release us all from what Augustine obviously thought was culpability, but rather in the light of the Psalms and prophets, and the words of the Lord Himself. The Church offers us help in this daunting task of making a Confession that is something more than self-serving: "I am heartily sorry for having offended Thee", she prompts. The Anglicans in their sturdier days used to say, "We have offended against thy holy laws. We have left undone those things which we ought to have done; And we have done those things which we ought not to have done; And there is no health in us. But thou, O Lord, have mercy upon us, miserable offenders...."

Now *that* is a bit much, surely? For one thing, we're no longer comfortable with that sort of thing. Besides, "studies have shown ...".

What have studies shown? Did the patriarchs and prophets and psalmists get it all wrong? Did our Lord miss something? Has the Church been too severe a Mother?

Interestingly enough, to read the confessions in the Psalms, and to hear how the Lord in the Gospels speaks of the sins that bind us all, and to listen in on Augustine's frank scrutiny of his own sins, is not at all to be left in despair or self-loathing. Joy beckons. Freedom and health and dignity lie that way. Dante had it right: He called his poem *The Divine Comedy*, even though he draws us through the most onerous sequence of penitentiality in all of literature. Comedy in the highest sense rises above mere chuckles: It historically refers to any drama that ends in marriage. The marriage of the Lamb with His Spouse the Church is a comedy in Dante's sense. Hence comedy, lo and behold, is deeper and higher and mightier than tragedy, which ends in death, and which is most certainly the most profound utterance we mortals can make if the grave is the end.

So. Augustine and his *Confessions*. It is the record of how a man came to sheer joy. I happen to be writing this on the Feast of Saint Monica, Augustine's mother, who hung onto God's garments for years before her son turned to God. And for 1,700 years now, the faithful have found solace and hope in the fruit of her prayers—in the life of the man who became Saint Augustine.

The Carolina Wren and Others

Running across the back of my house here in Manchester, Massachusetts, there is a narrow porch leading to a deck that looks out onto a lawn surrounded by hemlocks and rhododendron. My father was an amateur ornithologist—he thought of himself simply as a "bird-watcher"—so all six of us children, now in our seventies and eighties, have always loved the birds, particularly the songbirds and sea birds of the Northeastern forests, meadows, and beaches.

I have put up several contraptions for the birds and fastened these to the railing of the porch just outside the windows of my study. From one iron rod there dangles a little square cage for suet. The downy and hairy woodpeckers and the white-breasted nuthatches like this one. The woodpeckers sit bolt upright, clinging to the open work of the cage, and peck with serious vigor. The nuthatches like to feed upside down. Chickadees clutch the very bottom of the cage, craning their necks up to the side, and peck from there.

Next to this arrangement hangs a tray of safflower seeds. Tufted titmice, cardinals, and chickadees come here. The point of safflower is that the grey squirrels don't like it. They are oafish and pushy and ruin things for everyone else.

Next to the tray I have one of these transparent plastic tubes for thistle seed. It comes from Ethiopia and attracts the goldfinches. As it happens, we have just now had a

Reprinted with permission by CatholiCity, January 12, 2009.

three-day blizzard, and the goldfinches, usually demure, have come in awkward numbers and spend as much time skirmishing as they do eating. Obviously they think that, what with all of this snow and one thing and another, food may turn out to be scanty. The holes in this tube are so tiny that it is hard to see how anyone at all can get his beak in there.

A few inches outside my windows I have hung another tube full of mixed seeds. Everyone likes these, even the juncos, who, being ground feeders, usually don't do much perching. They usually feed on the seeds that I scatter on the lawn or the porch floor.

About twenty feet out on the lawn a feeding house sits on a pole. Again, almost everyone feeds there, and on the ground around it—bluejays, mourning doves, white-throated sparrows, and even a mallard couple. The bluejays look like dragoons or *condottieri* in their snappy black, blue, and white uniforms, and the doves are like someone's old aunties with their small heads bobbing over their plump grey bodies.

Once in a while an outsider shows up. The other day, a red-bellied woodpecker (who has no red belly) was in the tray. My favorite at the moment, mainly because he is so shy, is the Carolina wren, who, like his cousin the winter wren, has a loud, clear, crystalline song straight from the Garden of Eden. Flickers, chipping sparrows, cowbirds, catbirds, and even, alas, the crows, like great black clowns with their beady golden eyes—they all stop by.

These birds interrupt my morning prayers. One's eyes drift out there, and then it's, *What are these creatures?* Or rather, *Who* are they? Are they "who", anyway? What is going on in their heads, if anything, besides instinct—a more or less pointless word, since it lets us all domesticate an opaque mystery that suffuses the whole of nature. And fancy God decking them all with these coral, vermilion, olive, gold, dun, cornflower blue, rust, and white feathers arranged in patterns of such final satisfaction. And *crests*, forsooth.

Gerard Manley Hopkins gave glory to God for dappled things—trout, for example. The ancient canticle in use in the Church for centuries, the so-called "Song of the Three Children" sung by Daniel's friends in Nebuchadnezzar's furnace, calls upon *omnes volucres caeli* (all birds of heaven) to Bless the Lord, praise Him and magnify Him forever.

Two aspects of the thing become apparent here. First, *we* are invited to enter into the domain of praise and offer our songs to the Most High when we encounter the natural world. This is not difficult; it belongs to our creaturehood. Half the poetry of the world extols mountains, winds, clouds, sunshine, forget-me-nots, bluebells, heather, elms, oaks, beeches, the sea, and the meadows and forests. Anyone whose spirit has not been altogether debauched wants to laud it all, and something in him wants above all to offer his joy *to* something, rather than seeing it fray off into the ether. If he stands in the tradition of Enoch, Noah, Abraham, and all the saints, he will know to Whom to make his offering.

But secondly, if the Psalms and that old canticle are not talking nonsense, it looks as though the Creation itself somehow praises God. What—Alps and buttercups offering praise? They have no souls or brains or voices or even consciousness—at least in no manner discernible to our own species. So we can make it manageable by saying that just by being what they are—so mighty, so exquisite, so perfectly formed—they manifest God's handiwork and, hence, His glory. So far so good.

But surely anyone whose curiosity has ever been aroused by the sheer mystery rustling in things—not only what all poets have wondered about, but, say, the earth quaking and the sun darkening at the Crucifixion, plus all of those "thrones, dominations, princedoms, and powers" that seem to be in the cosmic cards—one would have to be a clod not to have his curiosity, not to say his terror, aroused in the face of such things. To be sure, it is the easiest thing in the world to lay it all to rest as "symbolic". Mere fancy. Poetic hyperbole.

A man who is satisfied with that has never, perhaps, been thunderstruck by the sheer *ineffability* of things. And if he is a Christian, he, of all men, should know that the scrim that veils from us titanic mysteries that would destroy us if we were suddenly hailed with them is a most merciful scrim. "Humankind cannot bear very much reality", said T. S. Eliot. He was right.

The birds outside my study window seem to me to be cases in point, under the species of created familiarity, of Glory. George MacDonald said that dogs behold the face of the Father. Who will lay it down that the birds don't?

Brokenness and Sin

A clergyman—an old friend, actually—remarked to me recently that he is inclined to view sin and hurt as synonymous. Such remarks arise, surely, from the wish to be compassionate. The idea would be that we mortals stagger along under such burdens and pains laid on us by heredity and environment that any "sin" that might be put to our credit—or debit, shall we say—is actually just a case in point of our "brokenness", as the saying goes now. We are "wounded".

Hence, we have no warrant to rush at someone and beat him about the ears over his sins—his irascibility or sloth or cruelty, or over some carnal false step. He is hurting. In the Dark Ages they did that sort of thing; in the seventeenth century, Geneva and the Plymouth Plantation belabored their poor congregations in just this ferocious way. Sin incurs guilt, they said, and the proper antidote here is punishment and repentance. Various texts in Sacred Scripture would seem to call for such an approach. The herald of the gospel—the greatest of men, Saint John the Baptist—started out with, "Repent!"

But this approach is not widely brought into play in our own time. It seems to run counter to all that our epoch has learned about the wellsprings of human behavior. It seems to bespeak a harsh and pharisaical attitude. Who is in any position to accuse another, much less to harry a man for

Reprinted with permission by CatholiCity, May 5, 2010.

his sins? Insofar as I take up such a fierce tactic, am I not like the man in the Gospel who pursued his neighbor for a small debt, when he himself had just been forgiven an enormous sum?

Well, yes. The situation that arises when my neighbor's churlishness or outright injustice cuts across my own path is a delicate one. What I would like to do is to knock him on the head and insist on reparation. Oaf that he is, *somebody's* got to sort him out.

That's as may be. But one thing is sure: *I* have not been entrusted with the baton of the Avenger. And then, let us be sure that it is a wholly just and wise man who undertakes the matter. Such a man will perhaps not start by railing on the offender. And the chances of my being that just and wise man are nil. Our Lord's approach at the Well of Sychar exhibits how perfect love handles such things. For all we know, the woman may have been a slattern of the most abandoned sort; but Love saw a woman in there—and Love also called her "life-style" by its real name: sin.

My friend is a minister in the Episcopalian church. Hence, he hears confessions. I have sometimes wondered whether he offers *pardon and absolution* to his penitents, as well as solace and the promise of healing for their hurt. (It is not, of course, my business.) I know him well enough to know that he is disinclined to speak of guilt. We mortals are, in his view, "hurting".

The difficulty here, surely, is that I don't need *pardon* for my *hurt*. What I need for that is comfort and healing. And it is perhaps worth noting in this connection that, as often as not in the *Confiteor* in contemporary Catholic liturgy, stress is laid on healing rather than on absolution from my guilt. A penitent who has heard all of the readings in which the Lord is spoken of as the Lamb of God who takes away the sin of the world, and as having been wounded for our transgressions and bruised for our iniquities, may be seeking some assurance that his confession of sin brings about forgiveness, pardon, and absolution, as well as healing for his brokenness as a mortal man.

I, like everyone else, find myself twisting my hankie when I come upon the theme of the *wrath* of God, which peppers the whole of Scripture. Surely if our human problem is merely our brokenness and hurt, "wrath" is scarcely helpful as the nostrum? Saint Paul, in his characteristically brisk approach, announces that "the wrath of God is revealed from heaven against all ungodliness and wickedness" (Rom 1:18). In the face of this sort of dictum, we may reach for various ameliorating suggestions: "Oh well, that's old Paul at it again"; or, "We don't so much speak in that way in our more enlightened era"; or, "Hah: Do you who cite such imprecations wish to drag us back into the thunderous days of medieval terror and Puritan hypocrisy? Come. We have long since found our way well beyond such inconvenient themes."

But if we are serious about such demurrals, then we will have to come clean and admit that what needs to be done next is to expunge the mystery of God's wrath, certainly from the New Testament. And such a task would oblige us to offer a new and fumigated Gospel. The blood of the Lamb, at least in the Gospel that we have (distasteful as it may appear to modern sensibilities), is for the remission of sin. There is the nub. "In Adam's fall we sinned all."

But sin. Such a hoary and barbarous notion. Don't we all agree now that, insofar as there is a fundamental problem in the human scene, it is to be found in the region of violence, hunger, greed, and cruelty? These matters are at the top of the list of the political, sociological, and charitable efforts to cut through our troubles—and the guilty parties are ordinarily spoken of as "they". The rapaciousness of big business, racial prejudices, stupidity, and parsimony on the part of the electorate—*here's* where the trouble lies. And none of these can be laid at *my* door (or so one likes to tell oneself). The villains are "out there". It is they who are at the root of humanity's problems now. I, surely, am free of taint ...

I know a man—a mild, amiable, civilized, amusing, well-intentioned citizen who, on the surface at least, could perhaps be exonerated in the guilt sweepstakes, if guilt is to be attached solely to the items listed in the above paragraph. But then he looked into his own heart; and over the course of some months, he wrote down what he found there. Here is the list: vindictiveness, petulance, irascibility, perfidiousness, arrogance, humbug, inconstancy, malice, vanity, fatuity, venality, cravenness, pusillanimity, parsimony, fretfulness, officiousness, duplicity, sloth, vituperation, pettiness, impatience, contempt, disdain, sullenness, gossip. These are the sins that lurk inside of an ostensibly nice and harmless man, and for them the Church offers *absolution*.

They are not mere "issues" or disorders or hurts. Certainly there is brokenness somewhere at the bottom of it all, if we find that word suitable. But the real point is that, if the Church and Sacred Scripture have not been deceiving us all for two thousand years, the man will sooner or later have to give an accounting for that list. He will be taxed about it at the Tribunal on the Last Day. His least favorite stanza in the *Dies Irae* is this one: "*Liber scriptus proferetur / In quo totum continetur / Unde mundus judicetur*"—"A book will be brought forth / In which everything is contained / From which the world will be judged"—the "world" in this case being he.

If this line of thought seems grotesque and archaic, we may all have to revisit the ancient gospel. A choice between that gospel and softer, more reassuring, more up-to-date notions may have to be made.

Bob Jones University et al.

One could be forgiven for finding that the above title gives him a start. Bob Jones University in the columns of *Crisis?* What ho?

What ho, indeed. And the et al. there: To whom might that refer? Well, Dallas Theological Seminary, for one. And Wheaton College in Illinois. And probably all Assemblies of God institutions, and most (or all) Southern Baptist seminaries.

What about them? They are all packed with zealots, that's what about them. Furthermore, they don't have to beat the bushes for postulants. They don't have vocations directors out plucking men by the sleeve, timorously wondering if perhaps these youngsters might think about thinking about a "vocation". They have admissions directors whose time is spent with tweezers, picking out the suitable candidates from the mountainous haystack of applicants.

Only a reader very slow to react to what he is reading will still be wondering where we are going here. We are talking about Roman Catholic seminaries, if anyone needs to have the topic spelled out. One is aware of at least two that are full. There are probably several more. John Paul II obliged the Legionaries of Christ to build yet another dormitory at their then-new Rome campus in order to accommodate what he foresaw would be a surge of applicants. At least, this is what I was told by my priest-guide as

Originally published in *Crisis* (October 1, 2005). Reprinted with permission.

I was being shown around the campus. And heaven only knows (maybe Rome, too) how things are going in Africa, Southeast Asia, and Latin America; but short of cold statistics, one at least has the impression that in some areas there is virtually a glut of men in the Catholic seminaries.

And in your average diocesan or archdiocesan seminary in Europe and the United States? I know from my own teaching experience of one that is (or was, anyway) emptying out in the bleakest possible manner. Buildings are sold off or entire institutions are shut down.

This jeremiad scarcely constitutes late-breaking news. We have all read a hundred articles, books, and columns about the "crisis in vocations". Lots of sociological reasons are adduced: The world is more secular (how can the world get more secular? Anybody remember his Latin here?). Boys and young men are so hag-ridden by the pressures of modern life and gainful employment that they haven't got time to think about such unreal options as the sacerdotal priesthood after the order of Melchizedek (whoever he might be). The Church jolly well has got to get with the times; what boy is going to opt for anything as stuffy and irrelevant as this Church that refuses, on point after point, to "respond" to the busy and urgent agenda of contemporaneity (this agenda comprising a rather short list of demands from half-a-dozen caucuses who are eager to redraw the moral and metaphysical map of the universe)?

I don't buy any of these reasons. The problem is not sociological. It's not even historical. It is, to put it baldly, spiritual. Period. Why should I, an eight- or ten- or fifteen-year-old altar boy, want to throw away my life in the priesthood, forsooth, when what I get in CCD is retailed for me by the dissident, and even angry, cadre into whose hands religious ed appears to have been placed in diocese after diocese, parish after parish? (And God bless the hundreds of godly, faithful, sacrificing, praying, and saintly folks who are teaching the ancient Faith with courage and clarity.) Or again, why should I be interested in a Faith that seems to be drawn mainly from Hallmark cards, if we're talking about homilies?

At Bob Jones et al., they teach a fiery gospel—for good or ill, from the Catholic point of view. Anything worth thinking about here?

Changing Times & Permanent Things

An odd sodality convenes at my house monthly. We are academics, which guarantees that we are all garrulous, for one thing, and, for another, that we are all vastly impressed with our own perspicacity. Everyone in the group (there are about ten of us) would lay claim to some sort of Christian faith. Although each one hails originally from the Evangelical sector of Protestantism, some have now opted for flat Protestant modernism, others are now Anglican, and at least one would find himself in the Ultramontanist (read "extreme") reach of the Roman Catholic Church.

At times the talk turns to the nettlesome moral questions that loom in the public mind now: abortion, homosexuality, contraception, assisted suicide, and so forth.

The approach on the part of one or two in the group when it comes to such points is one of cautious hesitation. Abortion? Well now, that's a vexed question. It's difficult to know quite what to say on the topic when one thinks of abused women, malformed infants, penury, quality of life, inconvenience, and so forth. Who would wish to be inquisitorial? Or again, homosexuality: We all, obviously, recognize the distinction between a man's coping with "same-sex attraction", on the one hand, and, on the other, his opting into an active "life-style" therein; but on this latter point, the house is divided. Contraception? Surely it has

Originally published in *Touchstone* (September/October 2012). Reprinted with permission.

long since ceased to be an issue? "Times have changed", and "we now know" that no moral category need be invoked in this connection.

Zeal quickly comes into play when such topics are mooted. "Well, X, or Y, or Z has the character of sin—even of mortal sin—that's pat." This from the Ultramontanist, or, possibly, from a few representing the classical Reformation tradition. Or, "No: these are delicate issues, and one can't be strident. Times have changed." This from those who wish to keep abreast of the times.

For example, one of us whose moorings are in a loosely structured but nonetheless ardent sector of Protestantism, observed not long ago that he has come to feel that homosexual practices ought no longer to be placed under the interdict. His motive here is compassion. He has been very kind—pastoral, actually—to a student who found his bottled-up attraction for other men to be crushing. It was our friend's experience in this connection that had obliged him to set the traditional Mosaic and Pauline canons on one side in the name of compassion. His student was clearly in agony.

Another, troubled by the conundrums raised in his own mind by hermaphroditism, urges a fundamental re-casting of Judeo-Christian moral notions: Such dismaying phenomena would seem to call for this. The patriarchs and apostles had never taken such anomalies into account. (I have not myself been able to get to the nub of his views here. But he urges that we must place the hermaphrodite at the start of any moral dicta we might wish to lay down. Somehow, on his view, the whole tradition is sadly flawed.)

Yet another would wish it to be understood that he is not, as it were, enthusiastic about abortion, but he passionately supports the present federal campaign to require every hospital, regardless of its religious foundation, to cooperate actively in making abortion and contraception convenient and available on demand to all women. He skirts the question of infanticide as perhaps an ambiguous but unavoidable corollary to the program.

As our discussions have proceeded (I almost said "ground along") month by month, I have found a question taking shape in my mind: What is it, then, that underlies this disparity of views on what have heretofore been assumed to be moral fixities, in a conclave of presumptively Christian scholars?

An answer to this question may possibly suggest itself in connection with the word "unnatural". For one of us to appeal to this word arouses unease in the bosoms of a few. Unnatural? The word seems to bespeak an attitude redolent of notions that have long since evaporated under the scrutiny of Baconian, Cartesian, Kantian, and Hegelian suppositions, that is to say, of the modern world. "The nature of things" is indeterminate, if there is such a thing at all. Hence, the word "unnatural" is otiose.

The word "fixity", with its strangling connotations, evokes pre-scientific ideas. In this connection, C. S. Lewis, in his inaugural address at Cambridge when he was installed in the new Chair of Mediaeval and Renaissance Literature, asked, "How has it come about that we use the highly emotive word 'stagnation', with all of its malodorous and malarial overtones, for what other ages would have called 'permanence'?" ("De Descriptione Temporum" in *Selected Essays* [Cambridge University Press, 1969], p. 10.)

"Change", "development", "progress": Such words form the axioms upon which the world now proceeds. So when one says, "Times are changing", what he may mean is: "Things are getting better."

If one is speaking of anesthesia or antiseptics or antibiotics, it would seem that he is on safe ground here. In other connections, a fugitive thought may flit through the mind of the man who is thinking of the actual good of the human race: Is it "better" to get from New York to New Delhi in a few hours rather than a few months? Is it better to have instant access to universal information at the click of a key? Is the internal combustion engine an undoubted good? Is the covering of the earth with asphalt and concrete an undoubted good?

Such questions seem capricious. Obviously, only an agrarian or a Luddite (I would be a camp-follower here) could raise such questions with any grain of seriousness. But even happily modern men may find themselves mopping their brows and asking, "Where is it all going?" What "it" do they mean? Well, development, change, progress, one would suppose. Might we not find some judicious charioteer to govern the hurtling course of this Icarian plunge? But who will nominate such a charioteer? And we are up against questions that overthrow all conceivable suggestions.

When it comes to the moral universe, however, it may be asked whether, in fact, "progress" is a word with any meaning. Obviously, the almost global modern decrying of slavery would seem to qualify as progress, although we may recall that ancient codes decried cruelty, under which rubric slavery would seem to appear. It is the violation of such codes (the Tao, that is) that has constituted most of the unhappiness of human history. From the beginning, the touchstone has been, "Would I be prepared to switch places with my slave?"

But, in the brisk air that now blows across contemporary thinking, may we, in fact, ponder some fundamental moral review?

Certain moral categories would seem stubborn here. Murder—that is, the gratuitous and unwarranted slaughter of a fellow mortal? Surely it will be some time before the

Tao will recommend this. Or lying. The lie is a most useful tactic in all sorts of situations, but when one comes upon a lie that has inconvenienced his own interests, he has difficulty being open-minded. Stealing? Again, most profitable for the thief, but hard to applaud for the man whose sapphires have been pinched, or, a fortiori, the man whose identity has been electronically purloined.

Ah. But might there be, after all, a candidate for review? In the "sexual revolution" of the 1960s et seq., it would appear that the protohistoric ban on adultery, and with it fornication and free sexual congress across all frontiers of gender, was lifted. (Sparta is often offered as an ancient precedent for altering common sexual codes. But did Sparta herself attempt a brief adjusting of the Tao? She would be part of the question here, and not of the answer.)

So—the difficulties encountered in the efforts to modify the Tao in the cases of murder, lying, and stealing would seem to arise in the sexual realm as well. The adulterer or fornicator will no doubt find vast gratification in his pastimes, but the offended party will take a dissenting view: "You have bedded my wife?" or "That was my boyfriend with whom you made free!" It is hard to gain a consensus, even in the realm of sexuality. Someone is sure to view the fruits of the revolution with the most somber misgivings.

But there are situations—millions of them no doubt, daily—in which no offended party would seem to appear. Just two people (or more, alas) in any mix of gender, enjoying a divertissement. No strings. No special commitments. No prior claims on either hand. Hence no offended parties. All would seem to be smooth sailing.

And here we find ourselves asking whether there is any prior court to which appeal to ancient taboos might be mounted in such situations. Will it be only on the level of common loyalties like family or betrothal or friendship that these taboos ought to be invoked? May the rest of us sail on at will?

It is here that I have found myself mulling over the views of my Christian colleagues. To remark "Times are changing" as the warrant for adjusting the Tao in the interest of sexual "needs" would, surely, find a stony response from the patriarchs, prophets, apostles, fathers, and the ancient Church generally. (Even sumptuously polygamous figures like Abraham or Solomon kept to fixed notions: "This woman is one of my wives or odalisques. You may not enjoy her." Pharaohs, khans, caliphs, sultans—they all appealed to some such canons.) There was clearly something prior to a man's desires, or even to his supposititious needs, when it came to ordering things in the sexual domain.

The ignoring of that "something" was, of course, and has always been, the fountainhead of half the fury, sorrow, and agony of the whole world. But on the workaday level of my desires, appetites, inclinations, and even "needs", might the time now have come for us all to invoke the canon "Times are changing", and to re-draw the moral map of the universe? Not a few of my Christian friends seem to see such a re-drawing as a step forward, certainly in the interest of compassion.

Such a move in the moral realm would seem both plausible and desirable while we are, in any case, overleaping so many frontiers. And surely it follows from the freedom that belongs to our human dignity, does it not?

To a mind formed by doctrines of progress and occupied with these proximate questions of our human desires and needs, all objections to updating ancient sexual canons will appear as obstructions.

On the other hand, T. S. Eliot spoke of "The Permanent Things". We could also speak of "the architecture of the universe" or "the bright fixities" or "the choreography of the Dance". We could even go so far as to speak of "the natural", and hence of "the unnatural".

We would be invoking the paradox, at work in every conceivable realm of reality, of fixity—immutable law—as being the very ground and donor of freedom. At one pole would stand the (briefly) attractive state of anarchy: no trammels, no tyranny, no checkrein on my impulses, convenience, and choices. At the other pole would appear the picture of the Dance: the stars in their courses; the mystery of time itself; the solemn choreography that yields the joyous freedom of the minuet, the waltz, and the ballet; the fixed rules that govern the training of the gymnast, the acrobat, and the athlete; the sovereign fidelity that beckons a man and a woman into the dignity of the nuptial state; the interminable self-denial and obedience to the rules that equips a Beverly Sills or an Itzhak Perlman.

When this sort of thing is pondered, it begins to look as though obedience, mastery, freedom, and joy turn out to be a seamless fabric. The very "thou shalt nots" of the Law look like guarantors of our authentic human dignity and glory. Basic training, as it were.

And we may ponder here the sacramental notion that the material world is the icon of reality. Silver aspen leaves, the song of the hermit thrush, the surf, Mont Blanc, the taste of raspberries, grains of wheat, the body of a woman and the body of a man: These are either neutral data, or they signal Something. The Christian point of view has always supposed the latter.

It all becomes almost clinical: The structure of the man's body bespeaks a creature whose nature it is to lift and haul and defend the city, and to go out from himself to seek the place—the body of the woman in the fruition of their love. The structure of the woman's body would seem to suggest that she is already there. She is "the place". Even though she was, in the ancient story, created after the man, she is "at home" in a way that eludes the man. He charges about the world, restless, clubbing mastodons, probing the seven seas, cobbling up his philosophical systems or symphonies, conquering kingdoms, and writing, writing, writing.... The woman does not seem quite so hagridden to get things under control. Her very breasts and womb seem designed to receive.

This line of thought is scandalous, of course. Can't a woman command a ship or "do" philosophy (Edith Stein) or govern an empire (Elizabeth I, Catherine the Great, Victoria) or fight? Of course she can, valiantly and wisely. But is there a difficulty here? (Is Penthesilea your archetypal woman?)

Perhaps there is a key word there: archetype. Obviously, a woman can do virtually anything a man can do, except to sire offspring; and so with the man: He can caress his infant with profound tenderness, but he can't bear or nurse it. The two genders are not, *pace* the 1970s, interchangeable, even with the best will in the world. Has the modern stress on equality and power in the public realm set on one side the most obvious Permanent Thing touching the phenomenon of Man, namely, man as Father, and woman as Mother? When these creational categories became "roles" in the 1970s, did we witness progress? Was it a Good Thing to muster out the notion of the natural, with its corollary unnatural?

Is it thus with the whole Tao? Do the canons, at work in all tribes and cultures from the beginning in some form or another (e.g., sheer promiscuity has never been extolled) point to Something unalterable?

Christianity has supposed that they do. It is for this reason that I have found myself curious upon hearing my academic friends proposing alterations under the ensign "But times are changing."

What My Children Won't Learn in School

Any Christian has an ambiguous attitude toward "the wisdom of this world". He has no doubt about holy wisdom—*Hagia Sophia*—which, in a manner of speaking, may be thought of as a sort of daughter of God himself and which was extolled by Solomon as being beyond price. It is something to be pursued at all costs. In the end, it seems to stand close to charity, very near the throne.

But what is called the wisdom of this world is another matter. On the one hand, of course, there is "worldly" wisdom—all the calculating and self-seeking and power-mongering that stand starkly over against the wisdom that is from above. This wisdom is pure and peaceable and gentle, and comes, often, out of the mouths of babes and sucklings as well as of sages and saints. There is also the luminous rationality of Athens, which, despite its prowess and sublimity, breaks down into scandal in the face of absurdities like the preaching of the cross.

But there is also that elusive prize that stands at the far end of the enterprise we call education. No one will insist that the mere piling up of knowledge will yield this prize. But on the other hand, none of us can quite escape the feeling that there is some connection between the increase of information and the prize. We pay tens of thousands

Originally published in *Christianity Today* (September 3, 1982): 26–27. Reprinted with permission.

of dollars to schools and universities—for what? For good careers, of course! I want to be a marine biologist, we say. I want to be a surgeon. I want to go into politics. I want to teach. Well, you have to have an education for that. So we embark. Sheer career considerations probably supply 90 percent of the answer to the question as to what we want from our education.

But there is always that further notion at the edges of our imagination: Isn't it *really* better to know than not to know? Am I not better off to have learned of Greece and Rome, and of quantum mechanics, and of DNA, than not to have learned? Doesn't all that contribute somehow to my becoming wiser?

There is the rub. Does it? There seem to be various jokers in the pack here. For one thing, you come upon super-educated old fools whose heads are so stuffed with data that it seems to pop out of their ears like bits of straw. Or, more alarming than this, you have the spectacle of the evil man whose knowledge greatly increases his power to work his evil. A bad ignoramus is to be avoided, but a bad Ph.D. is to be feared like the Devil himself. He has so much more at his disposal. So we cannot say that mere education will guarantee anything in the way of real wisdom for us if we use "wisdom" in its ordinary sense of implying knowledge that is being put to good use. Surely it is not going too far to say that wisdom and goodness find their habitation in the same place?

Yet another joker in the pack is the spectacle of the completely uneducated sage. We have all known some old person like an ancient nanny who filled our ears with homespun notions that turn out to be as enduring and pure as gold, or a salty old geezer who has learned a wisdom that outshines that of the academics from years of plain living. Does this pull the rug from under the educational enterprise?

Once or twice each year, I find a student in my office hemming and hawing, and presently it becomes clear that he has decided to leave school—not, he tells himself, because he does not want wisdom, but rather because he does. The trouble is, the halls of ivy are much too confining for him. He wants to learn wisdom in the real marketplace or in some quiet backwater in Vermont. There, he tells himself, he will be able to live close to the earth and have time to think. Somehow this type finds his way back to the halls of ivy after a year or two, and generally his testimony as to the worth of the interlude in the market or the backwater is very muted.

Clearly, then, the whole question of education is shot through with uncertainties if one wants to carry it farther than the mere question of job opportunities. Anyone who is raising children and paying for their education will want to peer narrowly at this extremely expensive enterprise.

And, of course, the questions become more acute for a Christian. Because he sees himself as only a pilgrim in this world, he does not look to the resources it offers for the things of final value. In past centuries, the Church was vigorous about teaching the notion *de contemptu mundi* (of the contempt of the world) to the faithful. Now, any Christian has got ringing in his ears such injunctions as "Lay not up for yourselves treasures upon earth", and "Set your affection on things above", and "Here we have no continuing city", and so forth, which seem to stress the ephemeral nature of everything here. One will thus always have some questions as to just how he is to understand the relationship between human culture and one's being a Christian. It is not an easy question. If anyone supposes that it is, he might begin by reading the works of Saint Augustine and Reinhold Niebuhr.

The question comes to me in the following manner right now, since my own formal schooling is over and since I am a father. Just what is it, in fact, that I want their schooling to do for my children?

Part of the answer is easy. I want them to be civilized and articulate members of their generation. I want them to be able to live intelligently in this epoch and to bring to the choices they make the judgments formed by eons of human experience. I do not want them to be trapped inside the airless hutch of modernity. They will be assisted here by reading history and poetry and philosophy. I do not want them to be ignorant as to the sort of conditions under which all mortal life must be lived. They will get light on this from physics, astronomy, chemistry, biology, botany, anatomy, and so forth. I want their capacity to apprehend beauty to be awakened and nourished and regaled. Hence, I want them to know about Praxiteles and Virgil and Giotto and Mozart. I do not want them to be traduced by the bestial view of mankind that is the specialty of our own century. I would like them to have Ulysses and Aeneas and Roland and Lear looming in their imaginations so that they will have images against which to test figures like Arthur Miller's salesman, or Andy Warhol, or Charlie's Angels.

And I would like to see developed in them a particular quality for which we have no word in English. The Greeks called it *aidos*. It suggests an attitude combining elements of honor, duty, and shame—not shame in the sense of grinding mortification, but rather of the capacity to blush; to be awe-struck in the face of what is awesome; to venerate what is venerable. It is not a frame of mind native to our own century. It would stand at a polar extreme from the egocentric ennui and petulant slovenliness nourished at the wellsprings of TV, new wave music, glossy journalism, and cinema.

I would also like to see them learn, during their schooling, something of that quality the Greeks called *sophrosyne*. Again there is no single English word for this, but it comprises temperance and gentleness and prudence and discretion. It has something to do with soundness of mind, self-control, and whole-mindedness. It is the opposite of hysteria and mania. It would stand in judgment, for example, on the "gut reaction" so lauded and encouraged by our own era. It would pause for a very long time before joining loud and popular political and moral fashions. And I hope to see their education introduce them to yet another quality extolled by the Greeks, namely, *arete*. Our words goodness, virtue, and excellence approach the idea. It bespeaks soundness of quality in a man, a sword, a horse, a servant, a ruler. It would not be embarrassed, for example, to be found cultivating virtue. The distance we have come from this wholesome frame of mind may be gauged by reflecting on how our contemporaries receive the words "virtue" and "wholesomeness". Try either word out in a group. You will get snickers, or else an embarrassed blank, or, worst of all, knowing and clever comments about the Moral Majority and Mrs. Grundy.

And (one more bit of Greek), I would like to see the principle of *meden agan* (nothing too much) at work in their imagination as a result of their education: moderation; sobriety; the middle way; restraint; temperance. It stands over against all excess, violence, indulgence, and licentiousness. But what box-office value has this notion got now? What lyrics to what songs by what rock groups extol all this? Will peer pressures or values-clarification classes press this on them?

By this time it will be clear that I am asking a great deal of my children's education. Besides the useful amassing of knowledge that will help them to be active and intelligent participants in their epoch, I am asking, in effect, that they become good and wise.

And at this point any Christian will demur. Education cannot do that, we say. There is no inevitable connection, alas, between knowledge and wisdom. "To know right" is very far from being synonymous with "to do right", on the Christian view. The tragic joker in the whole pack—if we may use such a figure as this—is that we mortals don't *want* to do right. Ignorance is not our problem. Our fundamental problem is sin, and for that we need redemption, not education. There is always this conundrum for Christians when they raise the question of education.

But the conundrum has another face to it. While Christians agree that the wisdom of this world does not yield sanctity—which is the only thing that matters in the end—nevertheless, it does seem to be the case, in the normal run of things (always granting that God can raise up children to Socrates as well as to Abraham from the very stones if he wants to), that the mind that has been honed and chastened by the rigors of education is in a strong position to apprehend and to articulate the Faith, once that mind has been enlightened by the Holy Ghost.

Of course there are always Saint Francises and John Bunyans, whose own sanctity and contributions to the well-being of Christendom owe nothing to education. But figures like that are excessively rare. Most of us, in fact, are better off if our minds have been enlarged by discipline. Saint Augustine may argue in his *Confessions* that he wishes he might dispense with all the pagan learning he had. But we are all the beneficiaries of the schooling that tutored his immense mind. And we may all give thanks for the ferocious old atheist Kirkpatrick who banged sense and discipline into the young intellect of C.S. Lewis. Who else has perceived and articulated for so many in our century the sheer splendor of the Faith?

And so I find myself back where I started. What do I expect, or wish, education to do for my children? Perhaps the answer should echo what Dr. Johnson said when they asked him, on his deathbed, whether such and such a pillow would "do". "Why yes," he said, "all that a pillow can do."

Education can do all that education can do for my children, and I want that. But I know that it cannot do what grace alone can do, namely, make them ready to enter into the Kingdom of Heaven.

Christ and the Psychedelic Vision

In recent months a curious phenomenon has engaged the attention of America. It is the widespread use of the hallucinogen LSD. Prominently associated with the movement is Dr. Timothy Leary, the former Harvard University professor, who has organized the League for Spiritual Discovery (the initials are obvious).

The use of LSD has aroused comment from nearly every group that is accustomed to offering opinions on public issues. Social agencies, governmental agencies, doctors, academic institutions, and churches have appeared as spokesmen for one opinion or another.

If it were simply a medical matter, one would be inclined to urge churches to remain silent on the issue. But since Dr. Leary has proclaimed it "a new religion" and since the movement uses Christian terminology, it should be of great interest and concern to the Christian church.

As I write this, Dr. Leary is holding a series of "psychedelic celebrations" in New York City. Thousands of people are attending—the sort of people the Church could never dream of coaxing into her doors.

Last night I attended one of these celebrations. It was called "The Reincarnation of Jesus Christ". The program for the evening took the form of the Mass. I sat in the theatre, with hundreds of students, intellectuals, mods, hippies, and teenagers, and heard the Gospel read, and the life, Passion, death, and Resurrection of Jesus Christ proclaimed,

Originally published in *Eternity* (May 1967): 26–28. Reprinted with permission.

and the invitation given to "go all the way". I heard the psychedelic experience explained in regenerative terms.

As the theatre was filling, there were bizarre, kaleidescopic slides being thrown onto two huge screens at the front. For perhaps half an hour there was nothing to do but watch these patterns shift, like the aurora borealis, in dazzling color. Then the lights went out, and two guitars began to play music of a distinctly East Indian flavor. Dr. Leary and a helper appeared in simple white clothes, barefoot, and seated themselves on a low divan at the side of the stage.

Dr. Leary explained that we were being invited to a celebration of the Holy Communion, the Last Supper. He himself, he said, had been a Catholic and had not found Christ to be alive in the churches. He remembers hearing people say, "Let's go to the seven o'clock Mass, so that we can get away to the beach early", or "Oh, let's go to the eleven o'clock, since we were out so late last night." Christ was dead, and incarcerated in ancient and shopworn structures.

But then six years ago, a friend brought a chalice to his house, and he was initiated, under sacramental conditions, to the ecstasies of LSD. He came to understand this as a mode of perception that brings one directly into confrontation with God. The expressions "turned on" is used to designate the state of perception under the power of LSD. Dr. Leary says, "To be turned on is to see with the eyes of Christ."

The "journey" (that is, the experience) is described as a trip into the inner universe through external sense organs, so that through the power of sight enormously heightened by the influence of LSD, one becomes intensely aware of the cellular structure of the body, for instance. One moves beyond the mind to the direct perception of structure as glory, and as one encounters the external world (passing faces, one's own face in a mirror, etc.), memory carries one back into the racial past, exhibiting the unity of one's own being with all other beings, of one's own father with all other fathers, and so on ad infinitum, so that one's response becomes "Glory be to the fathers, and to the sons, and to the holy spirits."

Dr. Leary opened the actual ceremony with prayer, asking God (Whom he did not address by name) to help us to use this experience, not for selfish ends, but to the end of realizing universal love, the kind of love embodied in Jesus Christ. He then expounded the Lord's Prayer, suggesting that the Father in Heaven is to be found in here (motioning to his heart area). Then he said we were going to witness the crisis of one Patrick Murphy, a Christian from Brooklyn.

Our attention was again directed to the screen, where shadow images of a boy and a man faced each other. The man, Christ, asked Patrick if he dared to go back to the beginning (it was left to the observer to decide whether this meant the beginning of time, or the sources of truth, or birth, or what). The boy hesitated, and the challenge was repeated.

Then the shadow of two hands in the act of elevating the chalice appeared over the figures, and descended to them, implying that Patrick was at this point making his communion. But it was a communion in twentieth century, or rather, psychedelic, terms. We were immediately switched to the screen, where we penetrated Patrick's consciousness.

For the next forty minutes, without cessation or alleviation, a torrent of images flowed over the screen. The background consisted of black and white footage of crowds passing and jostling along a sidewalk, much of the time in negative image, so that white was black. Superimposed on this, and traversing the screen at random, were icons and drawings of saints, martyrs, the Virgin, Christ, and unidentifiable figures and faces. Also appearing, swinging across the screen, were spots of viscera, representing, I take it, the "universe within the body" mentioned by Dr. Leary as the locale of the journey.

The phonic accompaniment to this spectacle consisted of a folk-rock Mass, sung continuously, so that one heard the Kyrie, the Gloria, the Credo, Sanctus and Benedictus, and the Agnus Dei over and over, in a severely modern idiom. And, superimposed on this was the reading of the Beatitudes, the Ten Commandments, passages from Saint John's Gospel ("Let not your heart be troubled. Peace I leave you"), and words from parts of a litany ("Saint Joseph, pray for him; all ye holy patriarchs and prophets, pray for him; all ye virgins and widows, pray for him").

At the end of this, Dr. Leary resumed speaking quietly. He explained that the experience of LSD was a sacrament of love, even as the Last Supper was. Since it is an awesome thing, which brings us to the frontiers of realities never before perceived by the human consciousness except in mystical ecstasies, it is not a lark or a form of mere pleasure.

Because of its grave nature, the catechumen must "tune in", that is, prepare himself. This will involve acts of Confession, so that he will be in a state of grace and will be worthy to receive the sacrament (cf. 1 Corinthians 11). He explained that if the sacrament is taken with known sin on the conscience, the experience may well be one of paranoia and terror, rather than bliss. He defined sin as "the times when you have moved the black pieces on your chess board", meaning the occasions when we have done things for which our own consciences condemned us. It could have been eating meat on Friday, or drinking, or smoking. Whatever was interdicted by our code was evil for us.

Of the experience itself, Dr. Leary said little. Clearly, here as in sexual ecstasy, the experience is of such a nature that description cannot approach it. The heightened perception involved brings one, according to the testimony of those who know, to the state described by saints and mystics as union with the divine. (Aldous Huxley wrote of his experience some years ago in a small book called *The Doors of Perception*, before anyone had heard of LSD. His experience was with mescalin, or peyote, which is also a hallucinogen.) It is, apparently, not of the same order of things as the experience conveyed by heroin or marijuana. It is a spiritual encounter.

Dr. Leary insists that it must issue in love. By this he means what the Christian means—true caritas. He is not announcing some new order of erotic freedom. When he is asked if he will initiate someone into the experience, he answers that this request is like asking if you may sleep with his wife or have his bank account. He holds that the only milieu for the sacrament is within a circle of trusting and intimate friends.

Various responses to this phenomenon are possible, the most obvious being, of course, dismay and hostility. Here is a new form of chaos and license, which has pirated the sacred rites and language of Christianity and has dragooned them to its own service. Here is blasphemy.

It seems to me, however, that here, as in a thousand other situations, the thoughtful Christian is called on to reject the hurried and frightened bluster that marks the pronouncements of those who, like Job's friends, are always quite certain of where the truth lies and of what is amiss. What is asked of us is something infinitely more telling.

In the face of this oddity, we must painstakingly form the questions, to be asked of ourselves, not Leary, that will help us discover the radical level on which we must dissociate ourselves from this exciting and appealing thing. Our response must not be the mere blundering and confusion of minds that, like a bull in the ring, suspect a danger and charge in all directions. Simply *because* it is new and threatening, it is not thereby wrong (devout people who were used to Ptolemaic cosmology damned the Copernican). We must go deeper than fright. If it is wrong, it is wrong on levels other than its newness and its mystery.

For one thing, we must leave it to medicine to tell us about its effects on the human body and psyche. For another, we cannot lump it together with the sort of dehumanizing demimonde that surrounds the heroin market. Dr. Leary's vision is a high one.

The following questions have occurred to me as those that might lead us toward some understanding of our own view of what is at stake:

1. We believe that the structure of reality is glorious and that it attests to the excellence of the mind of God. And we suspect that, if we were able to see reality not through a dark glass, we would see the glory of God. Since this sort of vision is what is claimed for LSD, and since we are not yet in a position to know that what is revealed to perception by LSD is *not* that glory, we must ask if there are grounds for resisting such a direct and "chemical" approach to dazzling realities. Do we understand a scriptural order that requires the enjoyment of glory to be earned, or at least not available without qualification?

2. Concerning the apprehension of glory, we must examine our ideas as to the *moral* prerequisites for ecstasy. Scripture speaks of Paradise but makes it clear that the road thereto is arduous. The notion of instant and gratis Paradise strikes us as being at odds with the nature of things. (But here we must be clear what we mean, else we will find that our strictures are cancelling the validity of, say, sexual ecstasy, which is obviously quite open to all men.)

3. What implications for this situation has the Passion of Christ? That is, we understand our enjoyment of paradisaical

bliss to follow upon faith in the unique and atoning efficacy of that Passion. Is it possible to show the hallucinogenic experience as an attempt to circumvent biblical strictures placed upon the vision of truth? Is it an attempt to bypass what God insists is the only gate to glory, the Cross?

4. Can we show by Christian categories that the highest good for man in this life is, oddly enough, to be found, not in visions of bliss (even supposing them to be true visions), but in the plodding acceptance of responsibility, and in faith, and in works of love, and in doing justice and loving mercy and in walking humbly with God? Can we show that this, and this alone, leads eventually to the true knowledge of God (i.e., bliss)? What were the foci of Christ's teachings? Can we re-assert these as the sole desiderata, so that the psychedelic pursuit of the beatific vision will emerge as misbegotten?

It seems to me that if we begin with some such questions as these, we will avoid the adolescent fright of mere religious zeal in the face of the unknown, and we may be able to reach an understanding of our own priorities that answers tellingly to the appeal of instant glory.

The Church as Participatory Democracy

The Catholic Church has traditionally thought of herself as having been constructed hierarchically. Jesus Christ, for example, is the head of this Church: He is not the chairperson of any revolving ad hoc caucus of the whole. He picked twelve men and endowed them with the unction to carry on His ministry in His Church with His teaching and ruling authority. This is not a question to be canvassed by endless symposia, colloquia, and dialogues. Otherwise, we would have to agree that a sea-change has overwhelmed the Church since the days of Ignatius of Antioch, Polycarp, Clement, Justin, & Co.

Back at square one, some questions of conscience arose over what you could eat, your purveyors of meat possibly having purchased some of their wares from heathen temples. The matter at hand would most certainly have promised a vigorous agenda for any lay caucuses that anyone wanted to float. My word—fancy the exchanges! "This kind of meat is nothing, since those gods don't exist anyway, and we Christians don't for a moment grant that any noisome effluvium lingers over the chops and filets, infusing them with hell's own gangrene. Eat what you want, and celebrate your Christian freedom."

But then the cautious souls venture to wonder whether the whole matter does not bring with it a certain blur: Are we sending out the message that pagan sacrifices are a

Originally published in *Crisis* (November 1, 2004). Reprinted with permission.

neutral matter from our point of view? Should we not put as much distance as we can between the Christian assembly and the cult of Diana or Cybele, even in so apparently an insignificant a matter as our diet?

The sketch is, of course, a twentieth-century scenario. When the question arose in the early Church, the apostles met, talked, reached a decision, and handed out the word. End of discussion, as we say now. You were Catholic (the word came into play early on to designate which Christians were in organic, obedient, and visible union with their bishops), and so you welcomed the manifesto from the apostolic council and went on your Catholic way.

Jump two thousand years. We have, in the archdiocese where I live, a number of high-decibel dissident caucuses (one claims to be the Voice of the *Faithful*, forsooth). The people active in these purlieus are most earnest in wishing to bring things up-to-date, but certainly not merely to "streamline" the poor, clanking old Church. The idea is to bring the insights and dispositions of contemporaneity to bear on what looks like a very dismal situation. Their fervent recommendations are certainly plausible: There's a shortage of clergy? Ordain women, for heaven's sake. Divorce and remarriage present obstacles? All you have to do is scratch the antediluvian rules. Sexual fashions? That topic needs some hard scrutiny, and the first thing to do is to jettison clerical celibacy *now*. The hierarchy is bogged down? Let's take our cues from some sensible citizens like Benjamin Franklin and Thomas Jefferson: Spread out the powers. Or again, traditional English-language usage was full of clever, scarcely noticeable pronouns that carried an immense freight of gender (so to speak) with it: Change the whole vocabulary. And God? Well, s/he certainly would be the first to encourage this grammatical leap forward.

Meanwhile, back at the apostolic ranch, the voice of Peter still speaks. Clearly. Authoritatively. Charitably (yes, charitably, believe it or not). In *Dives in Misericordia*, *Dominum et Vivificantem*, *Veritatis Splendor*, *Evangelium Vitae*, *Fides et Ratio*, and scores of other utterances, we have the faithful "handing on" (*traditio*) of the Faith.

And, just by the by, the updated church so sedulously sought by these caucuses is already here and in place. It is called Protestant.

Decay Invades My Bones

There's an inauspicious title for us all to mull over. Is it a complaint about lupus or osteoporosis? Is it the cry of someone reaching for a metaphor that will somehow answer to the despair that has overtaken him? Is it just a (slightly tedious) bit of hyperbole?

Its candidacy for any of these options would be eminently plausible, but as it happens, it is none of the above. The grisly picture is evoked by the author of the line—not, oddly enough, by way of complaint, much less of self-pity, but rather as an effort to get through to us the intensity of his reaction to the sight of God's coming to the aid of His people. "You tread the sea with your steeds amid the churning of the deep waters. I hear, and my body trembles; at the sound, my lips quiver. Decay invades my bones."

It is our friend Habakkuk speaking. If you read your breviary, you will come across this bit on Friday of week two, at morning prayer. Obviously Habakkuk's capacity to react to the arrival of God is enormous. There is nothing blasé or cavalier about this prophet's responses. (Alas: Where, on a scale of one to ten, might my own responses to the daily readings fall? Perhaps "fall" is the embarrassingly apt word here. How often have I found myself obliged to reach for such a violent metaphor in order to articulate the sheer force of my own response to the readings—to *any* of the readings,

Originally published in *Crisis* (September 1, 2005). Reprinted with permission.

up to and including the Creation, the Flood, the Annunciation, the Transfiguration, the Passion, and the Resurrection, not to mention the Apocalypse?)

In my own case, the difficulty of responding to the Word with anything even remotely approaching what might be called adequacy is, I would guess, greater than the difficulty experienced by cradle Catholics since, having been nurtured in Protestant Fundamentalism, I was drilled (and drilled, and drilled) in the sheer *content* of Scripture, day after day, week after week, decade after decade. It is a stark impossibility for us mortals to maintain a state of high responsiveness to any stimulus at all, and Sacred Scripture constitutes no exception to this lackluster capacity of ours to respond to things. If you live at the brink of Iguazu Falls or on the slope of Cotopaxi, your capacity for wonder exhibits a reverse ratio to the amount of time you have lived there. If you listen to the B Minor Mass twice daily for five years, your latter responses will be feeble in comparison to those aroused in you upon first hearing the Mass.

But back to this decay in my (or Habakkuk's, shall we say) bones. In at least two of his books (*Perelandra* and *Till We Have Faces*), C. S. Lewis has a mortal encountering a god. The sensation on the part of the mortal is of being naked: nay, of being ashamed. Ashamed because of his sin? That would certainly be appropriate. But it is worse than that: The shame occurs over the sheer fact of being mortal in the presence of the god.

This is not a stance that comes easily to us modern men. The therapy industry and all of the dynamics at work in educational theory, drummed into us from birth onward, have us getting comfortable with our feelings, or feeling okay about ourselves. The more we rummage in our emotional entrails (our very own mode of haruspication), the more fascinated and preoccupied with ourselves we become (not to mention our politics). There is no one in whose presence we are taught to bow.

If Habakkuk's dismay in the presence of the Divine Majesty seems fawning to us—or worse, masochistic and sick—we have a situation on our hands. The bald and eternal fact is that, one way or another, we are going to find ourselves faced with that Majesty one fine morning. How do we propose to get ourselves—and our offspring—ready?

Vogue and the *Waters of Siloe*

My current reading has me head over heels in Lord David Cecil's *Melbourne*, Lord Annan's *Roxburgh of Stowe*, Muggeridge's *Chronicles of Wasted Time* (all of them for the second, or tenth, time—it's the exquisite prose), and Thomas Merton's *The Waters of Siloe*, a history of Gethsemane and the whole Cistercian phenomenon.

But there is another item on the list. The other day I borrowed a copy of *Vogue's* maiden issue (if you can call it that) of a magazine for men. What is one to say? Page after sumptuous page after opulent page of Ralph Lauren, Valentino, Gucci, Versace, Georgio Armani, and the rest of them. Cuff links (sapphire and white gold to be sure) for $12,000, a portable telephone for—steady now—$30,000, shoes for $11,000, and so forth and so on. Not to mention the sultry, voluptuous, very Mediterranean young male models, or the female models draped in scant tag ends of diaphanous materials, daring the viewer in the most sulphurous terms to "come hither".

The thing is, one finds one's head spinning. Let us juxtapose only Merton and this magazine for the moment. Here are two worlds: As a Catholic, of course, I know very well which world I am bidden to by the Most High; but the other one is so dazzling. Or, shall we say, briefly dazzling. When one's head has stopped spinning, it turns out to be the apotheosis of fatuity. Who in his right mind

Originally published in *Crisis* (January 1, 2006). Reprinted with permission.

supposes for one moment that these people have found the Well at the World's End, much less the *Civitas Dei*?

One of the features in this pilot issue is an article on Swiss bank accounts and the sensationally wicked men who have many of them (no doubt a few honorable men also avail themselves of this luxury, but the article focused on the bad guys). As much as $1.3 *trillion* is *laundered* through Geneva every year. The point here is that, for recreation, these men seem to have little to do but pamper themselves aboard their yachts in the daytime (they don't all *live* in Geneva) and whore their way through fancy clubs at night. Surely a somewhat truncated view of what human existence calls for?

On the other hand, we have these monks. One's eyes pop out on stems at their draconian disciplines and endurance of hardship, although Merton is very good about insisting that it is the Divine Love that is the object of it all and that animates their whole life. Vegetables, water, black bread, no heat, straw pallets, up at 2 A.M. for Matins and Lauds—one staggers at the regimen. And I found myself asking: What chance have the rest of us grunts in the Paradise sweepstakes with comrades like this in the race? One has to hang on to the Church's teaching about the active and the contemplative life, neither one canceling the other, but the contemplative most surely being the superior way.

I suppose I must assent to this, since it is Church teaching. But I do not find it easy. It's all very well to recoil at the grotesque excesses of Geneva; nonetheless, I go to sleep betimes in a soft bed, in a bedroom beautifully appointed by my wife, and eat three meals a day with bacon, eggs, pastries, wine, meats, potatoes, rice, pasta, and so forth. And I do not arise in the small hours to say my prayers. Will I make it? To what extent do I know anything of the One who remarked about Himself, "Foxes have holes", and bade us follow this pattern?

Well, these two life-styles (more accurately, life-*substances*) are the extreme poles. Most of us have never fully weighed the options. We land at our station in life in a somewhat higgledy-piggledy manner, and we hope that God redeems and turns to our sanctification what must, upon scrutiny, turn out to be a bit random. But, we believe, that is what redemption does.

Ecce Quam Bonum

"Behold, how good and how pleasant it is for brethren to dwell together in unity!"

We hear this bracing sentiment often enough in musical and liturgical settings, most notably in the seraphic motet by Tomás Luis de Victoria or in the spare sequence of chant. When it is conveyed to us under these modalities, we are easily moved to concur. Ah. Indeed. Such a very good and pleasant thing it is—everyone offering courtesies and good cheer to everyone else, harmony flooding household and workplace tasks and all the common duties of the day. Hey nonny.

But the iridescent bubble pops at about this point. Who among us dwells in such a never-never land? Well, if one is a Christian at all, and has ever groaned out "Thy kingdom come", then surely it is a "not-yet" land. If it is really "never-never", then our faith is unavailing.

But was the psalmist speaking of a stark impossibility there? Had he ever seen anything in the real world that moved him to write down a line like that?

Well, he must have. But perhaps the more piquant question for us is, have we?

It is to be hoped that at least some (most? all?) readers of InsideCatholic.com are able to reply, "In my household." There, if anywhere, lies the kindergarten of caritas, greatly assisted by all the natural affections, thanks be to God. And

Reprinted with permission by CatholiCity, September 15, 2007.

some happy souls might also be able to answer, "Oddly enough there's a fairly amiable crew in my office. Oh, sparks fly intermittently, one must admit, but we bumble along most of the time." So: At least fugitive glimpses of that "good and pleasant" state of affairs are vouchsafed even in the workplace now and again.

But what really got me thinking about that line from the psalm was the parish. I have been a Catholic for twenty-two years now, and my wife for twelve. The people in various parishes where we have been are amiable and virtuous people, to all appearances. Most of them, at least the ones at daily Mass, are, like my wife and me, valetudinarians. But do we dwell together in unity? There is absolutely no way of knowing. Why not? Because things rarely get beyond a courteous "good morning", if even that.

After ten years in one parish, we knew the names of perhaps three couples. I do not think there was a notable fault here: My wife and I were not especially seeking bonhomie. Both of us grew up in evangelical Protestant churches and have known enough bonhomie. And I am sure that if one or the other of us had ever staggered and fallen, everyone would have clustered around with anxious offers of help.

It is perhaps not unusual, then, to find Catholics shuffling into Mass and out again, year after year, quite politely, once a week or more, doing their duty dutifully. And perhaps there is a sense in which the angels can see here a trace of that unity of which the psalmist speaks, which is so good and pleasant. Who can say?

The Church is, we are told, the sacrament of Christ in the world. The "sacrament"—that is, His presence, in a mystery. Faith has trained our eyes to see the inauspicious, tasteless wafer as a holy thing. Is this also how I see that bag lady there, and that unclassifiable old person over there?

What do my eyes see anyway?

I Will Go to the Altar of God: Worshipping in the Local Church

I will go to the altar of God. These are familiar words to us all, of course: They come from Psalm 43, and we have no doubt said them many times. For Christians, they have a double meaning. They call up for us the worship of Israel, when the people literally went "up" to the hallowed places to pay their vows, offer their oblations, and make their sacrifices to the Most High. But they also say what we might wish to say when we prepare to pay our vows, offer our oblations, and make our sacrifices to the Most High, in the act we call worship.

But, put like this, it might seem to have a strange ring to it. What is this about vows, oblations, and sacrifices? This, surely, is not the language of the New Testament. Are we not taught that sacrifice and oblation have been offered once and for all in the Passion of our Lord Jesus Christ and that it is inappropriate for us to speak of any sacrifice or oblation that we can make, since He has done all that can be done? Is it not closer to the truth of things to say that Christian worship is a matter of our expressing to God our feelings of gratitude to Him for what He has done and our praise of Him for His great majesty?

This, certainly, is indeed one of the elements of Christian worship, this pouring out of our expressions of thanks and praise. Christians believe that this is the principal

New England Journal of Ministry, June 1981.

activity of the creation—that those odd comments in the Bible about morning stars singing, and dragons and great deeps praising God, and so forth—that they are vastly true, even if no satellite that we can send up ever quite picks up this music, or if no bathysphere ever glimpses Leviathan. No one who has ever stood in a northern forest at dusk and heard the singing of the winter wren, the veery, or the hermit thrush can doubt that there is a music here so exquisite and so heartbreaking that the angelic Mozart himself would give his soul to know where it comes from. And, some of the sweetest sounds in the ears of the Most High must be the croaking of the frogs He has made, the braying of the jackasses He has made, and all the other bleating and hooting and trumpeting that goes up to Him from all these wonderful creatures of His.

For us mortal men, there is the frightening dignity that has been conferred on us like a mantle, that we somehow lead this chorus. This would seem to be hinted at in the creation story, where we find that our flesh is in some way the crown of Creation, and that we were made vassals over all of this, to name it, and rule it, and take care of it in the Name of the Creator Himself. Of course we botched it straight off in Eden, where we made our grab for whatever that poisonous knowledge was that would make us like gods. We got what we wanted, to be sure, but it killed us. Was it not at that point that secularism appeared? For what do we mean by "secular"? We use the word to refer to what belongs to this world only. We use it in contrast to the word "sacred" or "hallowed". But this is a ghastly mistake, says the Bible. All things were made by Him, and for Him, and it is all His. There is nothing "secular"—unless it is in my attitude. If I suppose that something is mine, then I am guilty of sacrilege—of rifling the sanctuary, so to speak, and of running off with the sacred things in an act of plunder. Is this not what we did in Eden? Did we not say, "Very well: Almost everything is Thine, O Lord; but this is one small bit we will seize for ourselves—this one small bit." The difficulty here is that the entire fabric ripped at that point. Heaven groaned. Earth felt the wound, says John Milton in *Paradise Lost.* Now we must live with this deathly gash, or abyss, in things, seeing them as sacred and secular: a division that did not exist for us in our innocence.

But how did we get here from our topic of worship and from the singing of the morning stars and the thrushes? Alas—it is all too short a leap, is it not? You and I believe that all nature praises the Lord; and we also believe that this is our principal business; and we also believe that we are appointed to lead that chorus somehow. And yet we find that we do not feel much like doing it most of the time. We are so besotted with worldliness; it fills us with anxiety about things (the Church used to call this cupidity—a good word) on the completely fraudulent supposition that anything can ever be ours if we scrabble and claw for it. Praise dies on our lips, and adoration finds itself extinguished. Why can't we just sing like these birds and be happy and full of innocent joy before the Lord? It seems that we must, if we are going to do it at all, gird up our loins and address ourselves, not always entirely easily, to the business of praise and adoration, that is, to worship. We even block off an hour that is called "worship".

And here we have it. Surely this is the point. We do, precisely, have to block off a time for worship. We did not have to do that in Eden. In our innocence there, everything that we did all the time was nothing but worship. Our eating and drinking and work and play and rest were all nothing but a continuous oblation made to the Lord. We were put into Eden to bless God for it all, and we did this without ceasing and without boredom. There was no liturgy in Eden—that is, no separate act of worship—surely. Adam and Eve did not need to block off an hour a week or an hour a day in which to praise the Lord: Surely all their activities went up in praise, always—the way ours will do when our Redemption is complete in the City of God, where we are told that praise is continuous.

But, because of our sin, we tore that seamless fabric of activity. We had to live with division. We had to leave Eden and walk out into the desert called history, where we would be taught, little by little, how to worship once more. But alas, we could not learn it all at once. It was like starting kindergarten lessons: Build this altar here. Make a sacrifice there. Remember the Lord. Pay your vows. Now build a tabernacle like this: Put it in the center of your camp; make it all of gold and purple and fine-twined linen; now bring your bullocks and heifers and goats and lambs—see to it that it is the firstlings of your flocks, and not the dregs and runts, that you bring. This spot in the center of your camp will hallow the whole camp; and this act in which you bring your sacrifices and oblations will hallow everything you do all week long; and this lamb that you bring will be the token that you and all that you have are hallowed—that is, that all belongs to the Lord.

And suddenly we are back home again in Eden where we belong! All belongs to the Lord, and what belongs to the Lord is holy, and where everything is holy, there is Eden, or Paradise.

Not so quickly, alas. We are still in history, still in school. We must learn to live with the division we have made—this division between sacred and secular, even though in the end it is a false division. It takes a very long time—a whole lifetime and more, for each one of us, and the whole history of our race—to learn the lessons. Bring sacrifice; make oblation; go up to the altar of God—and in so doing, learn little by little, by this discipline placed upon you, and by these offerings required from you—learn that these are only tokens—that they "stand for" the whole thing. All hours are God's; all flocks are His; more, you are His, all the time. But, being fallen men and not seraphim, we find it difficult to keep this vision in our minds. We get distracted. We get preoccupied; the cares of the day swoop in, and we lose the flush of euphoria that we felt when we sang our hymn of praise at the altar of God. Dishes and traffic jams and committee meetings and the telephone and getting the carburetor fixed and waiting in line in the post office behind someone who has seven packages to mail, each to a different country—all this clutters everything up and somehow the spell is broken.

Well, O man, return, then. Return to the altar. Go. Make your offering to the Lord—your offering of contrition, and of thanksgiving—at least the attempt at thanksgiving—even for these baneful and harrying things—and then make your act of worship once more, since that is what you were made for to begin with, and that is what you will be doing forever and ever, and now is the time to be learning, not just that it must be done, but that, lo and behold, it is indeed what we were made for and that this act of worship gathers up and glorifies everything we do all day every day.

But this is to have leaped ahead a bit. Two objections to this line of thought might have presented themselves to you. First, we seem to have jumped, without so much as a nod, from the Tabernacle in Israel over to the telephone and the post office several thousand years later. Haven't we ignored the great watershed of the Gospels here? Did not everything change when Christ came? Surely it is no longer a matter of paying vows and bringing oblations and sacrifices? The one sacrifice has been made, once and for all. And second, is it not odd to speak of worship as an act? Isn't worship an experience? You make it sound as though worship is something we can do in response to a command: But surely true worship ought to spring spontaneously from my heart. Isn't that what Christians mean when they talk about worshipping?

We may consider this second objection first. Indeed, the spontaneous overflow of joy or gratitude to the Lord, expressed in shouts and songs and the clapping of hands is one of the loveliest manifestations of praise. We do not need to be skilled in order for our worship to bring joy to the Lord. What earthly father would say to his small child who has brought him a drooping bouquet of wilted dandelions in a jelly glass, "Oh, but this isn't good enough. The florist does it much better." The very thought of a rebuff like this makes us wince. If mere mortal love can transfigure these dandelions into the very flowers of Paradise, how much more does the Divine Love transfigure our poor attempts to present something beautiful at the shrine. Our most exalted oratorios and cantatas, surely, are mere bleating and croaking compared to the music of the seraphim. But our gracious Lord asks it of us and rejoices in whatever is offered with a true heart, from a cracked and off-key shout of "Hallelujah" going up from a shanty somewhere, to the beating of tom-toms, to the solemn praise offered in the Church of the Holy Wisdom in Byzantium.

For what is the common thing in all of these efforts? Is it not that worship is being offered? It is not how gorgeous what is weighed in heaven may look and sound or even the intensity of exalted feeling that may have attended it.

You may sometimes have heard the phrase "a beautiful worship experience", perhaps from tourists who may have gotten themselves into some English cathedral late one afternoon. Here are these titanic columns soaring into the serene dimness high overhead, and these windows through which the twilight sun slants with subdued and multicolored majesty, and then—the organ pealing out, and the piping voices of the choirboys chanting the Psalter in a music so pure and pellucid that your heart breaks. You have stumbled into the ancient service of Evensong, and you stumble out at the end transfixed by the sheer sublimity of it all. "What a beautiful worship experience!" you gasp. And indeed it has been beyond what you can bear.

But this thrill and exaltation is not itself worship, of course, any more than the thrill and exaltation that surges in the breast of a young man or woman in love is itself love. The love of a man and a woman may be attended, God knows, by soaring and lyric ecstasies; but it is not those ecstasies that constitute the foundation stone of marriage. The foundation itself is a much more solid thing.

It is thus with worship. Worship may be attended, like love, with all sorts of exalted feelings and experiences, or it may not. That does not matter very much. For worship is primarily an act, and an act is something we do.

There is a very old word that catches this idea. It went out of common use among some Christians at the end of the Middle Ages, but it is a good word. You find it being used among the early Christians to denote what they did when they came together as a body to make their weekly act of worship. The word I am speaking about, of course, is the word "liturgy". Loosely translated, it just means "the work of the people". If we hear the word nowadays, it might conjure up a picture of a special kind of worship service that is excessively elaborate, marked with solemnity, pomp, ritual, and ceremony. Sometimes when we know a feast day of the Church is approaching, like Christmas or Easter, we try to ginger things up a bit with more music and slightly more formal dress than might otherwise be worn, and perhaps some candles and some response for the congregation to say printed out in the program. This is all most appropriate, but it does not make the service more liturgical, or indeed more "worshipful" necessarily. If you are anything like me, you like very good music well performed, and you like some formality and "atmosphere" in a special service like this. All of this represents an offering on the part of the church—someone has gone to some trouble and some time and some expense to put this together and to rehearse the singers and so forth. This is all part of the offering, and as such, it is received and transmuted by the alchemy of the Divine Love into pure gold.

But the word "liturgy"—this work of the people that the early Christians talked about—referred to the specific thing that they did when they came together. From what we can find out about what actually went on in the years when the apostles were still about, and the very early years of the young Church after the last of the apostles had died off, they seem to have focused their corporate worship on the Lord's Table. It is worth our noting one thing here that has always marked Christian worship as well as Hebrew. It is the element of structure, or formality.

There are a thousand different ways of organizing worship services, of course. But whether we are speaking of a solemn Eucharistic liturgy or an informal company of Christians gathered to sing and pray and break bread, there is always the element that something is presiding over the activity. It may look, to an outsider, somewhat informal: But the people gathered there see themselves as under a certain set of expectations—rules, even—that determine what they do. There may be an element of informality as to who suggests which song to sing at which point in the gathering, or who prays, and so forth. But everyone would know that something had been violated if someone jumped up and decided that they should all play hide and seek as the next item in the service. No matter how informal it may seem, everyone knows pretty exactly what is going to happen, and even when. Now it is a singing time, now it is a sharing time, now it is a praying time: that sort of thing. Of course, at the other end of the spectrum, the order is clear enough for any outsider to see: Every gesture and movement and word is strictly determined by the unseen order that presides over things.

There are two elements in this order that presides over Christian worship. They are ritual and ceremony; and both are worth our paying attention to, since they reveal something important about us ourselves and, therefore, about how we may come to this business of worship.

Ritual, strictly speaking, refers to the words used in an order of worship, and ceremony refers to the actions—the gestures and movements. All of us are familiar with the Christian use of hymns and psalms in worship, and in these we have ritual, that is, fixed, "secondhand" words helping us to worship. Left to our own spontaneous resources and devices, we often find it difficult to know what to say. But then we begin a hymn or a psalm, and we find that, far from cramping us or quelling the "liberty of the Spirit" in us, lo and behold, these words, written by someone else, and "imposed" on us, turn out to assist us in the very thing we would have a hard time doing left to ourselves. Which of us, asked to express our awe in the presence of the Divine Glory, will not be glad for the help of such secondhand formulas as "Holy, Holy, Holy, Lord God of Sabaoth; heaven and earth are filled with the majesty of Thy glory. Hosanna in the Highest." But that is a very, very old set of words and has been used daily in the Church for many centuries now. Ritual, then, turns out to be a liberating thing, not a cage that imprisons us. (Of course, when we gather informally to "share" our experiences of grace, or to chat and have fellowship, we do not use these formalities: But the Church, in her public acts of worship, has seemed to turn to psalms and hymns, not to reduce everyone's freedom, but to set us all free from the shallow puddle of our own resources.)

Ceremony might seem a bit more remote from us modern men, accustomed as we are to informality—indeed, we even find people striving to get things unstructured at times. Ceremony might seem to militate against the liberty of the Spirit.

But here again, we may recall two things: First, this Spirit of Liberty, the Holy Ghost, is the very architect of order. We see this in the Creation, and in the moral law, and in the serenity that fills the whole being of someone who is full of this Spirit. Havoc and confusion and clutter are not the marks of His presence. But secondly, we may recall an oddity about ourselves. We human beings always ceremonialize things. We set the table for breakfast: Dogs do not bother to do this. We organize a parade when we have won a game or when the hostages come home. We put on jeans for one event and coats and ties for another: These are ceremonial garments, indicating "picnic" or "the Boston Symphony". But it reaches farther than this: We really do reach for ceremony when we come to the central mysteries of our existence, namely, birth, love, and death. Obstetrics tells us a great deal about birth, but it cannot tell us why we want pink and blue and candles and cake. Again, sheer biology can tell us a great deal about the fruitful coming together of a man and a woman in the mystery of procreation, but it cannot tell us why this event should be heralded and festooned with processions and flowers and gifts and veils and winged collars. And again, medicine can tell us what has happened on one level when someone dies, but it cannot tell us why we should thereby hush things up and have music played and drive slowly through the streets. Ceremony seems, one way or another, to be a very crucial mark of the mystery of our humanity.

But there is more: We seem to ceremonialize things, not by way of beclouding them, or hiding from them, or escaping from them. Quite the contrary, we reach for ceremony when we know in the depths of our being that we need help to come at the mystery facing us. Ceremony heightens and intensifies our experience by bringing order to our feelings about it.

We do not, of course, have to have ceremony. We may ignore the significance we attach to things. Christians, because they have always attached the very highest significance to the worship of the Divine Majesty, have tended to ceremonialize this activity. We know that gestures and postures and bodily attitudes mean something. Words alone are very far from being adequate to our experience. Anyone who has ever loved knows that a kiss, which is after all only a gesture, carries vast significance. We shake hands, we wave, we bow our heads to say grace, we kneel to say our prayers; these are all ceremonial actions that help us by doing for us what words alone can never do.

This brings us around to the act peculiar to Christian worship, namely, the Lord's Table, where He meets His people in the Communion of bread and wine. Here, at the center of the mystery of the Church, we have ceremony. It does not matter whether we find ten thousand Christians at a great festival Eucharist or three Christians sitting on the beach with a paper cup of wine and some broken saltines. It is the same thing. But it is a ceremony—very different from a banquet or a picnic where that same wine and those same saltines might have supplied part of the menu. Now these humble things bear an infinite weight of glory. For the Lord Himself blessed them and said that when this was done in this way by His people they might be called His Body and Blood.

What is going on here? Do we not find in this ceremony the making present to us Christians the thing that was so dimly hinted at in the worship of Israel with all of its offerings and sacrifices, namely, that the place where God and man meet is the place of sacrifice and offering. But, there has only been one Sacrifice, of course—the "full, perfect, and sufficient, sacrifice, oblation, and satisfaction for the sins of the whole world" made by our Lord in His Passion. The blood of the bulls and goats signified the Sacrifice that was to come; and the Bread and Wine signify for us that same Sacrifice.

But what an oddity: It is no longer blood and gore and burned fat and ashes that is appointed. It is food. Bread and wine. The altar—the place where alone we mortals may presume to approach the Divine Majesty—has become a place of feasting. The place of slaughter and death is now also a table. The ordinary stuff that we bring to this table (and it is worth remembering that the early Christians made quite a point of this business of the laity bringing the bread and wine) is received by the Lord and given back to us, He says, as His Body and Blood.

In one sense we see enacted here the whole Gospel mystery. What have we got to bring to the Lord? Nothing, really—or, if it can be called anything at all, it is just the plain stuff of ourselves: "ourselves, our souls, and bodies, to be a reasonable, holy, and living sacrifice unto Thee", to use the language of one church's liturgy. What can we bring to the Most High? Ourselves—our life, our work, our praises and thanksgivings, our joys, our griefs and burdens and limitations, and our very sufferings: What can we do with these but lift them up before the altar and say,

"Thy servant, Lord, hath nothing in the house"—nothing but this. Bread and wine in themselves are universal symbols: They stand for the plain stuff in our lives—our Monday through Saturday lives, we might say. But when these are brought, and offered, our gracious Lord takes them and blesses them, and gives them to us as heavenly food.

Altars are places of death. Sacrifices are brought to altars to be consumed. Christians believe that it is only through the mystery of sacrifice and death that there is any life at all. Easter follows Good Friday. Resurrection follows the Cross. In the mystery of our Lord's Passion we find that the Sacrifice has been made and that now, all who will may unite themselves with that Sacrifice and find that life and nourishment and joy spring from this uniting. The altar has become also a table.

But the mystery goes on and on. We find that our High Priest, who is also the Victim at that altar, has called us His priestly people. What does this mean? Surely it must at least partly mean that, as He was broken for the life of the world, so we, His Body, are to be broken for the life of the world. And that, as He offered Himself in oblation to God, so we may find that when we offer ourselves in union with the one Oblation, we are taken into the mystery that stands somewhere near the heart of the Gospel, namely, that what is offered up—what is made a sacrifice—what is given over to death—is like a seed planted. It springs up into life—into corns of wheat from which bread can be made for the life of the world.

Surely Christians would see something like this going on in their worship. Rightly understood, worship is not a separate activity at all. It is a focusing of all our activity. Like the tokens in the Tabernacle, it stands for all that we are and all that we do. Here we begin to return, as it were, to the work for which we were made, and which we knew in Eden, of adoring the Most High in all of our work. We haven't learned it yet; but we are learning.

When we come to the altar of God, what do we Christians bring? Nothing much: just plain stuff. Bread and wine. Our songs and our prayers. Here comes a man with a week's worth of headaches and committee meetings in his hands. Can he offer this? It is all he has right now. Will it be received, if he offers it up? And here is a woman with a pile of dishes and diapers and a week's worth of chauffeuring children to and from music lessons, Scouts, youth group, and skating. Not very impressive. May this jumble be gathered up and offered, with her love, at the altar? And here is an artist. She has been working all week on one painting, and it is not even a religious painting. May she present her work as an offering? What good is it? And here comes a poet, and a ballerina: Is it all right? May they come? And here is someone who has just been stunned with grief. May he offer his suffering? Is the Suffering of the High Priest powerful enough to hallow and glorify this which is offered at His altar?

Surely we must say yes to all of this. Surely Christians, when they say, "I will go to the altar of God", know that they enter thereby into the place where ordinary things are transfigured and where all is holy, all is glory, all is joy.

Ex Aegypto

Ex Aegypto vocavi filium meum. "Out of Egypt have I called my son." We all know this quote from having heard, year after year, the Gospel readings in connection with Christmas and the events that follow it. The Holy Family had to flee to Egypt from Herod, who was about to mount the Slaughter of the Innocents to forestall any plot to supplant him on his throne with an upstart boy. Saint Matthew remarks that this all came to pass as a fulfilled prophecy, referring to Hosea's word that God had "called my son out of Egypt".

Not long ago, a Carmelite nun friend of mine in Philadelphia sent me a poem by her grandfather, Clifford J. Laube, with that Latin text for its title (the collection of his poems is titled *Broken Crusts* and may be obtained from Arx Publications).

There are not, so far as I know, many poems in the annals of Christian meditation addressed to Egypt. This one is an "apostrophe", that is, a line of thought addressed to something non-human: one's native country, a field of daffodils, a Grecian urn, or Egypt, in this case.

Egypt, from your silted dream the river-lily nods.
Dust is in your tabernacles. Death is on your gods.
Night is on Ikhnaton, but his spirit in your fanes [temples]
Was a witness to the truth, and the truth remains.

Reprinted with permission by CatholiCity, December 23, 2008.

Isis, Phthah, Anubis, and the rest of those gods have vanished from Egypt, and all is quiet in her hollow temples. Ikhnaton—the pharaoh who *knew* that there had to be One God above all gods who must be worshipped—is dead, too, having failed to persuade Egypt to abandon her throng of deities.

Egypt, by your sunken plinths the ibis wades.
Broken lies the obelisk, the hieroglyph fades.
Wilderness of ruin! But a live-forever blooms:
Starry hope deep-hidden in your death-denying tombs.

The ibis wading near ruined columns, the fallen obelisk—one is reminded of Shelley's Ozymandias, with his stone visage down in the sand. But, strangely, there is hope flowering among the tombs and pyramids and sarcophagi, with all of their unguents and spices, so earnestly brought in to fend off death and decay.

Egypt, on your templed towns a ten-fold justice fell,
Chastening your tyrant kings, avenging Israel,
But gratitude remembers how you gave a fronded path
To Three in holy hiding from the fang of Herod's
wrath.

The God whom Ikhnaton sought so sedulously visited a much later pharaoh, Rameses, with ten plagues when that king refused to release Israel, who belonged to that God. But blessings on you, Egypt, for having offered a refuge under your palms, much later still in time, to a man and woman and their endangered son. (Very odd—how the eye of the just sees a destiny undeflected by the indifference or inattention of earthly powers.)

Egypt of Osiris, let your phantoms sleep.
Egypt of Rameses, may your dreams be deep.
To Cleopatra's Egypt a long oblivion;
But starlight on the Egypt that shielded Mary's Son!

What we have here is a case in point of true—and, to my mind, striking—Catholic piety. For one thing, such piety sees the folly of schemes mounted to outwit God. "God is working His purpose out, as year succeeds to year"—this is plain Catholic belief. Rameses knew nothing of the God who could sink his chariots. Herod was mad to suppose that he could circumvent what the prophets had foretold. And Egypt, with her pantheon of gods, had no idea at all that she was protecting the One—the infant God come to be the Savior of the world.

What about that—the role that indifferent or hostile forces play in God's plan of salvation for the world? From Abraham onward—or, shall we say, from Adam, Abel, Enoch, and Noah onward—what has been asked of the just is that they lay their expectations wholly (and solely) in God, in spite of all. The Church finds herself in that lineage. And she is clear about the one final and undoubted thing: The God who made us will save us, calling Israel and then sending the Savior; and all of history moves toward its fruition in Him.

In all of her efforts to "reach out" and "dialogue" with other religions and philosophies, the Church has never put forward the notion that all roads lead to heaven, so to speak, with all religious founders and prophets equally testifying to the saving truth for us men. She has only one gospel: "But God shows his love for us in that while we were yet sinners Christ died for us" (Rom 5:8). That is the one gospel with which the Church is charged. Neither Rameses nor Herod—nor any other prince, dictator, or power—can frustrate this divine plan.

The poem "*Ex Aegypto*" testifies to this. It sees Ikhnaton as "a witness to the truth"; and Rameses himself became, ironically, a figure testifying to the grace of God. Catholic imagination, when it is suffused with the generosity that comes from the God who sent us the Savior, can, with true piety, say: Blessings on you, Egypt.

Finding the Way In

Every once in a while I pull out of its shelf my worn copy of Milton's poetical works. What can one say? To embark on any given line of Milton is to find oneself in a thunderous domain where language becomes the very avatar of bliss. *Paradise Lost* is, of course, Milton's crowning achievement, with *Samson Agonistes* right on its heels.

But there are dozens of short poems for one's pleasure. Near the top of this list, I would put the twin pieces "L'Allegro" and "Il Penseroso". In these two works, Milton mounts an "apostrophe", that poetical form in which the poet speaks to an abstraction: Shelley to the West Wind, Keats to Solitude, Shakespeare to "devouring time", and so forth.

"L'Allegro" hails happiness, "thou goddess fair and free", and "Il Penseroso" extols melancholy, the "pensive nun". When one has finished reading these twin pieces, one is in a quandary: Which *is* the better mood? On the surface, happiness carries the day—but upon reflection, one asks whether melancholy might not after all be a mood more fitting to our mortal condition.

> Haste thee nymph, and bring with thee
> Jest and youthful jollity,
> Quips and cranks, and wanton wiles,
> Nods, and becks, and wreathed smiles....

Reprinted with permission by CatholiCity, March 7, 2011.

In this happy mood, Milton conjures the picture of a country morning, where we hear "the lark begin his flight.... And at my window bid good-morrow."

It is, of course, sheer fancy. No one can possibly take it seriously. Aren't poets forever summoning us all away from the plodding burdens of real existence and off to a mere cloud-cuckooland? A lark on my windowsill greeting me indeed.

But upon reflection, do we mortals not yearn, in our very bones and marrow, for that realm where the barrier between us and the rest of creation is withdrawn? On a tour, say, through the great valleys and vistas of New Zealand; or among the little hills, meadows, brooks, and cottages of the Cotswolds, do we not, all of us—if our souls' nerve-endings have not been altogether cauterized by noise, speed, and machinery—find ourselves wishing that we could get *in*? To be whisked along in a great charabanc at sixty miles an hour *past* the scene sends us back to the inn at the end of the day vaguely uneasy, dissatisfied—wishing ... Or, among the giant firs of British Columbia or the spruces in the Swiss Alps, with perhaps—oh joy!—the glimpse of a fawn or a chamois: Would we not give a very great deal to be rid of *time*, which bundles us along our way so brutally, and even more, to exchange courtesies with the creature?

In all the fairy tales, such barriers have started to break down. Here's a robin trying to get our attention, or two beavers with their boiled potatoes and sewing machine, or a faun with his scarf and umbrella, or (better yet) a unicorn looking at us from a cool glade. Do we weary readers not find a fleeting sense in ourselves that it all might be beckoning us *on*? Surely the man who feels nothing but scorn and boredom at such fancies may be missing something?

Milton certainly entertains such a fancy quite seriously. On the porch and railing just outside the windows of my study, a Carolina wren comes from time to time to get at the feeders and scattered seeds that I have put out. But he never bids me good morrow. Neither does the little red-breasted nuthatch, or the red-bellied woodpecker, or the chickadees and titmice and chipping sparrows.

What if one of them *did* greet me one fine morning?

At this point, readers may be thinking, "Ah. Where have I come across this line of thought before?" You have come across it in C. S. Lewis' sermon "The Weight of Glory", which he preached in the University Church of Saint Mary the Virgin in Oxford:

> Apparently, then, our lifelong nostalgia, our longing to be reunited with something in the universe from which we now feel cut off ... is no mere neurotic fancy, but the truest index of our real situation.... We do not want merely to *see* beauty.... We want something else which can hardly be put into words—to be united with the beauty we see ... all the leaves of the New Testament are rustling with the rumour that ... some day, God willing, we shall get *in*.

We are told by Saint Paul of a "far more exceeding and eternal weight of glory" [2 Cor 4:17; KJV] that lies in store for us. It is immensely difficult to keep such a picture in focus if one is beleaguered with the clutter of ordinary life, or harried by tension and controversy, or weighed down with sheer pain. Our ordinary efforts to grasp the idea of glory as it comes to us from the Bible, with thrones and golden streets and cherubim, seem to have nothing to do with larks and fauns. It is sometimes urged in the name of piety that the larks and fauns belong either to childhood, to be firmly put away as we mature, or worse, to paganism, to be jettisoned.

But that lark at my window, whether he wishes me Good morrow or not, *does* stand on a threshold. On the hither side stands me, crowned with the dignity and mystery that belong to the species *Homo sapiens*. But beyond the lark stretches a whole realm to which I and my kind are almost total strangers. Oh, to be sure, we can observe the birds through our field glasses, or trap them and classify them and dissect them. But who knows what they know? What attracts them to a mate? What makes them build those elegant nests? What makes them sing? Dear *God*, what makes them sing?

If only we could get *in*—truly inside the world of porpoises and gazelles and ivory-billed woodpeckers—and angels and archangels and seraphim and red dwarfs and galaxies.

What does Redemption mean? Whatever else it entails, surely there will be a re-knitting of the frayed fragments of a Creation tattered and torn by us sons of Adam. Then, perhaps, the lark will not only greet me, but he will show me the way *in*. Then, perhaps, all the fancies that have broken our hearts in all the songs and tales from all of our tribes will come into their own. And then we may even find the spot where

> A tiny little man stands in forest dim,
> A cunning little mantle he wears on him.
> Who can this stranger be,
> Standing 'neath the forest tree
> With the mantle hanging down to his knee?

Gods, Heroes, and Arthur Miller

Having taught English literature and the Greek classics for about forty years, I have found myself from time to time mulling over some of the questions that seem to arch over the whole enterprise. One likes to let one's mind run along some of the thunderous questions of ultimacy that roll across the heavens under which English classes struggle along. Are the Greek gods good or bad, for example? Or—here's a poser—what is the relationship between the will of Zeus and "what happens"? After all, he is the king of the gods, and one would think he'd have the prerogative of calling the shots. But not so. Most things seem to go wrong for him, and he has no authority whatever over the Fates, who hold the shears that snip the thread of your life when they decide your hour has come.

At this point in the discussion, I usually make the obvious point that any Christian believer has got precisely the same riddle in his own lap. What is the relation between God's will and what happens? Attila the Hun. The Black Plague. The dismal slaughter of the world wars. Cancer. Stalin. Alzheimer's. Genocide. Abortion. There are, to be sure, reaches of "Christian" theology that have it all nailed down so that the human drama is nothing but the unrolling of exactly what the Most High has pre-programmed from all eternity. But mighty few readers of *Crisis* will be found in those reaches.

Originally published in *Crisis* (December 1, 2004). Reprinted with permission.

Nevertheless, a certain gloomy irony popped into my mind some years ago among my general musings about literature. It was this: When you get rid of the gods, you get rid of us. If we sup-pose that that is merely a platitude, we might reflect briefly. It happens to run exactly counter to the entire set of sup-positions that undergirds our epoch. It makes very little difference here whether we wish to call into play the word "modernism" or "post-modernism". (Plus ça change, plus c'est la même chose.)

Somewhere in the nineteenth—or eighteenth or seventeenth century, the idea began to percolate through Western imagination and philosophy that if we mortals are ever going to stand tall and rise to our true dignity and stature, we are going to have to get the gods off our backs. It trickled down (or avalanched, shall we say) to popular culture in the 1960s. We began to hear, "I make my own morality." "A pox on bourgeois [read 'my parents'] morality." And religious taboos! Gadzooks! Get these gods off our backs!

The idea was that as long as we have the gods—read "God"—peering over our shoulders and calling us to account, we're going to creep along timorously, a whole race of helots.

Very appealing notions. There is one small joker in the pack, though: It has been the epochs and civilizations that did think the gods were there—and most emphatically were calling us to account—that have drawn for us the titanic figures of the hero: Gilgamesh. Achilles. Hector. Beowulf. Roland. Lear. Even Henry V. But then a disquieting dwindling begins to take place in our protagonists. We get the courtier: Castiglioni's *Il Cortegiano*. And then the gentleman—often very admirable but scarcely heroic. And then? Willie Loman in *The Death of a Salesman*, who goes out with a whimper, not a bang. Or Estragon and Vladimir, waiting there for Godot, who never shows up.

There are a few figures from our century that testify to the thesis at work in this essay. Tolkien's figures (Aragorn, Frodo, and their fellowship) and Lewis' (Reepicheep, Puddleglum, and Peter the High King) stand before us as heroes in the ancient tradition, without the slightest blink of irony. Catholics, accustomed as they are to harking back many centuries for authority, will have no trouble seeing the point of this. Perhaps the most awesome figure conceivable is that of a great king whose majesty knows how to kneel in the presence of the god.

The Good Doctor Donne

Beethoven, Shakespeare, and the rest—how we extol them. "Oh, I do love his Seventh Symphony so much!" Or, "Oh yes—'To be or not to be ... '—so powerful. So immeasurably profound."

The thing about all of this, of course, is that once one has graduated from school, the chances of one's returning to the works of these gentlemen are sparse. When was the last time (even you music lovers who pride yourselves on having got beyond the golden oldies) that you listened—really *listened*—to Beethoven's Fifth?

In any event, among such works we would certainly find John Donne's sonnet, "Batter my heart, three-person'd God." When was the last time you mulled *that* one over? It offers the occasion for some salutary and brisk self-examination—an exercise that ought to be on the (daily?) agenda of any good Catholic.

> Batter my heart, three-person'd God; for You
> As yet but knock, breathe, shine, and seek to mend;

What's this? Ah: I am so besotted and slatternly that Your efforts to flag me down are far too gentle. You merely knock at my door, or breathe on me like a wooer, or illumine me with comfortable words from Scripture, or try to patch things up here and there. You are going to

Reprinted with permission by CatholiCity, December 1, 2008.

have to hammer on me if I am ever to start from my habitual torpor. (It's worth noting here that a very sharp awareness of one's own sluggishness is at work in these sentiments. Donne, not being modern, thinks of his condition as sinful unless grace intervenes. He is not merely "broken": He's guilty of the sin of Sloth—one of the Seven Deadly ones, remember.)

> That I may rise, and stand, o'erthrow me, and bend
> Your force, to break, blow, burn, and make me new.

The penitent warms to his task here. Dear Lord, don't merely knock: You are going to have to break down the door and throw me down (very brisk stuff here). Don't just breathe: *Blow*. And as for shining—it will take the fire of Your Love to rouse me. As a matter of fact, my condition is so pitiful that You are going to have to make me new. Tinkering won't quite do the trick.

If one is at this point inclined to palliate things by remarking that, well, of course Donne was a Puritan—he wasn't. He was a very Catholic-minded Anglican. The Puritans hadn't tipped their hand yet.

> I, like a usurped town to another due,
> Labor to admit You, but oh! to no end;

I am like a town that owes fealty to God but that has been conquered by a usurper and owes its taxes to the wrong lord now. In other words, without Your grace, Sin has me in thrall. I make attempts to let You in, but it's useless. I'm too feeble. Has any one of us ever found it a bit wearying even to pray? Or to keep our minds focused at Mass? There's so much else besides *the Lord* that crowds our thoughts ...

Reason, Your viceroy in me, me should defend,
But is captiv'd, and proves weak or untrue.

Sheer Reason, Your good gift, which should be ruling my thoughts and behavior in Your name, turns out itself to be in chains and unable to save the situation. It can even deceive me. It looks as though Grace is called for.

Yet dearly I love You, and would be lov'd fain,
But am betroth'd unto Your enemy.
Divorce me, untie or break that knot again,

The sad thing is that, in spite of all, I do love You, and want very much to be loved by You, but I seem to have betrothed myself to Satan. Again—violent sentiments these; but Donne was speaking from a mind saturated with Scripture, the Fathers, and the saints. Surely it's not quite that bad? But we need to consult sources more ancient than modern counseling if we are ever to make it to the dread precincts of holiness. Well then, grant me a divorce from this false spouse; undo my shackles; break the knot with which I have fastened myself to the enemy.

Take me to You, imprison me, for I,
Except You enthrall me, never shall be free;
Nor ever chaste, except You ravish me.

Heigh-ho. Prison again? Yes. It's the ancient and rich notion that bondage to God is the very, and only, state of true freedom. All else is illusion, like an *ignis fatuus* luring us mortals eventually into the dungeons of hell.

But what's this about chastity? Well, sin has fouled me. I have lost my virginity a thousand times over—not only in Eden, but by choices without number that I myself have made. And unless You, Lord, purify and ravish me with the fire of your Love (remember Bernini's sculpture of Saint Teresa?), I will never be pure enough to enter with Holy Church into the Marriage Supper of the Lamb.

A memorable sonnet, to be sure. But also, perhaps, a jolting reminder of the ancient and never-outdated exercise of fierce self-examination.

An Advent Note on Ikhnaton

One's thoughts don't ordinarily run much to the pharaohs in connection with Advent. Insofar as Egypt might crop up at all, it would seem more fitting to hold it for the Flight into Egypt after the Nativity.

In any case, I received a card this past week from a Discalced Carmelite nun friend of mine. She is an artist and photographer and had made up a sort of collage in which the centerpiece is the painting from the Boston Museum of Fine Arts of the Virgin and Child asleep in the arms of the Sphinx (referring, to be sure, to the Flight into Egypt). In the shadows at the foot of the Sphinx, one can descry, fallen, Cleopatra and Ramses and Osiris—pagan Egypt, that is, in ruins. But in the dark sky of the background—immense, haunting, and immensely wistful, it would seem—we find the solemn and magnificent head of Ikhnaton.

Readers will recall that he was the pharaoh who, alone in remote antiquity, was convinced that there *must* be the One above all the clutter of deities worshipped in Egypt's rites and sacrifices. He went to his grave, as far as we know, unsatisfied. C. S. Lewis poses the question somewhere as to which of us can think of that lonely king without saying a prayer for his soul.

The point is, there was a man whose whole being yearned for the coming of God. He would have given

Reprinted with permission by CatholiCity, December 3, 2007.

anything to have seen the Face of God. He kept Advent, so to speak. Do we for one moment suppose that he will be denied what he sought?

As it happens, I am writing this column on the Wednesday of the week between the Feast of Christ the King and the First Sunday in Advent. The First Lesson this morning at Mass was about another pagan king. The trouble here is that this king was most certainly *not* looking for God. He was frolicking in a great debauch. When the handwriting came on the wall, poor Belshazzar's knees knocked and his hip joints gave way.

Here, no doubt, we have two icons for Advent worth pausing over.

The hymns for Advent form one of the season's most salutary aspects, it seems to me. For one thing, there is the sixth-century Latin "Hark, a thrilling voice is sounding." The word "thrilling" is to be taken in both senses of "full of delight", since the news announced is indeed, for those like Ikhnaton and the saints, good news ("Christ is nigh"), and "full of dread", for those like Belshazzar and other distracted types, since the One drawing nigh is, alas, the Judge. The first stanza of this ancient hymn goes on to adjure us, "Cast away the works of darkness, / O ye children of the day." The very theme of the first weeks of Advent.

Then there is Saint Ambrose's *Veni, Redemptor gentium*—"Come, Thou Redeemer of the Earth." How Ikhnaton must have prayed that, or something not altogether unlike that. What note do we strike when *we* sing it? We know that He has come. Why sing it, then? Here lies the mystery of liturgical time: It transcends mere sequence and chronology. We enter into the region where the eternal touches history and the event (in this case, the coming of the Lord: His second coming, then His nativity—we mark them in that order in Advent, backward) becomes present. Or, put it the other way around: We are taken into the "present" of the event—the second coming, or the nativity, in the liturgical seasons and festivals.

And finally, among the great treasury of hymns for Advent, one other may be noted, namely the sixteenth-century "Remember, O Thou man". It is very solemn, indeed, or so it would seem from the first few lines, quite remorseless: "Remember, O thou man, / O thou man, O thou man, / Remember, O thou man, / Thy time is spent. . . ."

Not really very suitable sentiments for us twenty-first-century positive thinkers, surely?

But what is it we will wish to have been reminded of on that Day when *Liber scriptus proferetur/In quo totum continetur* ("a book will be brought forth, in which everything is contained")? Do we want to start our reflecting just then? Hey nonny!

Advent supplies us with this chance. It is indeed a thrilling season, in all senses. All of our fondest, purest yearnings are to be fulfilled, and we are invited to purify our hearts in order to be ready to receive the Lord from heaven—in His comings as Judge and as the Rose from Jesse's stem.

The Hallowed House and the Secular World

Thomas Howard is one of the most erudite and literate Catholic authors in recent history. He was raised in a prominent Evangelical home (his sister is well-known author and former missionary Elisabeth Elliot), became Episcopalian in his mid-twenties, then entered the Catholic Church in 1985, at the age of fifty. Dr. Howard was a highly regarded professor of English and literature for more than thirty years and is the author of numerous books, including *Dove Descending: T. S. Eliot's "Four Quartets"*, *Evangelical Is Not Enough*, *Chance or the Dance?*, *Lead Kindly Light*, *On Being Catholic*, and *The Secret of New York Revealed*. He corresponded recently with Carl E. Olson, editor of *Catholic World Report*, about the new edition of his book *Hallowed Be This House: Finding Signs of Heaven in Your Home* (Ignatius Press, 2012), as well as the state of American culture, secularism, Anglicanism, and great literature.

CWR: How did the idea for *Hallowed Be This House* originally come about? Do you think there is an even greater need today for a sense of the hallowed and the sacred than there was when you first wrote the book in the 1970s?

Editor's note: This interview with Dr. Thomas Howard, conducted by Carl E. Olson, was originally published by *Catholic World Report* on December 12, 2012.

Thomas Howard: I think the original idea for the book came to me gradually. It must have been the fruit of a lifetime of reading and teaching Western literature, where one finds, up until at least the Enlightenment, the assumption of an ordered, hierarchical, and blissful Universe. Even the pagans assume this. But in my young adulthood, I found myself moving from the very faithful and good Protestant Evangelicalism of my family into the Anglican Church, where at least the notions of hierarchy, sacrament, and liturgy are remembered. Also, of course, I became soaked in the works of C.S. Lewis, J.R.R. Tolkien, and their friend Charles Williams. In all of these writers, one finds the ordinary stuff of quotidian life treated as though that stuff bespeaks—what shall we say? Glory? Ultimacy? The Truth of things? Splendor? Yes—all of that. The ordinary is not ordinary. It trumpets joy, freedom, and virtue to us mortals if we will pay attention. Is there a greater need today to see things this way than when I wrote the book in the 1970s? Yes. In the decade of the 1960s, when my wife and I were living in New York, which became the eye of the storm, Western Civilization as it has been known for millennia collapsed. The moral order was overthrown with great zest, and this overthrow is always, inevitably, the prelude to the collapse of any civilization. I myself would see signs of hope, however, in the papacies of John Paul II and of Benedict XVI, with, in the latter case, the promulgation of the Year of Faith. This is a clear call to the Church to reassert, very strongly, the real substance of the Catholic Faith, which is more, far more, than a matter of "it's nice to be nice", which perhaps has been the impression conveyed to the laity in common parish homiletics in the wake of what obviously concerns the Holy Father at the moment—namely, the training of seminarians, for perhaps a century, in "the historical critical method" of reading Scripture.

CWR: Can you give an example or two of how our houses are, or can become, hallowed? How can we better develop a sense of sacramentality and an incarnational perspective?

Howard: How do we "hallow" the household? In one sense, we might repeat what fierce nuns used to lay upon young parochial schoolchildren to do when they skinned a knee or did badly on a quiz: "Offer it up!" That, like all such clichés, hints at something true. The business of "offering" touches on the very center of things. God "offered" his Son for our salvation. Jesus Christ always "offers" his whole being to his Father in the mystery of the Holy Trinity, and offered himself for us poor mortals on the Cross for our salvation. Anything that is thus "offered" can become holy, that is, "set apart" for God.

We see this in the Eucharist, and we are invited to see it in the ordinary routines (often, to be sure, dull or nettlesome) of common household life. The love of a man and woman in the nuptial mystery; the nurture and training of children; peeling carrots; carrying out the trash: All of these supply us with the chance to see ordinariness as the very sacrament of Love, that is, the chance to say to each other, "My life for yours", which is what Love says, e.g., "Here—let me hold this door for you." "Here—let me wash the dishes for a change." "Here—let me get up at 3 A.M. to give the infant a bottle, and let you rest for a few minutes." And of course, all of this is "sacramental" in that the sacraments themselves entail, in every case, a physical point at which holiness and eternal truth touch our mortal life. (Yes—even Confession: There must be a priestly set of ears and a penitent's voice box. We can't text or email our confessions.) So, by the same token, the small, unnoticeable routines and tasks of household life, being characteristically physical events (laundry, sweeping)—these touch on, and even "mediate" to us, the chance to take a small step into the Hallowed: Things become holy by being offered to God. I can do this with my daily household tasks.

CWR: Several of your books, including this one, analyze and critique and address the secularism that seems to infect and infest almost every aspect of modern life. When did you, as a young man, first begin to take the measure of secularism and skepticism? How has secularism changed in, say, the past fifty years? What can be done by the ordinary Catholic in the pew to cope with secularist influences and challenges?

Howard: I think my beginning to "take the measure of secularism and skepticism" came about gradually. The household in which I grew up was profoundly Christian (Evangelical), so the notion of holiness was, so to speak, in the air. One gradually becomes aware that what is at work in Christian love, which one slowly learns at home, is not noticeably at work out in "the world". People don't take God into account. This state of affairs, which has characterized the world of us men since the day after the expulsion from Eden, took an exponential leap forward, I would propose, in the 1960s, when the hubris, venality, lechery, vanity, and predatoriness native to our fallen humanity exploded out across society and became, eventually, sovereign in the public realm. Erstwhile canons of *politesse*, self-control, reticence, modesty, and integrity were overthrown. "Let it all hang out!" became the ensign under which we were told to march. For the "Catholic in the pew", surely the tactic for coping with this firestorm that rules the contemporary world is the old tactic: Stay close to the Center; walk with the Lord, in prayer, quietness (when possible!); the reading of Sacred Scripture daily (if only briefly); and, of course, "assisting at" Mass (that is the old phrase for it), at least weekly, and, if possible, more often. And of course it's not a bad idea to minimize the occasions (TV, cinema, and rock music plugged into one's ears) when that firestorm can assault us with particular energy.

CWR: Your book, *Chance or the Dance?* (Ignatius Press) was originally published in 1969 as *An Antique Drum: The World as Image*. It is remarkable in its insights regarding a whole host of problems, and it is already shot through with a deeply sacramental understanding of the world. How did you, as a young Evangelical, come to that understanding? What role did it play in your decision eventually to enter the Catholic Church?

Howard: I don't think I ever heard the words "sacrament" or "sacramental" in my family's household. The Protestant Reformers had pretty thoroughly evacuated the Faith of any such notion. They were certainly faithful to the Scriptures and the Creeds, as they understood them, and were stout defenders of the Faith. But Protestant religion is primarily a religion of "the Word". It can often seem as though God has revealed himself in cerebral, verbalist, discursive, propositional terms. Of course they believe in, and defend energetically, the *doctrine* of the Incarnation; but their worship and piety is virtually 100 percent focused on the text of Scripture, and on preaching. "Communion" is something of an embarrassment, and it was consigned to the margin of things at the Reformation, some denominations marking the Lord's Supper only four times a year.

So I think that, in my own case, the notion of the sacramental began to take shape in my young imagination by means of a desperate yearning. I was not at all sure what it was that I yearned for, but it seemed to lie vaguely in the direction of the liturgy of the Anglican Church. And it was during the twenty-five years of my life as an Anglican that I learned about the idea of sacrament. As far as my being received into the ancient Roman Catholic Church goes, I had, through reading (Newman, Karl Adam, Louis Bouyer, Romano Guardini) moved steadily in the direction of the Church until, in 1985, at the age of fifty, I was received. The question "What is the Church?" was the single, implacable, remorseless question that became the catalyst here. As an Anglican, I had the best music, the best vestments, the most beautiful church buildings, and the thickest incense that there was. But "*What is the Church?*" would not leave me alone.

CWR: As a student of history and a teacher of literature, how would you describe the current state of American culture in general? What bothers you the most about popular culture? Any signs of hope?

Howard: As far as "the current state of American culture" goes, I, having deep pessimism in my bones and marrow, would take the most melancholy view possible in this regard. Surely all the signs of a disastrously decadent civilization are there? I have nothing new to say here: The loud and brash "sexual revolution" would be the vanguard, I should think, with its concomitant collapse of the family, its assault on the most fundamental quality of our status as men and women—namely, gender—and the sovereignty of philosophical atheism, *and* now, the explicit attack on the Catholic Church globally—these would, to my mind, be the signs. I don't look to politics or education now as a remedy for our malaise. The Enemy is too strong for any human tactics.

As a Protestant Fundamentalist (i.e., Evangelical), I was taught to look for "the blessed hope and the glorious appearing of our Lord and Savior Jesus Christ". We believed, on tiptoe as it were, in the Parousia. As a Catholic, of course, I would not venture to attach any date to this event. But it's hard to fix much hope on human efforts to quench the firestorm, although of course I believe what the Church teaches, namely, that our task is always, always—no matter what century or civilization we live in—to alleviate human suffering and need and to testify to the only Anodyne for our troubles, Jesus Christ.

CWR: You were an Anglican for many years before becoming Catholic. Recently, the Church of England voted—to the surprise of many—not to allow female bishops. Do you think the inevitable has merely been postponed? What is the future, do you think, of theologically liberal, or "progressive", Christian groups and movements?

Howard: The Church of England (Anglican) has just now voted to deny the office of bishop to women. Is this a sign of that Church's orthodoxy and fidelity to the ancient apostolic Church's tradition? I myself would not attach much confidence to the move, since the power structure of the Anglican Church, namely, the bishops and clergy, voted in favor of opening the episcopal office to women, and it was the laity who blocked the move. In that church, the view is that "the faithful are not yet ready" for various moves "forward", e.g., same-sex marriage, women bishops, gender-neutral language, and so forth. But the inevitable forward movement of time will bring all that to pass (it already has, in some of those sorts of questions). Very much the same notion is at work in the American Episcopal Church. And when it comes to the future of liberalism and progressivism in Protestantism, again, I would not foresee any check in the surge toward hegemony of these -isms. What Pio Nono (or was it Pius XII?) saw coming and named "modernism" has burgeoned and flourished and gained almost total control in seminaries all over the world. This is what Benedict XVI is explicitly addressing. But even as the Supreme Pontiff, he has a staggering task facing him. Even Catholic faculties (I know this from teaching in a Catholic seminary) sometimes chuckle and wag their heads knowingly over the Holy Father's efforts. The academic dean at one seminary, when I pressed *Veritatis Splendor* on him twenty-five years ago, read it at my shrill behest, came into my office, and threw the booklet down with the remark, "The pope's exegesis is *so bad* that I couldn't read further." Period.

CWR: As a longtime professor of English literature, what are the essential works of literature you recommend every Catholic read?

Howard: What books might make good reading for Catholics now? I'd have to say that the reading of the Fathers (there's an Oxford paperback edited by Henry Bettenson entitled *The Early Christian Fathers* that contains easy-to read excerpts from these men)—that the reading of such volumes as this would provide a great rush of encouragement and fervor to any Catholic. In my own case, I was greatly helped by John Henry Newman's *Essay on the Development of Christian Doctrine* (Penguin paperback) and by Karl Adam's *The Spirit of Catholicism*. I would also recommend *all* of the works of Romano Guardini. His main book, *The Lord*, is (I tell people) "the best book written since the Bible". One can read only one chapter at a time, not because it is too difficult, but because it opens out on such gigantic vistas of the Faith and the spiritual life that one can take only so much at a given time.

And of course, we now have the works of Benedict XVI. They're not bedtime reading: But I can, I think, guarantee that any reasonably intelligent Catholic adult will find himself thrilled. Also anything by Josef Pieper. And then, naturally, any and all of the works of C. S. Lewis and J. R. R. Tolkien.

Harmonizing Athens and Jerusalem

I have just been re-reading an old book. Not old in the sense of its being eighteenth century—it is Dacre Balsdon's *Oxford Life*, which came out in the early 1950s. One does not have to have been a scholar or a commoner at one of the colleges in Oxford in order to find high pleasure here. For one thing, the prose itself is glorious: understated, droll, well-tempered, urbane, and what the English would call "spot on".

This itself raises one preliminary question, namely, how do we arrive at prose like this? Certainly it has nothing to do with one's trying to cobble up a "style". Nor can it be taught in any writing seminar. It is clearly the fruit of one's having been wholly at home, perhaps from childhood on, through school (an English public school) and university, in the centuries-old domain of civilized discourse. Such discourse appears to have disappeared from the American map. There is nothing in our journalism, television, politics, or education that remotely echoes such prose. It is difficult for a gloomy man not to suppose that somewhere in the last half-century we (America) have seen the collapse of discourse. To be sure, we muddle along through our exchanges of speech, somehow getting the idea across. But Dr. Johnson, or the nonagenarian president of Magdalen, Dr. Routh, would find our modes of discourse not only impenetrable but appalling.

Reprinted with permission by CatholiCity, March 3, 2009.

But a larger question presents itself in connection with the ancient topic that lies between Athens and Jerusalem, asked by Tertullian in the second century. What, in other words, do the very highest achievements of human culture (Athens) have to do with the Eternal (Jerusalem)?

The topic has been canvassed by theologians and philosophers for almost two thousand years now. How do we harmonize, or else set in opposition, the two regions of high human culture, on the one hand, and holiness, on the other?

Lest the word "holiness" appear to introduce a laughably capricious element into such an exalted topic, we may recall that the word bespeaks one of the only two options that we mortals have. Either we are going nowhere in the end, and art, music, poetry, drama, architecture, and civility must supply the only consolations offered to our brief moment on stage; or we are, in fact, going somewhere *else*, and the only route thence is the route of holiness. And this "else" itself, far from being merely a state of affairs somewhere over the rainbow, rustles and swells and whispers and oozes in every single detail of this mortal trek of ours—not only in Bach and Mozart, or in Caravaggio and Vermeer, or in Dante and Shakespeare, but (perhaps more crucially?) in every instance of generosity, fidelity, and purity that appears in the actions and attitudes of "holy and humble men of heart".

The question may be trivialized, of course. On the one hand, one may adopt the *merely* cultured attitude: I will become discriminating. I will surround myself with porcelains and fabrics and landscapes and friends of the most delicate sensibilities. Let Calvinists and Puritans and other riff-raff burden themselves with *virtue* and the terror of the Last Trump. So amusing. Or, on the other hand, one may announce one's disdain for all matters of culture: All questions of taste and discrimination and civility are beneath me. I am zealous for "the Lord".

The difficulty with both of these simplifications is that they are, well, simplifications. Neither has come to grips with what sort of creature we mortal men are. We are neither angels, who apparently can look straight at Reality and bear up, nor beasts, whose existence seems to be wholly material (although on that last point, I am one of the ones who hope that the animals are in on something that will only be revealed to us all at the Last Day, and that will turn out to be glorious). The first man, perhaps an aesthete, has impoverished himself by failing to grasp the mystery of our having been made for God, and the rigorist has perhaps failed to explore just how the truly noble achievements of human culture trumpet the *majorem gloriam Dei*.

But back to my book about Oxford. The book is the work of an Oxford man and is itself a very fine thing. And Oxford? Here, certainly, we find the highest order of scholarly and literate culture. This university stands as a sort of paradigm for all human inquiry, at least in popular imagination—and, to some extent, perhaps justly.

Is it a *good* place? Hum. Tertullian might find himself scrutinizing the matter. On Athens' accounting, we would all have to say yes, in that the university's contributions to human culture are undoubted. On Jerusalem's accounting, one will most certainly find centuries of true piety and virtue at work in the hearts of countless scholars there.

But then, Oxford is like every human place. It is made up of us mortal men. Hence the good qualities of Athens are to be found there: courtesy, gravity, genius, jollity, brilliance, hard work. But other qualities of Athens are also to be found there: jealousy, niggardliness, malice, vanity, venality, cravenness, pusillanimity, humbug, hatred. By Jerusalem's touchstone, these latter qualities spell, finally, damnation.

That seems severe. Only a prig would write off Oxford (or Padua, or Yale, or Tubingen, or Main Street, or your house or mine, for that matter) with such a compendious judgment.

So we end up with a platitude (the platitudes are true, come to think of it). Our mortal scene is a jumble, not to be unscrambled until the Day of Wrath (and Mercy). Athens and Jerusalem locate themselves not so much in Greek or Levantine geography as in the inner man. And who but an oaf does not wish to find some testimony to Athens in his own imagination, while he makes his way along toward the only City that will finally survive the Shaking of the Foundations?

How I Changed Churches

My own pilgrimage has led me in the direction of the Catholic church. By that I do not mean to specify, at this point, the Roman Church. Rather, I mean toward the church understood as one, holy, catholic, and apostolic.

With respect to the first of these words, "one", I find the state of schism in which the church exists to be genuinely agonizing. This was not always so; but for any seriously catholic Christian, it becomes a matter of great anguish.

As touching the second word, "holy", I have come to an Augustinian view as opposed to a Donatist view. That is, the holiness of the church is not restricted to the few who exhibit manifest godliness in their lives. To believe otherwise leads to the interminable proliferation of schism, and you get sects, cults, and little denominations, cropping up left, right, and center, with no reference to historic continuity.

Which raises the third point: catholicity. The guarantee that the early church had against heresy and schism was the teaching authority of the church catholic, which meant the bishops in consultation interpreting the Scriptures and defining dogma. (It is to be remembered that in church history, leading heretics all believed in the inspiration of Scripture. Hence the church needs something more than earnest individuals with their New Testaments in hand.) This hierarchy of authority is no medieval development.

Originally published in *Eternity* (February 1977): 16. Reprinted with permission.

One has only to read the Fathers of the second and third centuries to discover a vision of the church that would be thoroughly astonishing to modern, independent, individualistic, American Christianity (which cannot be called "churchmanship" since it is precisely individualistic and has no doctrine of the church).

Which raises the fourth point, "apostolic". The church is founded by Christ on the foundation of the apostles. Into their hands he gave the teaching authority, and they passed this on to their successors. There was no mistaking in the early church who were the appointed successors to the apostles. There was no question of self-appointed bishops. (If any such appeared, they were denounced by the orthodox bishops.)

If anyone points to the muddle and struggle in the early church as evidence that Christ could not possibly have meant that sort of thing to represent the continuity of his body on earth, it can only be pointed out that he did the same sort of thing with his word, the Bible. From a human viewpoint, it is a mish-mash of literary forms written by dozens of people; but through it we have the Word of God. Through the poor job the early bishops and councils did in their quarreling and infighting, we have the orthodox church. The treasure is in earthen vessels.

I am an Anglican, then. There are all sorts of Anglicans. I am one who is vastly thankful for my evangelical nurture and who believes that the liturgical, sacramental life of the Catholic church is the fruition that evangelicalism longs for passionately.

Isabella and Angelo

A very tangled situation arises in one of Shakespeare's lesser-known plays, *Measure for Measure*. This is to say nothing particularly arresting; after all, what do we come upon in any of his plays *but* tangled situations? We all know the agonies and cross-currents in *Hamlet* and *Macbeth*, of course. (To my own mind, *King Lear* is the greatest of all of the plays; but who will quarrel when it comes to these daunting sweepstakes?)

In any event, in *Measure for Measure*, we find that things lie on the hither side of tragedy. Readers will recall that a tragedy is a story that ends in death; a comedy, strictly speaking, is a story that ends in marriage (or, we may say, in everyone living happily ever after). In his later years, Shakespeare moved on past tragedy and sheer comedy to some plays that have been called "late romances", or, sometimes, "problem comedies". What you find in plays like this is a situation that threatens to whirl down into tragedy but that is plucked up in the nick of time and salvaged.

Measure for Measure is such a play. The Duke of Vienna has decided to go off for a break from his onerous duties and appoints one Angelo, whom he seems to trust, to be his deputy. The joker in this pack is that Angelo, while a generally admirable man, has no self-knowledge. When he steps into power, he suddenly becomes an inquisitor, blithely unaware of his own feet of clay. He sets about rooting up all sin from Vienna.

Reprinted with permission by CatholiCity, September 1, 2008.

Now this might seem all very well in theory. But such a draconian scheme has never, alas, worked in our mortal situation. It can't be done. And, to add to the fun, Angelo falls into the very sin on which he has fixed his scrutiny, namely, sexual immorality. He wants to expunge all harlotry and fornication from the city—and then does his best to seduce young Isabella, a very pure maiden indeed. She has come to him to plead for the life of her brother Claudio, who has got a certain Juliet with child, and of course he hails Isabella with the predictable bargain: Favor for favor, lady.

And we are off and running. Angelo is, for the moment, omnipotent, so Claudio is doomed unless Isabella cooperates with Angelo's cynical proposal. At first she is cold. Right: Claudio has sinned, the law looms, so there we are. She, a virgin herself, is not eager to beg on behalf of carnal squalor. But then pity for her brother percolates into her mind. Oh, Angelo ... In the course of her efforts to plead with Angelo, we have some of the most touching lines in all of Shakespeare.

She mounts a plea for mercy (at which point we hear Portia's "the quality of mercy is not strained" echoing across from *The Merchant of Venice*):

> No ceremony [symbol of power] that to great ones
> [be]longs—
> Not the king's crown, nor the deputed sword,
> The marshal's truncheon, nor the judge's robe—
> Become them with one half so good a grace
> As mercy does.

Not a chip flies from the enamel of Angelo's rigor. "Your brother is a forfeit of the law, / And you but waste your words."

Whereupon Isabella reaches for eternal fixities:

Alas, alas! Why all the souls that were were forfeit once,
And He that might the vantage best have took
Found out the remedy. How would you be
If He which is the top of judgment should
But judge you as you are?

Outside of Sacred Scripture it would be hard to find a more succinct summary of the human situation and the grace of Christ.

In our own mild and amiable epoch, one does not often hear preaching that so starkly grasps the nettle. We sinners are doomed, having "come short of the glory of God", as Saint Paul puts it. In the days when the *Te Deum* was still sung in church, Catholics heard the phrase, "We believe that Thou shalt come to be our judge." This is not a favorite theme in modern catechesis. Our forerunners feared the Last Judgment. They were encouraged to think of the Four Last Things (Death, Judgment, Heaven, and Hell).

Isabella obviously was well catechized—and she assumed that Angelo was, too. But that story—our story—did not stop with judgment. The remedy was found—by God, not us. The very One who had the warrant to take the most dire advantage of our plight was the One who offered His mercy. It cost Him His life (what is that in the Chalice which is offered at Mass?). So, dear Angelo (who comes around in the end) and me: Bring that to mind when you judge another mortal. And recall it often in your prayers, with thanks.

The Italian Concerto

Very often, if my wife is out doing errands in the middle of the day, I will make up my lunch on a tray and carry it into my study. There I can put a CD on my portable player—it is the only system I have, and it sits in a shelf behind wooden doors at the bottom of the built-in bookcases. Almost inevitably I will pick something from either Mozart or Bach. Within the last year or so I have been given both of those boxed collections, which offer us, they say, every note that either of these gentlemen ever wrote. One approaches such a collection with misgivings: Who knows what performers have been rounded up for such a compendious piece of work? As it happens, in both cases here, the performances do, in fact, compare splendidly with the best single CDs I have.

In any event, the other day I decided to see what this version of Bach's Italian Concerto for harpsichord sounded like. I was pleased: Here were all the vigor and authority that this concerto calls for, but without the corybantic fury with which it is sometimes hammered out—viz. Glen Gould's piano rendering, which must surely leave poor J.S.B. aghast, if strains from our planet get as far as the Elysian Fields where, we must believe, he is at peace.

But since music rightly ordered is a case in point of all things beautifully ordered—the movements of the stars, for example, or the grace of dolphins streaking through the

Reprinted with permission by CatholiCity, May 5, 2008

water, or the way of a good man with a maid, or of the bees with their honeycombs, or the sun in its polychrome sinking each night—one's thoughts find themselves responding to the old bidding, "Will you, won't you, will you, won't you, will you join the Dance?" as though all things have in themselves an eagerness to participate in some overarching, solemn, joyous choreography that calls out the perfections in each.

While I listened to the concerto, I thought of the straitened limitations of the materials Bach had at his disposal when he set about composing it. Just an unwieldy crate for an instrument, to begin with, strung with wires (and gut? how do they make harpsichords?), and fixed with little claws to pluck the strings with. A lesser man who supposed that to do justice to his freewheeling genius he would need endless resources might complain: Are they asking *me* to crowd my creativity into *this*? Come.

But Bach sets to work with what is at his disposal. And of course he has another obstacle: They have told him that, whatever it is he wishes to create, he may not reach outside of the same old twelve tones that every penny-whistler has at his disposal as well. No privileged resources will be trotted out for your mountainous genius, sir. It's just the routine stuff you've got to coax into some form here.

Very well. Let us see what can be done. *Chum!* I'll start with that very unsurprising chord, and build the whole thing on that. Why not? It is a chord so hackneyed, and so worn thin by every tinker in the trade, that nothing but ennui can be expected to arise from it. Never mind—let's see what can be done here.

And we are off and running with one of the most glorious works for keyboard ever achieved. At no given point does Bach seek to shock us with anything that does violence to what are clearly the demands of his plan here—what I myself have often thought of as *tact*. No frivolous skidding about, no cheap showmanship, nothing ill-gotten. But what we have—in its pure integrity and obedience to the given choreography, so to speak, which he is sketching out for the notes—regales us with its energy, its decorum, and its harmonious inventiveness. He doesn't need to reach for jolting effects that might call forth mere gasps from his hearers. We gasp here as we gasp at the sight of the dolphins and the sunset—at perfection, actually, and not shock.

But aside from its effect on us listeners, we may observe that, within very narrow limitations, old J. S. B. has created an artifact that may take its place among the greatest achievements of mankind. He has not asked for bizarre resources, or special privileges. He has worked with what any little plucker of strings has to work with.

My mind made the small shift, as I listened, to the saints. Very few of them had anything particular to "work with". Drab circumstances, unlikely settings, poor resources, humdrum endowments—these seem to be the materials that are offered to our humanity. The artist and the saint may rouse us, if despondency or *accidie* threaten to convince us that we have nothing to work with. We have no more, and no less, than anyone else.

The Last Day will scrutinize what we have been doing with it.

Is the Jig Up?

When I was small, back in the 1940s, there was a lovely weekly magazine called the *Saturday Evening Post*. It was the publication that ran all of those Norman Rockwell covers that had the art critics breaking out in pustules and carbuncles. They grimly dismissed Rockwell's entire oeuvre as insupportably sentimental—a little grandmother, say, at a gingham café table with her skinny-necked, jug-eared grandson, folding their hands and bowing humbly, saying grace over their Thanksgiving blue-plate special. What brought the lump to your throat was the question of where the old family farmhouse might be, all full of cousins and aunts, and the table laden with apples, pumpkin pies, mince pies, cranberry sauce, and a great turkey.

There was lots of drollery in the *Post*, and I remember one article that was canvassing (jocularly) various crises in the world. Among other items, the author reported that a hen in Kansas had laid an egg with the motto "The Jig Is Up" inscribed on it. Clearly, apocalypse was imminent.

This prophetic bird had merely delivered the latest in an ancient lineage of sibylline and melancholy messages. Doom has lurked and leered at us from behind every bush since the day after the expulsion from Eden. If it wasn't the Amalekites, it was the Hittites. If it wasn't the Assyrians, it was the Chaldaeans. Philip of Macedon, the Caesars,

Originally published in *Crisis* (January 1, 2005). Reprinted with permission.

the Goths (Ostro- or Visi-), the Saxons harrying the poor Celts with fire and sword in the fifth century, and so on and so on. Has any epoch ever had the luxury of settling down in bucolic serenity? Some threat seems always to have been gathering itself on the borders.

In our own epoch we have seen the Kaiser and then the Fuhrer. Pearl Harbor. Ho Chi Minh. The Ayatollah. Osama. Some of these latter, who often appeared to be kindling only local brushfires, seemed to have a disquieting way, sooner or later, of threatening global conflagration. Everyone has to take sides. Allies shift and shuffle like the shards of glass in a kaleidoscope. Heaven itself only knows where things are headed as this column is being written.

But our hen, were she to re-lay such a cryptic egg now, might well have her beady eye on things much closer to our own shores—indeed, within the homeland, despite all of the security gauntlets through which we must all jump now (e.g., I find myself in my stocking feet in airports). The "jig" might well refer to such seismic technological and moral waves as stem-cell harvesting (are these little bits of tissue people?); cloning (the English Parliament voted to permit human cloning last summer on the very heels of disheartening reports that cloned sheep have an unhappy way of aging almost immediately, so that you get a lamb exhibiting all the debilities of a valetudinarian mutton); bishops undertaking to redraw the moral chart of the universe so that sodomy shifts from the taboo to the virtue column; and "marriage" becomes a word impossible to define. Teenage argot now speaks insouciantly of "hooking up" (the old word was "fornication"), and discourse collapses. When was the last time you heard any talk show or political speech that exhibited a cogent line of systematic argument that actually affected the listeners' categories?

But a new columnist can't push out from shore with a mere jeremiad. The jig won't really be up until "the day and the hour" arrive when the Master of the House suddenly returns to shake the heavens and the earth, the sea and the dry land, and all nations. The dominical and apostolic word here is "Awake!" Blessed is that servant whom, when his Lord returns, will be found watching.

The Last Lecture: Class of 1979

A week or ten days ago, my wife and I were talking as we tend to do from time to time. I remember only the following fragment from our conversation, but judging from this fragment, the conversation must have been about doom and one thing and another, which conversations with me tend to be about. I remember saying to her that the thing I fear most in life is chaos—the breakdown of order so that we get down to everyone screaming and clawing each other's eyes out in grocery stores, scrabbling for the last dirty celery leaves in the corner and the last wrinkled potato and finally the last bits of chewing gum and fake butterscotch topping—anything to fend off starvation, especially for one's children. Then starvation: lines of refugees slogging along country roads pushing wheelbarrows and rickshaws piled high with saucepans, rocking chairs, stuffed animals, and quilts. Why do refugees have so many quilts, I keep asking myself? I've been looking and looking at pictures of refugees all my life—Belgians and Poles and Estonians when I was a little boy, then later Koreans and Pakistanis and Nigerians, then later Vietnamese and Cambodians and Laotians. There are always bedrolls and quilts around. Why? Come to think of it, I suppose the reason is obvious, isn't it? What does life come down to when we have been dispossessed? If we can only have a saucepan with, pray God, something to put in it and a place to lay our heads

Used by permission of Gordon College.

like the foxes in their holes—that's the last ditch. After that you sit on the ground hollow-eyed and ghostlike and wait for death. Anyway, I was visualizing all of this as sort of a final horror. When my wife got a chance to say something, she, because she is wise and because she is good and because she's a woman and therefore sees more clearly than I do, said that the thing she fears most in her imagination is having our children taken away forcibly and taught things that are monstrous and grotesque—Marxist doctrines of man, for example, and cruelty and cynicism or the bitter, harsh, and sordid vision of life proclaimed so fiercely by prophets like the Reverend Mr. Jones or Vanessa Redgrave and Germaine Greer. When she said this, I realized that she had, in fact, touched on something that was, if possible, more frightening than the visions of horror I had conjured. But in what sense was it more frightening? After all, one can imagine one's children lined up outside the commune dormitory in neat grey tunics, hair brushed, cheeks scrubbed, singing in a great chorus, "Onward and upward with liberty, equality and fraternity!" and on cue from the matron in her tunic, raising their fists in the air with a shout of victorious scorn, "For God, mother, apple pie, and the boy scouts." What emancipation! They'd be healthy, busy, and disciplined. Who can wish for more? But Christ and all his holy angels defend us from the advent of that vision!

Now at this point you may be murmuring to yourself or your neighbor, "What's going on? The man's got his cues wrong. He's pulled out the wrong speech. He thinks he's at the Annual Joint Banquet of the Daughters of the American Revolution and the Society for the Preservation of the Prayerbook. We asked him to make us a speech as a sort of a 'last lecture', and here we are two minutes into the thing head over heels in wheelbarrows, proletarian communes, and paranoia. Come, somebody signal the

MC. We can't go on like this." But, if you'll hold off your signal to the MC, I'll try to explain why I've conjured these pictures, especially the latter one. As I mulled over what I ought to say this morning it struck me that you, you seniors that is—the rest of us are in a sense eavesdroppers here—that you will be hearing a number of solemn charges and commissions in the next few days. You're graduating, and this is one of those occasions that gives your family and your friends and your teachers and your baccalaureate speaker and your commencement speaker and the "last lecture" man a chance to offer you eager gifts of wisdom and warning as you disappear over the horizon into life. And let's face it, this is in the nature of the case, the way hugging and backslapping go along with a victory, or kissing and champagne accompany a wedding, or waggling your fingers and saying coo-chi-coo are necessary at a cradle. That is what is done. So, offering advice is what I am doing this morning.

But I thought that rather than coming straight at you with a sheath of salvific maxims (you can look that up if you want), I would ask you to join me in looking at a question that presents itself to me as well as to you. It's this: What on earth is it (now I seem to have the phrase "when push comes to shove" here, so I offer my apologies)—What on earth is it, when push comes to shove, that I want my children to know? Why does it matter so much to me that J be given the chance to teach them? Why do I recoil at the idea of their learning a whole different vision of things from somebody else? And it will be clear that it is not just biological children who are at stake here. It's anyone that we love and for whom we find ourselves responsible. In the next ten years probably more than half of you seniors will, in fact, of course, find yourselves with your own children; but there's not one of you who won't be responsible for somebody in some way or another, unless you opt out entirely and choose to become solitary and besotted; and I don't know anybody here who's going to do that. Life bundles us into these dread and wonderful responsibilities either by giving us our own children or by putting us into positions where somebody looks to us for the cues and for an image they can follow. To ask the question, then, with reference to one's children, or to the people one is going to be responsible for, is to raise the stakes high indeed. Then it's no longer merely a question of me thinking to myself, "Well, I suppose someday I'd better pull my socks up and get my act together." It's difficult to avoid this sort of procrastination, of course, especially when there are so many things about that are so much more attractive than sobriety and sanctity.

Sanctity? How'd we get here so fast? Who's talking about sanctity? Well, we are, aren't we? I mean if it's not sanctity toward which we must move on pain of our lives, then what in the world is it? Press the question on yourself. What is it that I'm going after? What do I think I want? Where am I headed? There are various possible answers, of course. Money is an obvious one; and which of us does not find this one attractive and hence tempting? Money does so many things; it opens exciting doors. It'll help me get to know the people I need to get to know; it'll help me get the house I want and the style of life I want; and it'll educate my children; and above all it will give me at least some security. With inflation and no jobs and peril of one sort and another looming upon us so frighteningly now, who's going to say that money isn't an enormously attractive buffer between us and the ragged edge? Or fame. Some people are not as interested in this as others; but probably for most of us the idea of being widely respected and sought after by all sorts of fascinating people and of being thought to be a fascinating person by everyone—that's very attractive. Who wouldn't like to hear the phone ring and find out that it's NBC or *Time* magazine on the line wanting us for a prime time talk show or a cover story? Why the very thought of it makes us start preening and looking in the mirror. Or fun. Seeing as life is so harrying and ambiguous these days, one may as well try to crowd in as many jollies as he can while it lasts. Eat and drink and be merry, big gang, for tomorrow comes the paper for Professor Spires or the exam for Dr. Wilson. And let's face it, the wish to have a bit of fun and to kick up one's heels on the brink of the abyss is not all bad. God defend us from the gaunt and solemn people who will spoil every jollity and every festivity by walking about with placards announcing the Trump of Doom. And after all, the Prophet we follow helped the merriment at Cana of Galilee by setting the whole party up to six fresh kegs after everyone had had quite enough. Or just plain security and stability and peace. (We're still talking about the things we might list before we get around to putting down sanctity as the thing we're after.) Heaven knows this last one, security or peace, is attractive. With the walls crumbling about our ears, and the economy collapsing, and oil disappearing and energy and environment emerging as apocalyptic problems and violence washing up to our very doorsteps—please Lord, just give us peace and security. One begins to appreciate some of those litanies they used to say in churches beseeching the protection of heaven against one threat and another. They used to say, "From the fury of the Norsemen, good Lord deliver us." The Anglo-Saxons prayed that one. Or you all know: "From goolies and ghosties and long-legged beasties and things that go bump in the night, good Lord deliver us." The Cornish men prayed that, and we might add, "things that go bump in the day or the night" like nuclear plants melting down, or muggers' blackjacks landing on our skulls. Or here's one for you Protestants: "From the tyranny of the Bishop of Rome and from all his detestable enormities, good Lord deliver us." There was a time when Englishmen saw their greatest peril as coming from the Catholic Church in Italy, France, and Spain. Which is all by way of saying that security is a thing most earnestly to be longed for at any time in human history and certainly in these days. And hence it might well siphon our attention away from the thing, sanctity, that alone matters when the chips are down. Or shall we say, when death wedges his way through the door we thought we had gotten bolted and barricaded and grins down at us. Hold it! Death? How did we get here? You're always landing us suddenly in topics that don't seem to have much to do with your assigned task: refugees, sanctity, death grinning at us. Come, what is your subject? My subject is the important things, and to come at it we need to tick off the things that aren't important but that might fool us into thinking that they are. Sanctity is the important thing, and money, fame, fun, and security are strong bidders for the title. And death is the thing that once and for all will sort out the candidates and hand the prize to sanctity.

If nothing else gets our attention, death does. I heard this past Tuesday of a girl at Gordon College who said, "I'm not into the Christian thing this week." Well, honey, you'd better say a prayer to Zeus, then, asking him to do what he can to keep the fates from snipping the thread of your life; cause when they do, you'll want all the Christian thing you can get. My favorite set of last words are those attributed to one of the medieval popes: "Wait! Wait!" he said. Who of us won't feel like saying that? "Just give me a little time to get my act together."

The students who land in my office during the ninth week of term, wondering whether there might not be some arrangements we can make, since somehow the preceding nine weeks seem to have gone by without their having thought much about this paper that's due tomorrow and the exam next week. I had a phone call last night: "Could we possibly ...?" And I must confess this never happens without my sitting there imagining myself with more or less the same plea on my lips when I'm hailed up in front of Saint Michael the Archangel and the Divine Tribunal. "Wait! Wait!" The great Saint Augustine once prayed in his younger days, "Lord, make me holy, but not yet." You see pictures from the Middle Ages and the Renaissance of saints sitting in their caves and cells with a skull grinning at them from a shelf or a tabletop. Why did they keep that sort of bric-a-brac around? Because, they said, it was a good *memento mori*, a good reminder of death. Not because they were morbid, but because they thought they needed some sort of a reminder of what lay ahead, so that they could keep their wits about them and not get too distracted by the clutter of distractions that tends to distract us most of the time.

So, with these considerations in mind, what shall we say? The question comes to me and to you alike, except that I have a good twenty years less time now than you do. What is it that we'd like to say to our children or to the people we are going to be responsible for? What shall we leave them as a legacy? How shall we help them to live? Or to put it yet another way, what on earth should I, or you and I, be learning today and tomorrow and everyday that will equip me to be a good and wise and strong parent or teacher or colleague or helper, one of the ones people will fly to when the foundations are shaken and not one of the ones screeching and squalling in terror and self-pity?

I myself, for one thing, would like to teach my children to be awake. And in order to do this, it will be necessary for me to make sure that I'm not slipping into a stupor. This is not as easy as it might sound. There are a number of stupefying things around now. The sheer force and noise under which we live batters and stuns us into imbecility. I'll give you a test to try sometime. Stop wherever you are, outside or in, and count the different noises you can hear. If I stopped here for a minute, you'd hear a loud buzzing noise for one thing. If you're outside, you'll be able to hear trucks on Route 128. If you are inside, you'll hear either somebody's stereo pouring out noise at a shattering decibel level or, almost worse, the saccharine and treacly lullaby of Musak. I spend my summers in a place that, short of sheer wilderness, is about as rural as you can get east of South Dakota. I've counted the following noises that are native to this pastoral countryside where I go to get away from noise: Trucks—gravel trucks, oil trucks, and the pick-up trucks of all the local handymen—hot rods popping and slamming up and down the roads, dirt bikes, chain saws, bulldozers, small aircraft, Air Force jets—they maneuver directly over Sugar Hill, New Hampshire, every day stretching a roaring canopy from horizon to horizon. And that's in the country! What shall we say of the cities and suburbs where, besides living with far more noise than that, people never turn off the TV? The TV. Is this a pestilence worse than the Black Death? I'm not sure. I wonder seriously whether it is not a twentieth-century variation on the theme of what we did in the Garden of Eden, where we made a grab for a knowledge that we were not made for and that hence turned out to be crushing. It killed us. We're not made to bear the knowledge of good and evil. Only gods can bear that and live. We thought we could shoulder it, and it killed us. I wonder if television is not our own special technological variation on this theme. For what does it do? It pours avalanches of data at us with a force and speed that can only destroy us psychologically, morally, emotionally, and spiritually. We mortal creatures were not made to bear instant, vivid, and gigantic spectacles of chaos and suffering and strife in every corner of the world—in Uganda, Ireland, Southeast Asia, Iran, Rhodesia, Italy, and in all of our own cities. If we think we can, then we're guilty of the sin that we were guilty of originally, namely, thinking that we can be gods. We can't. Saint Francis himself could not bear the spectacle—not because his heart did not have enough charity in it, but because he would have known that the poor and the lepers and the hungry he had as his neighbors were a load heavy enough for any mortal charity to bear. Do I mean, then, that we should shut our eyes and our compassion and lock ourselves away from the suffering of the world? Surely not, but the spectacle of universal suffering beyond our fingertips, universal suffering and chaos pouring into affluent American living rooms hour upon hour every day, year after year can only have the negative effect of getting us accustomed to the spectacle. We get calloused. Our threshold of shockability goes up and up, until we are blasé. The thing that we thought was consciousness-raising turns out to be consciousness-blunting. We turn out to be spectators like Romans in the arena ... and God help us all. We have news and entertainment TV to thank for this. And, of course, add to all this the bogus violence that comes at us in what is called entertainment, where we're glutted still further with violence dished up for its own value—people being blown to bits, guns blazing, knives flashing, cars careening, marriages breaking down and breaking down on thousands upon thousands of tedious soap opera afternoons. And topping all this up the Neanderthal throb of acid, punk, and funk rock blatting and yelling in our ears, stunning and cudgeling our sensibilities until they are flat, flat, flat. Does it surprise you then that high school kids sit in class paralyzed by boredom? That nothing is relevant except powerful kicks? How would *you* go about flagging down their attention with such hot topics as sanctity, grace, courtesy, charity, joy? Or Mozart, Rembrandt, and Shakespeare? How will you do it, big gang? What will you say to your children? How do I propose to keep alive in my children some rag of grace and tenderness and agility? Some quality of being awake to the texture and fragility of life? Some capacity to adore what is adorable, and to extol what is praiseworthy, to hear and see nobility and perfection and beauty wherever it appears—in one of the Brandenburg concerti (that's Bach) or in the rescue work of Mother Teresa in Calcutta or in some golden retriever wagging his plume of a tail or in someone's picking up a gum wrapper thrown down on campus by some clod who doesn't give a tinker's curse for the rest of us. Well, I'd like to teach my children to be awake. To be able to do this, I must myself stay awake. To stay awake myself, I must turn down the volume somehow and slow down the hypnotic speed. "Come out of the bustlings, you that are bustling", said old George Fox, the founder of the Quakers. And even though I am very far from the Quaker point of view on most things, I know that Fox was on the target here. I tend to bustle. Our age bustles, to put it far too mildly. It slams and rockets and careens. Somehow or other I want my household to be marked by order and peace and grace, so that my children's ears will still be able to hear a Mozart flute concerto or the song of the winter wren or the olive-backed thrush. Not, by the way, that we have only Mozart flute concerti in my house. It's not a home for aging grand duchesses. There are baseball gloves and a bit of John Travolta and the odd dirty sock dropped here and there. I want my kids to be normal, but I don't want them to be stupefied. I suppose the question I'm putting to you seniors here is this: Are you staying awake enough to be able to help your children—or whoever you are going to find yourself responsible for in five or six years—to be able to help them to stay awake?

Second—and I've already intimated this—I'd like to be the sort of a person who can teach his children what courtesy and grace are. Now it's easy enough to see how impossible a task that is nowadays by simply looking at our own reaction to the words themselves. Courtesy? Grace? Ouch! The very words make us wince. We think of nineteenth-century ladies' finishing schools and pinkies extended over bone china cups of Darjeeling tea. And pursed lips being dabbed demurely with lace hankies. Great Scot! What in heaven's name have courtesy and grace got to do with anything in this hey-hey-hang-loose era we live in? Well, they have something to do with something, I suspect. And that something must be the old, worn-out notion of charity, a notion that no Jew and no Christian can give the back of his hand to, no matter what era he lives in, since charity was commanded, proscribed, and spelled out in the law on Sinai, and taught in the Sermon on the Mount, and enacted and incarnate for an example for us forever and ever when the Most High came to visit us. Yes, but what on earth is it supposed to look like now? I mean, you can't have your kids sweeping and bowing and salaaming all over the place. Everyone would think they are crazy. No, I suppose I can't have my kids sweeping and bowing and salaaming all over the place. But surely, somehow, I can teach them what that was all about, namely, to honor the other person and to be kind and generous even in the smallest exchanges of ordinary life. I'd like to see in them some alertness to other people, some quick and thoughtful courtesy that is finely tuned to people who need help, whether it's simply a matter of quickly and unobtrusively offering a chair to a lady who comes into a room or giving someone a hand with a bag of groceries, or sitting up for hours with someone who's going through some "dark night of the soul". And it may be another index of how difficult a task this is going to be, for you and me, when we hear shrill and angry voices telling us now that that old business of offering a chair to a lady, indeed the word "lady" itself, is an insult to modern womanhood because it implies that women are the weaker sex and therefore not equal to men. Alas, what on earth does that fierce political frame of mind know about the ancient business of offering honor to something that is honorable? What do they know of the grave and joyous courtesies exchanged between our great lord and father, Adam, and our great lady and mother, Eve? Do we think they scrabbled at each other for equal time and droned away at committee tables making sure no gesture or phrase implied any inequality? Politics and justice in the public domain do have to work away at that sort of thing. But love and hence grace and courtesy know nothing of that calculating and squinting approach. I hope somehow I'll be able to keep alive in my children some notion of the exquisite and noble mystery of other selves, so that they will abhor all the forms of rudeness and discourtesy and self-interest by which we brutalize each other these days—all the forms, I say, from the lechery that calls itself free love and that has long since forgotten the mystery of the other self in its hot pursuit of bliss to the slogans that reduce us all to frightened and angry pawns in a wearing game of egalitarian chess.

Third, I hope I'll be able to keep alive in my children the capacity of contentment and delight in the utterly ordinary. This isn't going to be easy. It's not easy for you or me, I dare say, to keep this capacity alive in ourselves which is one reason I put it to you this morning. It's difficult because we are told in a thousand talk shows and a thousand books and in every journal and seminar and in every magazine and TV ad that what we want is something else. If you drive a Pinto, what you want is a BMW. If you drive a Peugeot, you need a Mercedes. If you shop at Lechmere, you need to move up to Bergdorf and Hammacher Schlemmer. If you go to the Cape for your holiday, you ought to try the Caribbean. If you're a mother, you ought to be an investment banker. If you work 9-5, it's a drag, and only dull people do that. If you're middle class, you need to get emancipated. Upward mobility, self-actualization, self-assertion, self-discovery, self-realization, aggression, kicks, travel, diversion, the beautiful people, the radical chic—anything but where we are. Nothing could be as dull as this. But how in the world are you and I, much less the people we're going to be responsible for, going to preserve the capacity for contentment and delight in sheer unvarnished ordinariness and routine when this is the mythology coming at us so dazzlingly? To have caviar and salmon dangled in front of my nose all the time has the effect of making me, sooner or later, think that the brown bread and butter on my plate is a bore and that to be happy I've got somehow to get hold of caviar and smoked salmon for my daily fare. But caviar and smoked salmon are not the staff of life. They're wonderful garnishings. I happen to love them. I don't get much of them, though. Precious few of us mortal creatures get at them very often. The Caribbean is there, heaven knows, and it's beautiful. But have the ads for the Caribbean, with willowy women and lithe men draped languidly on the deck of somebody's ninety-foot ketch with tall glasses of rum and tonic, and everyone tripped out on Nieman Marcus and Lilly Pulitzer—have those, or something like them, blunted my taste for walking through the woods to Chebacco Lake? Madison Avenue is doing what it can to bring this off, and they know how to administer very affective doses of their magic. Somehow you and I have got to stay in touch with simplicity. What are our demands from life? Is daily routine a form of joy for us because it gives us the thing that all exiles and prisoners and dying people would give the universe to get back, namely, the chance to go about the plain tasks of the day? Or is it a drag? I must say, when I say goodnight to my children in the evening, I think to myself: "Well, we've been given a gift of inexpressible worth here, namely, one more utterly ordinary day, unmarked by tragedy or sickness or accident." God forbid that I should neglect to offer up the sacrifice of thanksgiving for this. I don't want to wait until it's taken away before I look at it and assess its infinite worth. I myself am glad that I grew up at the end of the depression and during World War II. Luxuries were just not around then. Or rather, they were, but they were very, very small. And I think that did something wonderful for us all back then. I can remember my father taking his pocketknife and ever so carefully cutting a Milky Way bar into about five pieces for some of us children and passing them out. This was a great treat. The idea of eating an entire candy bar was something I never came across until I was an adult. Now, my children have more than one piece of Milky Way. So do I, and so do you. But have we still got the capacity to delight in one piece of Milky Way? If not, where are we? How much do we want?

Fourth, you and I have got one way or another to keep alive the capacity for sheer merriment and joy and to pass that long to others. We have got, in other words, to know how to laugh. Now that sounds like an obvious thing. But let me ask you an odd question. How many people do you know who have a wonderful, hearty, big capacity for plain laughter? Think through the people you know. Do they, can they really laugh? Do they love merriment and wit and the ridiculous? Is there laughter lurking in their eyes? I myself have wondered, now and again, whether a sense of humor is not a sort of natural capacity in us humans that's some sort of a reflection of holiness. Humor has something to do with humility—pompous people can't laugh. And with simplicity—sophisticated people can only offer tinkling and silvery mockery. And with purity of heart—lechers and gluttons can only leer. And with grace—clods and oafs can only grunt. And with charity—egotists are seldom amused. I think the saints are full of merriment. I want to introduce my children to at least the early reaches of those hilarious regions that we call Glory.

Fifth, I would like to be that sort of person who will be able to pass on to my children a capacity to endure suffering. Now, this sounds morbid, sadistic, even. What should I do? Should I thrash them and make them sleep on the floor? Or feed them hardtack and water in order to steel them against adversity? No! But somewhere in there I want to be giving them whatever it is that will make them strong and good and that will supply them with the sort of resources that can be drawn on when adversity does come. Surely, this too has something to do with charity, with one's focus being on something other than one's self. If my whole approach to life is to have my own self affirmed and to indulge my own preferences and whims and inclinations, then when something—sickness, grief, or trouble—comes at me, where am I going to be? Whereas, if I have been learning the disciplines of life, learning what vigil means and fasting, maybe, and renunciation, then, somehow, the sinews of my soul will have been toughened. Not, again, that I intend making my children kneel on a stone floor somewhere all night in order to teach them what vigil is all about. But can I, somehow, instill in them the habit of watchfulness and of self-discipline and a keen interest in the welfare of others so that there is heartier material making up the citadel of their souls than the soft mud of indulgence and egocentrism, which will surely be swept away at the first wave of trouble?

I used to know an old woman who had everything against her. She was a widow. She was poor. She had to work. She had an ungrateful wretch of a thankless son. She was stone deaf and she had all sorts of arthritis and rheumatism. But that woman was, and remains—and she's long since in Paradise—for me and for my whole family probably the most glittering example of sheer, simple joy, happiness, and contentedness that any of us has ever seen.

Again, five or six years ago I was visiting a church in Connecticut, and in the middle of the Eucharistic liturgy, when the whole congregation was kneeling and singing "Alleluia", I saw a woman near me with her hands lifted in praise. The thing was, those hands were terribly twisted and gnarled and she had a pair of crutches next to her. "Dear Christ!" I thought. "What makes Christians sing 'Alleluia' anyway?" Clearly, there was something besides self-interest welling up from that woman in that act of praise.

Well, this is the end of my speech. To whom have I been talking? You seniors? Yes, I hope so. Everybody else in the gym? I hope so. Me? Yes, me at least. What have I been talking about? Some of the things that would seem to me to be important. But, you say, I've left out two items that one might have looked for in a "last lecture" to seniors at a liberal arts college, namely, the curriculum that you have spent tens of thousands of dollars on over the last four years and, more important than that, the Bible. Have I no text? Have I no verse to leave with you all?

On the first point, I'll say what I think all of my colleagues on the faculty will most earnestly join me in saying, and that is that if the curriculum of which we are stewards has not enlarged, sharpened, and toughened your capacity to think and to reflect and to examine and to weigh the issues of human existence soberly and intelligently and to sift out the important things from the unimportant, then we have all failed you. No course in biology or music or economics or elementary ed. or history or doctrine is irrelevant to that.

And on the second, what is my text? I suppose the Law and the Prophets and the Gospel is my text, and the Histories and the Wisdom Literature and the Epistles and the Apocalypse. For what are they? What do they speak about? Look and see. Do they not tell us how to live? Do they not point out to us what is true? Do they not hail us with righteousness and joy and freedom and wholeness and sanctity? What else are we after in life? If I want to be a faithful follower in this way, faithful as all the train of patriarchs and prophets and saints before us have been, then I will point those who come after me to the important things. I have no charge to give you seniors that is not a charge to me. I applaud you, and I encourage you in the way you have begun, and my prayers are with you as you carry on. Thank you.

A Diva's Sentiments

Some time ago, I happened to hear a recital by one of the great Metropolitan Opera mezzo-sopranos. Opera lovers will know her name well. When my wife and I lived in New York, she was one of our favorites at the Met.

The nice thing about a recital like this is that you get to hear all of your favorite arias all in one swat. It can, of course, be argued that this isn't what opera is about—all icing and no cake, so to speak. It does a disservice (so the objection might run) to the real genius of opera to lump miscellaneous arias together like this, cut off from the whole musical setting that should draw the audience along toward the thrill of the aria. Nevertheless, such recitals are a great source of pleasure.

At the end of this performance, the audience rose for a standing ovation, which was quite the right thing to do in this case. The clapping and cheering went on and on, and the grateful soprano bowed again and again. Finally she signaled for quiet, and made a little speech, the theme of which was her overflowing love for the audience. "I love you", she told the people. "I love you."

One of the pleasures attending on these occasions—opera, theatre, ballet, concerts, recitals—is this intense and happy exchange between artists and audience. We step out from the rigorous protocol that presides over the performance itself and give spontaneous voice to our joy, one of

Reprinted with permission by CatholiCity, June 2, 2008.

whose aspects seems to be this effusion of mutual affection. We feel that we do indeed love the artist, and she us.

The phenomenon raises an interesting point. The "love" that suffuses things in such a situation rushes upon us the audience in response to something gloriously executed. For the artist, it overflows in response to the outpouring of adulation certifying the splendor of her achievement. Most of us mortals will never know quite this happy experience since our own work is, more often than not, somewhat humdrum and rarely entails much of an audience.

I found myself mulling over that "I love you." No doubt the woman expressed, quite sincerely and accurately, the feelings that suffused her whole being in response to the ovation. Why—all of these people here are clearly wonderful people, full of happiness and love, and they are so very generous in their appreciation for my own work here on the stage. How can I not love them?

Who will cavil?

The dynamics might possibly alter somewhat if she were to encounter me under other circumstances. She loved me while I was clapping: What about when I cut off her car in traffic, or cut into the line at the grocery store? (This imagines that she drives herself and does her own shopping.) She loved me while I was clapping: Suppose her desk were next to mine month after month, and she found me querulous, petty, vain, and altogether tedious? She loved me while I was clapping: What if she discovered the sort of a person I really am?

She is not likely to be put to this test. But it does raise some piquant questions about the conditions under which we find ourselves able to say that we love someone else. For her that night, all was bliss, as it was for us in the audience. Love seemed to preside over the whole glorious occasion. Love was, shall we say, easy.

But would this love (our adulatory love; her grateful love) have sustained the tests that love worthy of its name is asked to sustain? Saint Paul's porcelain filter might bring on somber reflections.

Love is patient, he says. But the lady hadn't been asked to put up with me. Love bears all things, hopes all things, endures all things, believes all things, and never ends.

Oh.

It may very well be the case that our mezzo-soprano is filled with just the sort of love of which Saint Paul speaks. But her pledge to the audience that night scarcely needed to draw upon this heroic and selfless love—a point with which she would no doubt agree.

In the ordinary run of things, the school of love may or may not offer to us the blissful and intense moments on whose wings we may breathe out such happy and spontaneous exhalations. Nevertheless, to enter the long school of this love—it is the love of God shed abroad in our hearts by the Holy Ghost—and to reach the end of the course is to find a bliss unimaginable even to the happy moments like that recital, when "love" did not seem to make any very searching demands.

Noise

I grew up in a white clapboard house in Moorestown, New Jersey, just outside of Philadelphia. In those days, it was a quiet Quaker town with broad, silent streets lined with huge oaks, elms, and maples, and venerable houses presiding on each side. One still heard the Quaker thee's and thou's routinely, especially at the Friends' School where I was a pupil. You could distinguish the old-fashioned Quakers from the up-to-date ones: The former said to my father, "Good morning, Philip Howard, how art thou?" The latter said to my mother, "Good morning, Katharine Howard, how is thee?" To this day, I speak the "plain language", as it was called, with my oldest friend, who comes from a very old Philadelphia Quaker family.

My memory of those streets, even Main Street, calls up a picture of emptiness—no cars at all. It was during the war (for people my age, "the war" means World War II), and no one could get any gasoline. My mother did the grocery shopping for six children on a bicycle that had a great wire basket attached to the handlebars.

The town was utterly silent. Even the soft hum of a passing sedan was rare, and no one had heard of hot rods with their mufflers altered to produce a shattering roar. Motorcycles—either gigantic, satanic Harley-Davidsons or smaller, ear-splitting Yamahas—were unknown. I now live in a small, seaside town north of Boston, and we have all of

Originally published in *Crisis* (February 1, 2006). Reprinted with permission.

these vehicles in more or less unsparing procession, almost twenty-four hours a day. One thing that stumps me about these loud vehicles is the question as to why the men (and they are men) operating them feel the need to gun their engines every five seconds or so. You feel that perhaps you could sustain a general roar; but to have it punctuated with these hammer-like explosions makes things difficult when you are sitting in your study.

But these are only the beginnings of the noises we treasure in Manchester, Massachusetts. There are no days when immensely heavy trucks are not abroad, gunning their own engines. We also take care of our streets: There are no days without heavy road machinery bulldozers, backhoes, and derricks—lining the streets with their din. And then there are the airplanes. We live under the flight pattern for Logan airport, so we have huge passenger jets sending down incalculable decibels at all times. But they are not as nettlesome as the one-engine pleasure crafts that arrive over our heads and circle and circle—and circle. (One little plane circled my house eighteen times. I counted.)

Perhaps the greatest and most unremitting sources of noise for us are the myriad small gas engines that every man now uses for all of his garden work. You start with power mowers. Then Weed eaters (my father and all the men in the neighborhood in Moorestown used sickles and hand clippers). Then chain saws (people didn't cut up so many trees when I was small, or if they did, they used an ax and a manually powered crosscut saw). Then circular saws: Everyone remodels his house perennially. Then leaf-blowers with their high whine. And leaf-vacuums (I don't know what they are called, but they make more noise than our old bamboo rakes did). In the winter everyone turns out with his snowblower (we shoveled with only a small scraping noise).

I calculate that there are a hundred houses within earshot of my house. Multiply that by, say, six or eight noisemakers, and you have a great luxuriance of sound.

Well, hey for the din and nonny for noise. Why tell *Crisis* readers about it? We are all Catholics, I suppose, and hence en route to sanctity—eventually, to be sure. Noise offers the near occasion for sanctity, or at least for the humble virtue of patience.

A Note on the Dark Night

For a time last fall, the press, and therefore to some extent the public, was briefly yet intensely occupied with the publication of some letters of Mother Teresa. Readers of this column will know of these letters, of course. The small Albanian nun had never supposed that they would be made public, since they had been written to her confessors over a period of some decades. I think that she had asked that they be destroyed. But she has been betrayed.

Or at least so it would have seemed, at least momentarily, on the surface of things. I know nothing of the details of their publication. Perhaps there was no betrayal at all. And, as happens anyway in the annals of grace, the letters appear themselves to be proving a fountainhead of help to some people.

The point is, this diminutive woman had suddenly become a sort of world icon—very oddly and ironically, as it happens—in the late twentieth century. As far as one can tell, it was at least partly the work of the British journalist and television personality Malcolm Muggeridge—himself at the time still very skeptical about Christian, and especially Roman Catholic, claims—who went to Calcutta and made a film about Mother Teresa that he titled *Something Beautiful for God*. The thing caught hold, and the world decided that it had a saint on its hands.

Reprinted with permission by CatholiCity, February 3, 2008.

I say "ironically", since sainthood was, and is, scarcely an item in the agenda of contemporaneity. But perhaps it is not altogether ironic. Vanity Fair, and perhaps even Babylon itself, has always kept in small reserve the capacity to breathe out a short "Oh! A saint!" when it comes upon such an oddity. If the figure becomes awkward, and eventually inconvenient, these cities have ways of coping. There were, to be sure, grimaces, and some baleful mutterings, when Mother Teresa spoke in Harvard Yard. But since she issued no call to arms on the spot, Harvard remained its (then) civil self.

But these letters. In them we find an aspect of the interior life of the Catholic that will not surprise Catholics who have been "walking with God" for many years with any sort of attempt at fidelity. The files of the Church are stuffed with the records of the souls—virtually every soul who has ever put down in writing any record of his interior life—who have striven to know God.

I say "striven". There is an eighteenth-century German hymn for All Souls' Day that says, speaking of the souls who appear before God's throne to receive their reward at the Last Day, "These are they whose hearts were riven, / Sore with woe and anguish tried, / Who in prayer full oft have striven / With the God they glorified." If you have been in the school of prayer for very long, and especially of intercessory prayer, you will know what that hymn, and what all spiritual autobiographies and letters, are talking about.

Actually, I suppose there may be a further irony even here. For Mother Teresa, it is almost as though the "striving" itself went dry. Her letters record years—decades—when God seemed to have withdrawn altogether. She had no word from heaven. Where was He? Where was her beloved Jesus? Even the Eucharistic Jesus seemed to have vanished.

But she soldiered on, with her prayers and with her work.

There, to me, is the great point. And there, to me, arises a somewhat piquant topic for reflection upon one's own state of soul.

One hears a very great deal now from those who "identify" with these letters. There is almost, it would seem, a sort of espousing of doubt abroad, as though it were the very cockade of authenticity.

But I find myself mulling. Here we had Mother Teresa—the courage, solitude, austerity, fidelity, perseverance, hardihood, struggle, valor, purity of motive, ardor, agony, and heroism that may claim to have entered "the Dark Night of the Soul", and if you are Saint John of the Cross you may speak of it. But the distracted, intermittent, flitting, hummingbird-like dabbing at existence and the thunderous mysteries of the Faith, which darts away at supposed difficulties and presently is seen no more, and then tells us of its experience of that Dark Night—one finds oneself embarrassed in the presence of the latter claim.

Look at Me!

The local Community House in Moorestown, New Jersey, where I grew up, used to sponsor a little parade on their grounds each year at Halloween. We would all line up in our costumes and file past a table on the lawn where the judges sat deciding which costume was the best. The great thing was to show up in what one hoped would be judged to be the most original, amusing, or beautiful costume.

One year—I was perhaps ten years old—I cobbled together a miscellaneous get-up with bits that I thought were amusing, other bits that I thought original, and even an item or two that I thought might qualify as beautiful.

The judges were not swept away. To my hopeful eye, they never gave even a moment's attention to me. (This corroborated a lifelong conviction that I had, in any case, that it was my lot in life to be passed over.)

The prize went to a boy who showed up riding an ostrich (his legs were the ostrich's legs, and he—or his mother—had rigged up little stuffed-stocking legs that dangled over the ostrich's homemade sides). Even the most envious of us had to admit that there was only one real candidate for the prize.

This wish to be noticed and applauded and, perhaps, accorded even fame is of course not universal. I often wonder whether men are not more susceptible to it than are

Reprinted with permission by CatholiCity, October 31, 2008.

women. We all have to cope with various forms of vanity, but men appear to be driven in this respect more urgently than is the case with most women. In all of us there is the desire to be known, in the sense of wanting some attestation from outside of ourselves—at the least, the attestation of a parent, a spouse, or a friend. It all arises from the sort of creature we are. If one is a person and not, like the poor wildebeests or herring, merely one of the multitude, then that personhood cries out for some recognition.

From the small girl in her frilly white First Communion frock, shod in black patent-leather Mary Janes and white socks, to the schoolboy who has worked long over a tiny wooden cart in Manual Training class, to the adolescent girl arising early to get her make-up just so, to the college prof preening his feathers at the lectern, to someone who finds to his delight that a TV interviewer has waylaid him—we mortals most earnestly wish to be known, and perhaps (for some of us) lauded and garlanded.

It is understandable. After all, we are made by God in His image, and He is, in a mystery, a threefold unity in which the Persons "know" one another in perfect bliss. We are addressed by Him as *thou*. We are not seeds in a granary.

But this desire to be known is prey, alas, to the warping effects of evil. It can become tyrannous and turn into egocentrism—pride, in other words, that will send us to hell if we finally insist.

So there arises a paradox, it seems to me. On the one hand, the desire to be known belongs to our very personhood, which is the gift of God; but, on the other hand, Scripture, the Church, and the saints, not to mention our Lord Himself, would appear to cut across this desire. Deny yourself, we hear. You cannot even be my disciple unless you "lose" your life. You must be "crucified". It sounds as though we are to forswear the very thing that seems to belong to our personhood, if we want to be whole and free. What is one to do?

For one thing, we may recall the "great multitude which no man can number" from Saint John's Apocalypse, whose whole joy is to adore the Lamb. Here there is no plucking of sleeves with, "But look at *me*!" Bliss and fruition for every single individual seem to attend this self-forgetting adoration. It is what we were made for in the first place, this adoration of That Which (He Who) alone is finally to be adored—by seraphim and the whole angelic hierarchy—and by the whole creation: winds, dew, whales, frost, the sun and moon, clouds, us men. *Benedicite, omnia opera Domini Domino.* They all look as though they have forgotten themselves.

But how shall I ever come to such a state of affairs?

The answer would seem to lie along the track indicated by the saints when they talk of renunciation, retirement, withdrawal, detachment, stillness, and poverty. Daunting words. But (they tell us) joy lies at the end. And not only that: It turns out that, as one trudges along that track, joy very gradually begins to dawn upon one. What I thought I had to secure by anxious efforts comes as a by-product of my having given over my anxiety.

For presently one finds oneself addressed by the One who says, "Behold I stand at the door and knock: if any man hear my voice, and open the door, I will come in to him, and will sup with him, and he with me." It is the One of whom the psalmist was speaking when he said, "Thou knowest my downsitting and my uprising; thou understandest my thought afar off." Even poor Hagar had a just inkling when she said, "Thou, God, seest me."

That day at the Halloween parade was big with the promise of this.

An Odd Reminder

Well brought-up children are taught to say thank you, along with all of the other greetings and responses that attend polite life. Such responses must be imposed at first, of course, and learned by rote, but soon enough they become habitual and virtually unconscious. This does not, however, mean that they are fraudulent. Somehow the authentic idea of gratitude seems to work its way in, by a sort of osmosis, to the young person's inner being, so that the imposed and learned response gradually flowers into the true generosity of spirit that animates good manners. At least, this is how it seems to work in good households as often as not.

But because we are all mortal (and fallen), things are never altogether ideal. The best of us wake up from time to time, embarrassed at some ghastly solecism into which we have blundered simply through inadvertent ingratitude or some residual oafishness. A letter not written; a phone call delayed too long; a friend's kindness stupidly overlooked.

The region of experience in which this sort of thing is egregious is, of course, our prayers. We make our petitions, heaven knows, and rightly so, since we are bidden by God Himself to do so. And no doubt we often do add our thanks for God's blessings. But if our prayers are hasty, the chances are that what gets huddled *in* is our list of petitions, with our thanksgivings left by the wayside.

Reprinted with permission by CatholiCity, April 7, 2008.

It may be for this very reason that the Church has frequently kept before our eyes in the Breviary and the Lectionary the words in Psalm 92: "It is a good thing to give thanks unto the Lord: and to sing praises unto thy Name, O most Highest" (this is a 16th-century translation). It seems odd, but it may, alas, be the case that we never quite get beyond needing to be reminded to "say thank you."

For my own prayers, I have found that one's acts of thanks are assisted, and somewhat vivified, by picturing with each item its opposite, or its lack. That is, if we tick off before the Throne the general categories for which we owe thanks, we may arrive at the end of the list in the rather mild frame of mind with which we embarked. We thank the Lord for freedom, peace, food, shelter, health, friends, the beauties of the world, His providence, and so forth, all of which suffrages are most salutary to be sure. But where has our mind been all along?

I have found that help is supplied in one's struggle on this point if one pictures, at each point, the situation if the blessing in question were absent.

For example, freedom: When one gives thanks to God for freedom, one may try to imagine what life has been like, for most of history, for people who have had to live under khans, sultans, pharaohs, commissars, and dictators—not to mention life in gulags and prison camps and exile of all unspeakable descriptions, or in galleys or under slavery. At this point the single word "freedom" takes on some bite, and one says it with fear and trembling.

Or peace: One thinks of trying to piece together one's house and family in the wake of Goths or Huns or carpet bombing or Sherman's march through Georgia or any scorched-earth policy or under any reign of terror when the Gestapo or the NKVD might knock on your door in the small hours, and there would be the end until the

Last Trump of your family circle. The one-syllable word of thanks suddenly looms like the archangel himself.

I myself include in my attempts at thanks to God the ancient list of the four elements, earth, air, fire, and water, since, obvious as they are, we do count on them, and they are after all gifts straight from God's hand, and one does not always think of thanking Him for such omnipresent bounties.

Earth: Think of a moonscape; then think of this fecund, fructifying place, such a riot of fruit and forests and meadows and loam and fauna and vegetation—the nursery of all of us and the lions and the arctic terns and the dolphins and ruby-throated hummingbirds and so forth. *Benedicite, omnia opera Domini Domino!*

Air: Think of smothering, or of being shut in a fetid dungeon, or of gasping in the final throes of emphysema. Air.

Water: Think of parching under a merciless sun in the Kalahari or the Sahara; then think of an icy brook in the Alps or a burn in the West Highlands or a glittering pool high in the Rockies, or a glass of water got by merely flicking a spigot when your mouth is dry.

Fire: All fire—from the sun down to the blue flame on the stove to the fire I never see in the water heater and the furnace in the cellar. When there's a power failure, pray God that the electric company will get things going again. And meantime, thanks be to God for this lovely roaring maple fire in the fireplace.

I also add light to this list and try to imagine blindness. My father had lost his left eye when he was twelve in a Fourth of July accident. I had imagined that things would "look" dark from that eye, and I can remember how bemused I was when he told me that he could see out of that eye no more than he could see out of his ear. Blindness. Or even the interminable Antarctic winter. Darkness. Thank the Lord for light.

And so it goes: food, shelter, clothing, health, work, friends, family, the pleasures of this life—"But above all for Thine inestimable love in the redemption of the world by Our Lord Jesus Christ, for the means of grace and for the hope of glory...."

Every one of us will fill in his own list. The main thing to remember: "It is a good thing to give thanks unto the Lord: and to sing praises unto thy Name, O most High."

Dr. Oz and the Fountain of Youth

The melancholy truth of the matter is that history has now taken us all quite beyond the tranquil days of fountain pen and writing paper and quiet hours at one's desk. One has to have that grey machine, with all of its ancillary machines, dominating one's study. I have managed to limit things to a small laptop on a corner of my desk, and a demure little printer in a corner behind a door, but there is no going back. I am still typing this on the laptop.

With the vanishing of paper-and-ink letters to one's friends, we have the culture of technology, which it is fashionable to lament, but we all fall in line nevertheless. One of the hazards of this culture is the matter of advertisements, which have taken on a particularly sinister aspect now. They not only appear on your screen unremittingly: They unfurl themselves in all the margins; they wink and flash, and *dance* forsooth; and worst of all, they plant themselves on top of the letter you are reading or writing. They invite us to look young, or join a scheme that will offer your photo to long-lost friends, or gain a B.A. with no work, or skirt the economic slump and amass a quick fortune.

I find myself particularly nettled in this connection with an offer that comes from someone called Dr. Oz. He smiles from the screen. He has developed a nostrum that will reverse the deathward plunge of your cells and

Reprinted with permission by CatholiCity, July 6, 2009.

thereby restore your youth. He tells us that we will look like teenagers. (Sans pimples?)

At least two questions present themselves here. For one thing, do we believe the man? Does anyone believe him? *Can* anyone believe him? For a man to have found the Fountain of Youth, that hidden spring sought with tears and high hopes for millennia, and to have bottled the water, is surely news next only in importance to the Trump of Doom.

But obviously such questions are frivolous. The only worthy question here is the one that inquires into the desire that prompts the offer. Advertisers have to offer products that we want—cars, cruises, laxatives, hair oil, fried chicken. What wish of ours stirs Dr. Oz to work up his elixir?

We mortals don't want to grow old. That's patent. Shakespeare's "Seven Ages of Man" comes to mind, ending with the lean and slippered pantaloon and second childishness, sans teeth, sans eyes, sans everything. We scarcely need to descant on the topic.

Or do we? Is there an alternative to that sort of lament?

My wife and I visit some cloistered Carmelite nuns from time to time. Many of them are aging now; some are bent over. And of course every one of them has given up father and mother and houses and lands, so to speak, and certainly nearly all of the distractions that the rest of us have at hand. Death is not far off for some of them. We go to their funerals when that arises. But nothing but delight, intense interest, eagerness, and great cheer pour through the grille that separates us as we sit and talk.

We also knew a local man—an energetic saint, a great sailor, and, like Saint Barnabas, an encourager. I went to see him in the Veterans' Hospital in Boston as he lay dying. He was "way up in his eighties", in my mother's phrase. When I appeared in his door, he raised his arms into the air and said, "Thank the Lord! Thank the Lord!" I knew him well enough to know that this wasn't merely an enthusiastic, much less pious, way of assuring me of a warm welcome. He was just *saying* that, since that was all he had left to say. It was a general salute to the situation.

We had a cook when I was young, an old white woman, widowed, with one churlish and ungrateful son who never visited her. She lived alone with a moldy and decrepit dog and a great forest of potted plants in an ice-cold flat on the ground floor of a house straight out of Poe. She was stone deaf and greatly crippled with heaven knows what all. I liked to ride along as my father drove her home on winter nights. As I would take her up the steps to her porch and front door, she would get the key into the lock, and, pushing the door, unfailingly say, "Oh! All to the good!"

Dr. Oz would have trouble getting up much business from any of these people. Something had long since summoned them from the common state of affairs where a man is, in T. S. Eliot's words, "distracted from distraction by distraction". Such a man might be attracted by the notion of regaining his teenage years. But why? What does he want? What is he afraid of?

Ad te omnis caro venit. Unto Thee shall all flesh come. That note can be either a grim one, if I have opted for a life of distraction, or, if I have come out of the jail of myself, it can be a sweet trumpet call from the precincts of Joy itself.

The nuns, and our old cook, and the man in the Veterans' Hospital hear it as that sweet trumpet. My teenage years, my young adulthood, my middle life, and my creeping old age will decide how I myself may hear the note.

Of Abbots and Actresses

It is recorded of the Abbot Pambo, of whom I know nothing at all except the following anecdote, that, upon a visit to Saint Athanasius, he came upon an actress—not, I would suppose, inside the good saint's cell. (I have only very dim notions as to what sort of women these Egyptian actresses were.)

In any event, Pambo broke down and wept. They asked him why. He said that two things had upset him: first, her perdition; and second, the fact that he himself didn't have nearly as much zeal to please God as she had to please vile men. I think we all find ourselves stricken with his second point. It is his first point upon which I briefly ran aground.

Perdition? This actress? Did he mean she was going to hell? How did he know? Well, I doubt that he would have passed a final judgment on her eternal destiny; but on the other hand, these grizzled fathers lived in frightening proximity to the divine holiness itself, and he recognized the precincts in which the poor woman had her being. He wasn't regaled by the fantasies in which these women live—then and now, one supposes.

He was looking at things from an odd angle. Was it his fancy? Was he morbid? How goes it with the souls of actresses anyway? Is all well? Who is to say? It's always a sticky wicket, this business of talking about the welfare of others' souls. I myself belonged to a profession during my

Reprinted with permission by CatholiCity, November 13, 2007.

own working life that shared none of the glitter but most certainly all of the fantasy of the theatrical world, namely, the academic. There is no employment in the world that offers more chances for vaingloriousness than scholarship, and collegiate hallways heave with portly coxcombs as vain as all of Egypt and Hollywood taken together. (I know this because I knew one of them as intimately as I knew any colleague, alas.) Pambo, being a very holy man, was no doubt on a far surer footing than the rest of us from which to discern matters of perdition.

But he scarcely gloated over other souls' danger; it brought him up short. Oh, she was eager to please men, to be sure, but an actress can *see* such an audience and hear the applause and the shouts. That's entirely understandable. Who can resist such pleasures? How sore a blame is to be attached to this level of venality? And what if she allows herself a bit of lewd leeway now and again? Have not women been doing this from the beginning? Is this not only human? Shall any given woman be damned for merely catering to well-paying, loud, and lusty men? Or, at least, so goes "moral theology" as it is often loosely and happily aired over convivial drinks.... Not really the drift of Pambo's own self-scrutiny, however.

He, rather, is jolted awake, thinking: If this woman is in danger, poor soul, where does this put me? She does what she does to make a living, no doubt, and perhaps picks up spicier motives that bring along more somber peril, alas. Well, she will find herself in God's hands one fine day. It is interesting that he does not for a moment sentimentalize things, as would most certainly be done in our own time—the strumpet with the heart of gold and all that. All will be accounted for—by her as well as by me, much as we quail at the thought. What she will owe is none of Pambo's (or my) business. Pambo turns fiercely to his own case: He has everything. He is the recipient of all the largesse of heaven. But he is doing a poorer job serving his Master than this actress is serving hers. What about that?

What conceivable case can be made out for Pambo? Most of us will not worry for long over him. We may well scrutinize our own case.

Open to Experience

Some years ago I heard a young man—actually, he was a teenager at that time—remark that he wanted to be "open to all experience".

I am pretty sure that I know what he meant. He was an intelligent fellow and eager to distinguish himself from people whose minds were, he felt, narrow. He saw various sorts of religious people about him who were not as sure as he was that the direction in which civilization was headed was altogether a promising one. They might wonder, for example, whether the much-praised "sexual revolution" was a movement forward in the annals of the human race, or whether it might be the beginning of the Gadarene Slide. For heaven's sake (he was thinking), we're grown up now ("man come of age", a popular theologian had suggested): Surely we do not need moral busybodies hampering our right to make our own decisions in such a matter as this? Has the human race not lumbered ahead for long enough under the strictures imposed on us by pinched moral codes that treat us all as children?

But I think my young friend was not speaking solely of matters entailing the big moral questions. His was a generation that looked back on the preceding generations as having been somewhat disfranchised by the mere lack of the chance to enjoy all this "experience" that he felt was the very precondition to full and authentic adulthood.

Reprinted with permission by CatholiCity, January 3, 2011.

Modern travel and communications had, it seemed to him, opened up whole vistas of "experience" to everyone. You could find out all about wine now by visiting endless chateaux, vineyards, and cellars as you frolicked across Europe with your knapsack on your back. You could climb Kilimanjaro or Chimborazo with your friends now, not merely read wistfully about it in the pages of Ernest Hemingway as your fathers had done.

And music: Technology was making the entire universe of music instantly available, from Praetorius to U2, so that you could enter knowledgeably into high-level discussions on the matter, whereas your fathers had had to scrape along with their paltry collections of 78's or 33's. And *food*—my word. Now we had rare sauces *drizzled* on our arugula and endive, whereas our forebears had to make do with iceberg lettuce and creamy ranch dressing. Or so it all seemed at any rate to my friend.

The great thing was to be "open to all experience". Why were one's elders forever hesitating before taking the plunge into that which was new and exciting? When a revolution announces itself, why dawdle on the sidelines? The Bastille in 1789, the Barricades in 1858, Chicago in 1968—*get into it!* Or, after World War I, go-ahead types took up martinis, twelve-inch cigarette holders, short skirts, cerise lipstick, marcelled hair, and cloche hats: Hey nonny! Free love! Aldous Huxley with his peyote and Timothy Leary with his LSD: Hurrah for heightened awareness! One was in a race to gain sheer quantity and variety of "experience". Who will carp?

Presently I found myself wanting to put a question to my young friend: All of experience, you say? *All?* Well, let's see. What about the experience of living your whole life in penury on a drab street at the edge of an industrial city? That would be experience, surely? Or shall we consider paraplegia; or blindness; or MS; or ALS? These certainly would qualify as experience, would they not?

Or again: finding oneself betrayed by one's spouse, or jilted by one's beloved, or sacked from one's job, or refused entry to the university of one's fondest hopes? Or (yet again)—how about starvation? Half the world seems to live perilously close to that. Or life in a Marxist state? There's experience for you, if that's what you are so eager to savor ...

Perhaps we need to modify the word "experience". Would "pleasure" be closer to the mark? Or diversion? Or ecstasy?

What constitutes experience, actually? To find an answer to that, we might consult a sampling of people from across the human scene and ask what their experience of life has been. An old Berber sitting at the door of his tent; or a coolie dragging scows up the Yellow River; or a mother of ten ragged children; or a London cabbie, or a shopkeeper in Guayaquil. Here's a wrinkled crone in black stockings, black dress, and black babushka. She will have missed quite a few of life's "experiences". But what do all these people know of this mortal life of ours? Poverty? Yes. Unremitting toil? Certainly. Endurance? Sacrifice? Motherhood? Small pleasures in local wine, home-baked bread, greens, tea? No doubt. Laughter over the antics of children? Surely.

At this point, of course, we have steered perilously near the bog of sentimentalism. Summoning this parade of people from all across history and the globe could easily regale us with mere emotion, the way candlelight and plaintive violins can play on our emotions. We do not have to go so far afield to consider inner-city schoolteachers, mechanics, salesmen, clerks, housewives, secretaries, managers, executives, and a host of others whose range of "experience", to a casual glance, might look less than thrilling.

Are they cut off from the experiences that offer us all the chance to grow into the wisdom, virtue, charity, courage, and endurance that alone mark the authentically human man or woman? A vast breadth of pleasures and diversions may or may not have come their way. But what will they have missed in missing such pleasures? Nothing, surely, that pertains to the dignity that crowns our true humanity.

Rethinking the Global Village

I happened upon a strange television show recently. (Like every man of a certain outlook, I have to hurry in here and urge that "I never watch TV", which is true, actually.) It was a Disney production, I think, and it had been prepared for children. It was set in a sort of Hogwarts school—shadows, a touch of menace, crosscurrents of evil in the air. The "plot" escaped my grasp altogether. I seem to recall a plump lady teacher with wings of some sort—not angelic. The pupils were youngish teenagers representing a sampling of ethnic groups. Somehow they began to encounter Evil, the avatar of which was a blond boy who looked somewhat like your archetypal English choir boy.

The program reminded me of a DVD I saw once, again meant for children. The tots in the story kept encountering all sorts of beings who, on first glance, would arouse terror in any ordinary mortal: great grinning pterodactyls, for example, and an elephantine purple blob with one eye coming at you, and tarantulas, basilisks, anacondas, and cockatrices. But they all turned out to be not only harmless, but positively companionable. *Sympatico*. Allies. Fun.

An agenda was clearly at work here on the part of the producers of the little drama: Exorcise the bugbear of *stereotypes* from your child's bosom. Stereotypes spawn terror, and thence hatred, and thence cruelty. One's soul

Reprinted with permission by CatholiCity, November 9, 2009.

becomes sullen and niggardly if one looks at life through the baleful lens of stereotype. You can't tell at all what someone will turn out to be merely by glancing at his clothes or weight or stature or color or features. Ugliness may cloak generosity, trustworthiness, innocence, and heroism as often as not.

Developing such an outlook in children becomes critical in the epoch of globalism that has rushed upon us. We mortals lived for millennia in surroundings that were hedged in by geography, distance, custom, culture, religion, and blood. Suddenly we are all thrust together. Hitherto, Watutsi, Danes, Celts, Samoans, Aryans, and Chinese lived under a canopy of expectations and assumptions that had been settled long since by their historic and anthropological locale. They rarely had to cope with the "others", and when they did, as often as not trouble broke out.

The treasure that is to be attributed to these limited cultural situations is rich beyond counting. Every museum and library in the world testifies to this. All music, painting, architecture, sculpture, poetry, and dance testify to this. "Multiculturalism" has not had enough time yet for us to decide whether it will join the antique train of these limited cultures with their rich dowry. Limitation seems to have been the very mother of peace (such as it ever was) and creativity.

But children are no longer born into Montenegro as such, or Java or Baffin Island or Nepal or Germany. They are now born into the world. Information in tsunami force and quantity, traveling at light speed, and instant communication with all six billion of us—and hence the vision of multiculturalism—form the landscape in which we all live now. We must come to terms with it one way or another.

The question that now appears on the horizon is: What, exactly, is the footing on which we will raise the new world? The cultural millennia that have preceded us all drew upon certain fixities. When you sift through matters of ethnicity, geography, climate, and so forth, you come eventually to the fixity that undergirds any culture: It is the notion of the gods. Many or One? Malign or benign? Personal or abstract? If there is a culture somewhere that has never acknowledged any transcendence at all, it is hard to find.

And from that transcendence there has issued what we call morals. Ethics. The awareness of Good and Evil. Taboo. Manners. All myths and fairy tales testify to this, as does history.

And Good and Evil are recognizable to us mortals. From the beginning, just men have responded with joy to the joyous, and with outrage, horror, and disgust in the face of the outrageous, the horrible, and the disgusting. We recoil at what threatens—at first even by its appearance. If what we feared as a threat turns out not to be so, then joy knows no bounds. This irony shows up in the fairy tales and myths—the Ugly Duckling or the Frog Prince. The Elephant Man turns out to be sheer beauty in tragic disguise.

But Good and Evil, and the cultural forms in which they present themselves, evaporate when their source in transcendence is banished.

This has happened in our own time. The modern age testifies to this in its painting, its poetry and fiction, in cinema, and in public morals. Questions seem to overthrow what had been thought to be the fixities, and you get first uncertainty ("But *is* that, after all, so bad as they thought?"); and then experiment ("Ah! Let's leap over this quaint taboo here and authenticate our autonomy"); and then bravado ("Let it all hang out!"); and then the loss of memory ("It was only poor Queen Victoria—or the

Puritans, or the Catholic Church—who came up with all these strictures"); and eventually squalor, bathos, and ennui. Babylon, Sodom, and the Rome of the late Caesars do not appear in our imaginations as icons of authenticity.

But what about the DVD with the peaceable monsters? Clearly the point there is to dispel stereotyping so that children finding themselves on a globe rather than in a village or a kingdom will be predisposed to discount appearances and to learn that ancient and universal cautions are to be set aside in the interest of a new innocence and freedom.

Would that the fruit of the effort would turn out to be global neighborliness and peace all round. But one wonders whether there is not a tincture here that has tainted all utopian schemes built on the notion of the good will, not to say innocence, of us mortals. The globe isn't Happy Valley. Who knows what evil lurks in the hearts of men? Appearances most certainly do not tell the whole story—indeed, they may brutally falsify the story (think of the Elephant Man or Kafka's Gregor Samsa the cockroach). But Brook Farm and all communes trumpet the sad story of efforts to set aside the protohistoric cautions and hesitancies.

Do we do children a favor by dissipating for them the cautions, even fears, that arose from our local, cultural insularities by pressing upon them a global insouciance, so to speak? The way through such cautions and fears is a hard and long way. They may turn out in the long run to belong to our very humanity. They may guard our limitedness, which itself may belong to our humanity. Paradise is the locale of universal trust and affability. Catholic imagination does not suppose that it will be gained on this globe by programs. Conversion—the very rebirth of every one of us—and not programming, is the precondition for universal trust and affability. The joker in the pack is called Original Sin. Prejudice and ignorance are merely fruits of that tough root.

So: What shall we say? Two cheers, perhaps, for the DVD? I myself would think so. But it's two cheers leading to some long reflecting on how we're doing in the global sweepstakes.

Saturday Morning, April 2

I was in my study in Manchester, Massachusetts. It was 10:30 on Saturday morning, April 2, 2005. I, like the rest of you, had checked the television (I use Fox) as soon as I had gotten up earlier that morning. The Holy Father was still *in extremis*—still bound in this mortal coil, and none of us knew when God would say to him the gracious "Now!"

The TV anchormen and women heroically kept up their running commentaries and endless interviews with everyone in and out of the Vatican whom they could round up over those last couple of days. There were a few moments on Friday when the word got out that he had died—quickly corrected and reversed. No: He was still with us, and they had not closed the shutters on the windows of his apartment up there above Saint Peter's Square. The TV people would have been more than human if they had not found the thought, "Well—when is he going to *die*?" flitting through their heads during that long vigil.

Was it grotesque to embark on encomia then—before the pontiff had died? I don't think so. Now, not being a great "figure" in contemporary Catholicism—neither a prelate, nor a theologian, nor a pundit, nor an author of any special note—I can only reflect as a common layman on what this pontificate has meant to me.

Originally published in *Crisis* (May 1, 2005). Reprinted with permission.

I was an Anglican when John Paul II was elected to the See of Peter. In God's good providence, I was not long thereafter (at the Easter Vigil of 1985) received into the ancient Church. But even before being received into full communion with the Church, I had been sharply aware that we—all of us Christians—had been vouchsafed a very great gift from the Most High. A great and good and wise shepherd who had had long experience in leading his flock through the rockiest and most perilous terrain: the Poland of the Nazis and the Bolsheviks, not to mention that elusive historical phenomenon, "the modern world". What was the ensign fluttering from that crosier of his?

Holiness. Intrepidity. Valor. Fidelity. Brilliance. Tenderness. Perspicacity. A fathomlessly rich humanness. Suffering. (You can't be Polish, it seems to me, a Saxon, and not know more than most of the rest of us all about suffering.) And a glorious, unapologetic, articulate, undiluted orthodoxy. This, I think, was what gave me the greatest hope when we found this man presently sitting in the *sede* in Rome.

The encyclicals began to appear. As the new boy in town, I was under the illusion (sadly mistaken, I soon discovered) that Roman Catholics snapped up papal encyclicals and read them with great zest. Alas. Even my priestly colleagues on the faculty of one of America's major theological seminaries looked at me with sad incredulity when I would rush into the hallway after having read (and underlined, and filled the margins of) the latest encyclical or pastoral letter or *motu proprio*. "Hey! Get a load of *this*!", I would gasp. Patient shaking of venerable sacerdotal heads.

Nevertheless, I read them. *Redemptor Hominis*; *Dives in Misericordia*; *Dominum et Vivificantem*; *Redemptoris Mater*; *Veritatis Splendor*. Oh, *laudate et superexaltate Eum in saecula!*

Evangelium Vitae. Fides et Ratio. Those were the ones that brought particular joy to this new Catholic.

My wife and daughter and I met him once, upstairs in that parlor where he would greet small groups of guests. By that time he was bent over, clearly in terrible pain. His face sagged, and he could only groan his greetings. Perhaps that was his greatest gift to us: He showed us how to suffer.

Songs of Absurdity

To worship God at all is to find oneself on a very odd frontier. Here we are, addressing all sorts of fervid sentiments into the ether—or so it might seem to a chance observer. A passerby might ask, "To whom are you talking, pray? God? But you have never once seen him or heard his voice. Nor has anyone else, for that matter. What makes you think that what you are doing isn't merely whistling in the dark?"

Well, we and everyone from Adam, Noah, and Abraham on down—all tribes and cultures—have always done this. It belongs to our humanity. That God is, and that He hears us and loves us and is worthy of our praise—all of this seems to be inscribed in our very being.

But, our inquirer might object, can't you hear the absurd claims you make when you worship? Take, for example, that song that the Virgin sang, and which you have picked up and made a staple of your own praises. How do you relate all of that to what seems obvious if only one takes the trouble to look around at how the world just forges on its grim way?

What about, "He hath scattered the proud in the imagination of their hearts"? Can that be said about the Virgin's world—or ours? It always looks as though the proud rule the roost. Heads of state, chairmen of boards, tenured professors, financiers, pundits, authors—how many of these

Reprinted with permission by CatholiCity, August 4, 2008.

are to be found among the meek and humble of the earth? Has God scattered them?

Or again, "He hath filled the hungry with good things; and the rich He hath sent away empty." Take a look at the world, man. Are you talking fantasy?

Or there is that staggering canticle, chanted in the Church for centuries, sung by Daniel's three young friends in Nebuchadnezzar's furnace. It sounds particularly far-fetched. It summons the Sun, Moon, and Stars with, "Bless ye the Lord: praise Him and magnify Him forever." But we all know that those orbs have no intelligence, much less mouths to sing with. What sort of a cosmology is this?

And it proceeds to even greater absurdities, calling upon Winter and Summer to praise God. No one supposes, surely, that there is an entity "Winter" that can join in lauding this God of yours? Not to mention Light and Darkness, Fire and Heat, and Dews and Frosts. Not to mention *Whales*. You call to them all, "Bless ye the Lord: praise Him and magnify Him forever." What is in your mind when you descant this way?

For a reply, of course, we have to recur to the plodding notion of Faith.

Faith pierces the scrim of *appearances* and rests its gaze on the reality that has been unveiled for us in the Incarnation of the Word, and in His life, Passion, death, Resurrection, and Ascension. *This* is the everlasting drama that arches over our mutability—the mere rise and fall of empires, and the evanescence of philosophies and fashions, and the contingencies and sufferings of our individual experience.

But to lay hold of all of this is a tall order for faith. Appearances hail us unremittingly. Sheer circumstances, for example: For most of us they are far from triumphant, or even noteworthy. And for many of us mortals, circumstances are grim: sickness, bereavement, failure, poverty, debility. And yet, like the Virgin, we keep on saying that God has blessed us lavishly.

Obviously what we say draws upon what we (Christians) see, which is precisely the *unseen*. No one now can see Christ risen from the dead, much less ascended into heaven and sitting at the right hand of God. None of this will yield itself to any poll, research, or telescope. It is all foolishness, as Saint Paul observed about the preaching of the gospel.

But Christian faith exults in it all. It says that God has raised us with Christ and made us sit in heavenly places (Paul again). It sees death as already conquered, and it sees a creation where indeed the dews and frosts and nights and days and the whales *do*, in a mystery, join us mortals and the angels in lauding the Most High. How do they do it? We have no way of grasping it yet. But depend upon it: In a sense that eludes us so far, the whole creation does, in fact, praise God. We mortals do so with words and voices and liturgy, and in some sense it is our praises that articulate and "lead" the praises of creation. The mute creation has other modes (merely by being the exquisite things that they are?), and when all things are made clear at the Last Day, we will perhaps discover what those other modes have been.

Meanwhile, we address the Most High with language that outstrips mere common sense and plain observation and rests on the bedrock of faith.

Themis

Most of us, unless we have been steeping ourselves in Greek drama lately, will draw a blank when we come upon that word. *Themis*. Not really a household word nowadays.

But it ought to be. It bespeaks, really, the whole shape of life for the Greeks. For them, it constituted the touchstone by which a man tested his own attitudes and behavior. If he was a good man, before he acted or came to a decision he consulted a certain "senate", we might say. He asked himself, first, about *custom*: What were the canons governing right action in his city-state? He submitted his proposed action to *that which is permitted*; and again, to *that which is correct*; and to the demands of *the holy*; *the way of our ancestors*. *Themis*, in other words.

But of course it was not only the Greeks who bowed to such overarching considerations. Every tribe, culture, and civilization of which we have any knowledge at all seems to have known that *themis* is in the cards, so to speak. *Themis*, of course, is the foundation of taboo, which is the guardian of order in any civilization. The prophet Jeremiah adjures the Hebrews, "Stand by the roads, and look, and ask for the ancient paths, where the good way is; and walk in it" (Jer 6:16). The Old Testament is laced with such adjurations: Repeat the Law to your children—line upon line, precept upon precept. There are things that you must do, and things that you cannot *ever* do.

Reprinted with permission by CatholiCity, May 5, 2011.

I find myself from time to time in conversation with some old friends about the great moral issues that beleaguer us all now and that would seem to raise the question of *themis*, or as the Hebrews and Christians might call it, "the will of God"—notions that heretofore have been thought of in those quarters as moral absolutes: gender, the sanctity of human life from conception, sexual behavior, and so forth. My fellows in these conversations are, to a man, believing Christians—all of them hailing eventually from the conservative wing of Protestantism. *Sola scriptura* would be the ensign under which they march.

I have been startled to discover, however, that my friends are, to a man, innocent of what the Greeks would have called *themis* and the Hebrew prophets and the apostles and Fathers of the Church the will of God. I am aware that these two categories are not synonymous. Greek wisdom was, of course, pagan, and hence questionable, in the last resort. Nevertheless, the idea of there being great fixities arching over our mortal life seems to be omnipresent in all cultures. T. S. Eliot called these fixities "the Permanent Things". C. S. Lewis would have referred to it as the choreography of the Dance.

For example, one of our number has concluded that, in the light of "recent studies", homosexual practices are now permissible. He adduces "compassion" as the operative word here. Who will be so callous as to forbid the only form of sexual bliss available to people with same-sex attraction? Scrupulous exegesis, on this view, can always remove any difficulties offered by the very few scriptural texts that might seem to rule out such practice (e.g., the astounding exegesis that arose in the palmy days of early feminism in the 1970s, which turned on its head all that the writer of Genesis and Saint Paul had to say about husband and wife).

Or again, another member in our group will have it that "times are changing." In his view, this is the nonnegotiable starting point: Times are changing—which, then, calls for a complete overhaul of all traditional moral ideas. It is all merely a matter of "society's stereotypes" for this man; it is not an ontological question. The notion that the feminine and the masculine are epiphanies of bright fixities that are written into Creation is simply outdated. "Science has shown", they say. Hence marriage can no longer be governed by antiquated ideas as to who may marry whom. Times are changing.

(To be fair, this man does, in fact, cling to the idea that marriage presupposes one man and one woman—he is an altogether moral man. But he cannot see that the matter has anything to do with the nature of things, so to speak. These ancient ideas have no grounding in eternal reality. Bible verses are all that he has to cling to. Lewis' "Dance" is not invoked.)

Virtually all of the men in the group have a difficult time being clear about abortion. Oh, to be sure, we're (more or less) against it. But scientific research has altered the whole matter. We must first consider such awkward factors as the hardships that impoverished women face when they have pregnancy thrust upon them, or the inconvenience that pregnancy holds for so many busy and affluent women, or the quality of life ahead for the fetus, and so forth. These factors now have priority.

But again, these men are not secularists. They are Bible-believing, "born again" Christians. They are also academics who, over the decades, have taught thousands of Christian students. When I have raised the idea of a fixed moral order arching over our physical life—which order itself, from the sacramental point of view, bespeaks the blissful nature of ultimate Reality—my protestations merely arouse incredulity. Times are changing.

"She Knows Who I Am"

On several evenings recently, my wife and I have gone around the corner to our son's flat overlooking the harbor in our small town here on the Massachusetts coast. He had invited us to watch a television series that takes us into the day-to-day workings of Windsor Castle over the course of a year.

For monarchists like me, it was all quite splendid. But I think the interest one finds in castles and monarchs—in this case, the queen—is not solely romanticism and sentimentality (though a lot of that is at work). For any Christian, there *is* monarchy at the back of everything. God is not the chairperson of an ad hoc caucus of the whole. In our century, and most especially in secular, pluralistic democracy, the whole panoply that hailed the human race with intimations of thunderous realities (yes, even under khans, pharaohs, and tsars, grotesque as all of that may have been) has been flattened out. The notion of majesty is impossible for democratic imagination to grasp, and this is going to be a problem when the sky is split open and the mountains flee away and the King appears "robed in dreadful majesty".

In this series on Windsor, you see the maids on their knees polishing the waxed floors in great gilded rooms of cavernous length and height. Or men in felt socks up on the banquet table set with gold service for 150. Or the

Originally published in *Crisis* (January 1, 2007). Reprinted with permission.

upholsterers, the clockmakers (for four hundred clocks), the "fender men" (for the fenders on the eighty hearths), the footmen, the chefs, the stable boys, and the game wardens. Gasps, here, of, "But that's slavery. That's atrocious."

Well, perhaps so, on some hasty egalitarian and political accounting. However, every single servant, indoors or outdoors, who spoke to the camera exhibited a curious dignity, a noble sense of proud responsibility, and a disarming love (it is the only word) for "Her Majesty". Just to be in her service was, obviously, a cockade of glory. More than one spoke of a lifetime of dreams having come true—even the ones who had worked in the castle for decades.

This is hell to all Marxists. But there is, apparently, another view.

Whatever one may make of all of that, I found myself brought to a halt by a remark made by the old geezer whose job is (solely, I think) to hoist the royal standard at the top of the great tower when the queen takes up residence. Since there are more than three hundred servants at Windsor, obviously the sovereign can't know each one personally. But this man, with apparent joy, finished with the remark, "But she knows who I am."

All Catholics at this point will take off their hats and laud this old servant for having uttered a sentence that any doctor of the Church would be happy to have made. *My great joy is that the Sovereign knows who I am.* Readers may recall that in the *Narnia* chronicles, the tiresome boy Eustace Clarence Scrubb, now redeemed, when asked whether he knows Aslan, the sovereign Lion, replies, "Well—he knows me." That is very good theology. Our Lord said to the obscure Nathaniel, "I saw you under the fig tree."

One fine day, we hope, all of the fever that has attended our own frenzied efforts to erect a place in the sun will have been abated. Sennacherib, Cyrus, Philip of Macedon,

Napoleon, Hitler, and Stalin all seemed to suppose that the abating of this fever is to be found in conquest. I (an academic) may suppose that it will be found in published articles, books, speeches, endowed chairs (or even a footnote citing my work, alas). But this is all specious coinage at the end of the day.

The servants at Windsor know something that eluded the conquerors (and too many of the rest of us, most especially us academics). What my soul most yearns for is that the Sovereign know me.

Thoughts on My Fortieth Birthday

Arriving at forty is a bit like having the ashes put onto your forehead on Ash Wednesday: That is, it is a vivid, real, harsh reminder of some pretty bleak data, namely, that one is mortal. "Remember O man, that dust thou art, and unto dust shalt thou return", says the priest; and your fortieth birthday cake might as well have this written in icing across it.

Youth is gone, there's one thing. Oh, to be sure, eight out of ten people will quarrel with this. What with health spas and health foods and jogging and saunas and calisthenics and sunlamps, to say nothing of Man Tan and Queen Bee Jelly and after-shower sprinkles and washes and dashes and lotions and unguents, and all the ho-ho about life beginning at forty, and singles and swingles and fortyish marrieds all coming suddenly alive via consciousness-raising and encounter and liberation and open marriage and so forth and so on—good heavens! Who is the curmudgeon muttering about youth being gone?

But it is, you know. Four/sevenths of your allotment has gone by you. (Oh—you are one of the ones who'll make it to ninety? Right then: four/ninths, which is, let's face it, half, give or take a ninth.) And, let's face it some more, it's not as though your next thirty years are going to be anything like your first thirty (or forty), if we're

Originally published in *Eternity* (April 1975): 21–29. Reprinted with permission.

thinking of vigor and spring and bounce and energy and beauty and that sort of thing.

And if we *are* thinking of that sort of thing (as who can't upon reaching forty), we're thinking about our bodies, and there's where the rub is. If we were gnostics or Manichaeans or Platonists, and could take the serene view that flesh doesn't matter since it's unreal, or second-best anyway, we might be able to rally a sort of insouciant frame of mind about it all. But if we're Christian, and believe that flesh and blood are not to be swept under the rug (because of the Creation and the Incarnation and the Resurrection of the body and the Eucharist—we *do* affirm these doctrines, remember), then we feel keenly the mortality of the flesh. For it is here that we experience both the glory and the tragedy of our humanness: glory in bearing the Imago Dei; tragedy in being part of the fallen order of decay and death.

My body, then. It is there first, and not in my mind, that I feel the bite of arriving at middle age. It's not a young body any more. I am one of the ones who (they tell me) looked young for a long time. Until I was thirty-five or so, people kept gasping and exclaiming when they found out I was more than twenty-five. Then the gasps and exclamations trailed off. They didn't seem to be particularly surprised to learn that I was nearly forty. Nobody said any more, "But you look so young!" The message was clear: I didn't. I wasn't. My jowls puffed out, for one thing. Not exactly a double-chin, mind you. But here were the cheeks and chin of a middle-aged man now. I had looked with horror in 1967 at the photographs in my college alumni magazine of my classmates at the tenth reunion and saw how the men had become bald and puffy-faced. Then somewhere along in there it happened to me. I had had a portrait taken for the jacket of a book in 1967: the face of a young man. When people buy that book now, they cannot believe that it is I. They do not recognize that young man.

I look in the mirror and try to see where the difference is. "Ah: just a bit of weight there. A little dieting will get me back to that 1967 picture." But it's no use. I took off fifteen pounds this last summer, and I look older than ever. It's a question of vague and general sag, not just in the face but everywhere. Things aren't trim and firm any more. And there's not that clear, smooth look to the surface: Somehow one's skin gets complicated as middle age comes on—freckles, dots, patterns, hues, and worse. It's all rather grim.

But, someone objects, this is all grotesque. This is no Christian meditation on the passing of years. This is the sort of thing one might hear from some pitiable pantaloon applying to Elizabeth Arden for the magic week in Arizona.

And of course something is wrong if I find myself galvanized by the merely superficial aspects of the business, and if I hope to retrieve something by poking into formulae in tubes and bottles, and by offering myself, supine, to the sun god. But this much, and no more, I have to admit: that it is in visible, measurable, weighable (alas) terms that Middle Age presents its mask to me. But I've got to look farther than the mask. What shall I say about this Visitor who is here now to stay, having bundled Youth out the back door, and who will not budge until Old Age (I will not allow Senior Citizenship in my door) arrives—provided, of course, that we ever get that far.

What shall I say to myself about my new Visitor? Well, youth is gone: We've got that item down. And debility is just barely beginning to show itself: We've got that down, too. Is there more? Well, for one thing, there is the whole question of expectations. In one's teens and twenties, there was always the bright spectacle of achievement ahead to spur one on. There were endless variations, in one's reveries, on the theme: travel; fascinating and sophisticated and aristocratic people in one's circle; the esteem of one's peers; celebrity; and, mainly, influence. Mind you, it was all well within the pale of "the Lord's will". Perhaps it would be missionary achievement—the big conference speaker, or the apostle to the natives of Borioboola-gha with thousands of converts in his tally. Or the great champion of Christian orthodoxy, slaying with the jawbone of an ass all the devils of secularism and the traitorous churchmen who tag along in their train. Or the scholar, or the author, or the whoever—all of it in the service of Christ and His church, to be sure. But something big in any event.

Expectations, then. They dwindle.

Then cynicism plucks your sleeve with tiresome urgency. "Well now! Let's see where we are! We haven't made such a big splash after all, have we? No, of course not. That's all just pipe dreams for youth. It's all rather plodding, isn't it? Grey, really. Pointless. And seeing as how you've discovered this at long last for yourself, maybe you'd better do others the service of extinguishing the stars from their eyes. Take up a patronizing and avuncular attitude when some younger person gushes about how terrific everything is going to be, or when some earnest type shares his huge burden for mounting an enormous new global Gospel push."

Cynicism. To be rejected like heresy and avoided like the pestilence.

Then there's fear. All kinds of fear. What will happen to the world? This question has more teeth in it for me now than it did when I was twenty, since now there are houses and lands and children to lose. Oh, dear—my children: What will happen to them? What sorts of heartache and failure will be visited upon them? Will chaos and tribulation fall on them in this apocalyptic century of ours? Will life be brutal to them? Perhaps I could suffer myself, but dear God, how shall I contemplate my children wandering about in sheepskins and goatskins.

And my job: With the Arabs squeezing the economies of the West to the last drop, and ruin and depression looming—will I be selling apples on the street corner? Will my wife have to fight other women in the A&P to get a loaf of bread? Will I find myself in bread lines, or worse, in straggling refugee columns, looking for fodder somewhere for my children? Oh, help, Lord. And the whole question of health—mine, my spouse's, my children's. We've been spared so far: The law of averages must have something awful in store. And what happens if I become an invalid?

But wait. We're back where we were a minute or two ago—head over heels in grotesqueries. There it was a matter of looking *back*—at lost youth. Now it's looking *ahead*—at all the dreadful things that may lie in ambush. "Give us this day our daily bread." The manna went rotten if you hid it in a pot for future use. Grace is given today for today.

E'en down to old age all my
people shall prove,
My sov'reign, eternal, unchanged
-able love;
And when hoary hairs shall their
temples adorn,
Like lambs they shall still in my
bosom be borne.

Ah. How's that? Old age? Hoary hairs? Yes, old age and hoary hairs, and all that goes along with that: increasing weakness; the years of achievement gone by; enforced leisure with its corollary of more time to worry. All of that.

But what *is* it that this great company of "all my people" has proved? That life begins at forty or at eighty? That Senior Citizenship is a ball? That you can get your youth back? That danger and illness and loss can be fended off?

No. None of that. It's only sovereign, eternal, unchangeable Love that they've proved, that's all. They all learned the simplest (and hardest because it is so simple) lesson there is: "Trust ye in the Lord forever, for in the Lord Jehovah is everlasting strength." "Some trust in chariots, and some in horses [and some in Medicaid, and some in a stable economy, and some in health foods], but we will remember the name of the Lord our God." That's a hard lesson to learn (let me remember, when someone hands me back what I've written here, and asks how things are going on the trust front). We never quite learn it, perhaps.

Perhaps that is one reason why we need to remember "the blessed company of all faithful people"—this great train of men and women, from the patriarchs and prophets, down through the apostles and fathers and martyrs and virgins and widows and confessors. It's not as though I were being asked to blaze some trail. It's new for me, to be sure: I've never been middle-aged before. I've never been anything but a youth before.

So what do I *do* now? Is it *all* a matter of girding up my loins and bracing myself for decline? Do I visualize a graph, with the line going from the top left ("Youth") to the bottom right ("Old Age")? Surely that's a faithless picture when, unfolding into flower and growing into fruit within me, are the buds and shoots that appeared and were so carefully tended and watered and nourished back then in my youth? (Tended and watered and nourished, mind you, by others—my parents and my friends and my counselors and fathers in God: Left to my poor gardening, we'd have cracked clay and dry stubble now, nothing more.)

Am I allowing myself to fancy that youth is somehow really "where it's at" and that when that is over, we settle into the long trek to the tomb?

This won't do. Is there not one splendor of youth, and another of middle age, and still another of old age? The splendor of youth must have something to do with smooth skin and apple cheeks and lithe bodies and stars in the eyes and energy and promise.

And then, blossoming from that, isn't there the splendor of maturity, with marriage and all that comes with it of love and sex and new parenthood? Or, if marriage and parenthood are not in the pattern for me, of the settling into service and living, with the fulness that youth can't quite bring to the business? Then the years of child-training. What years they are, filled with the daily lessons of fatherhood and motherhood—great metaphors of the Divine Love, dropped in our laps.

And then the splendor kept for old age—the splendor that all story and poetry and myth have always celebrated about old age. Experience and grace and wisdom. Things brought to their ripeness. The crown that no younger head may wear. The back bent, perhaps, or the finger gnarled; but a seat at the top of the table. (This whole way of seeing things is almost impossible for us to keep alive nowadays, I realize, what with our having decked old age with the imagery of fun and games.)

And how does the splendor of middle age present itself? It appears in several ways, most of them ways I couldn't have imagined when I was younger, or, if I had, wouldn't have found appealing at all. Domesticity, for instance. Home night after night. The gradual discovery that the real locale of human life is at the table and at the hearth. Whatever parties or trips or evenings out may come along, the place I want to be more than anywhere else is in my own house, with my wife and children. If you had told me this ten or twenty years ago, I would doubtless have thought, "Excellent. Have it that way if you like, but I want variety and dazzle and excitement." And that would perhaps have been fine for a young man.

But there is a different thing going in middle age. There is the growing conviction that the ancient, quiet rhythms of ordinariness and domesticity are what one wants to be finding out about. Insofar as I must be out speaking, or at some committee meeting, or at a party, it is at the price—the fairly heavy price—of an evening *not* at home. This is something I would not have imagined in my youth.

And responsibility. Responsibility for my family, and for my work, and for my church. These are all things that "tie me down". But lo and behold, they are not forms of bondage. On the contrary, there is the sense that, via responsibilities like these, one is slowly moving toward one's authentic and ultimate freedom—the freedom in the City of God, where one's appointed task and one's bliss are synonymous. Surely these lessons in fatherhood and work and prayer and so forth are dim foreshadowings of the Real Work that I was made for. First steps in the Dance. And the better the steps are learned, the more joyous does my participation in the Dance become. My whole notion of freedom is different from what it was when I was twenty.

And, strange as it may seem, monotony. I do not say boredom. Far from it. By monotony I mean simply sameness: the sequence of day after day, week after week, in the place that has been given to me, with the excitement of possible change just around the corner that spiced my youth having receded, and, in its place, the long lesson of contentment. Not just a passive contentment, either, but an active, positive happiness that I have been given this freedom to pursue my work. Do I not have everything that any man in exile, or any prisoner, or any invalid, would give the whole world to have? I have my health, my work, my family, my responsibilities—dear God! Make me treasure these, and may I offer them up to You daily, as a sacrifice of thanksgiving. They may be gone twenty-four hours from now. My lot may change suddenly and violently. Or I may be given years of this. But whatever the schedule holds, in my middle age here, I am thankful for what I have been given.

So—what does it all come to, all this reflection upon having arrived at middle age? The jolt of realizing it; the backward look at what has gone; the forward look at what is coming one way or another; and the look at what is here, in my lap as it were. "What have you got there?" says God. "Not too much, Father. My fortieth birthday is about all." "Who brought you there?" "You did." "Why?" "For Your Name's sake, I guess." "You guess?" "No. I know. Thank You."

The Three Monkeys

Trinket shops at roadside tourist spots used to sell items like shellacked coasters cut from cross sections of white pine or birch logs, or faux-bark mottoes inscribed with uplifting sentiments, or bawdy farmyard postcards. That sort of thing. Perhaps they still do.

Among the trinkets, one could always find the three monkeys telling us to "Hear no evil, See no evil, Speak no evil." I always found the business infinitely depressing for some reason. Whether it was the simian ambience, I don't know. I don't think I had any fierce schedule myself that entailed some furtive hearing, seeing, and speaking. It just all seemed squalid to me—as did these trinket shops to begin with, actually.

But those monkeys were in a very ancient tradition. I recently came across one of the Desert Fathers who gave a young inquirer what seemed to be a blanket warning against all hearing, seeing, and speaking. If the poor boy had tried to take the old hermit at his word, he would have been left deaf, blind, and dumb, of course. Those grizzled Egyptian Fathers were not given to softening their maxims. They snapped out what they had to say and went back to plaiting their palm mats, and God help you.

What did the old man mean? Is there a trace in what he said for our profit? It would seem so. Hearing, for a start: such an innocent faculty, the very gate of a thousand

Originally published in *Crisis* (September 1, 2007). Reprinted with permission.

pleasures; the voice of my beloved; the music of Mozart; the sound of wind in the spruces high on the White Mountains; the song of the hermit thrush. Indeed. But also the funnel for all that titillates: Aha! How's that again? He what? Say that again? Oh, I'm so saddened to hear that!

No, my soul. Before the Dreadful Judge, I am not saddened. Nothing has given me a greater frisson than to come upon this hint that my colleague (or parson, or friend, or enemy, or neighbor) has purportedly faltered. Just the merest rumor. What hell in my soul—and how I lard it over with oleaginous piety. I'll just mention it to so-and-so, so we can pray together ...

Hear no evil, my soul. Flee it. Expunge it. Loathe it. Detest it. Hate your delight in it. Kyrie!

Seeing: such an innocent faculty. The very gate of a thousand pleasures: the face of my lady; the books on my shelf; the curtain going up at the opera; my dog looking sheepish. But also hell's own periscope. Did you happen to see that? Well, I mean. It can only have been ... I've noticed several times lately ... Oh, I'm not drawing any conclusions, but ...

How beady are my eyes? What is my scope peering at? I have come across that text about the pure finding all things to be pure. Have I ever even so much as approached those quiet waters? Or have I brought perspicacity to a highly wrought art, like the Accuser of the Brethren? Am I massively astute when it comes to "reading" situations? The great difficulty here is that all of this astuteness may well be turned back upon my own case in the end. My skill will be obliged to go to work on the only task I have: to give an account of the one person in the universe for whom I am answerable, alas.

Speaking: not such an innocent faculty. The tongue is a great evil that no man can tame. Most of us will go to our graves still struggling. God bless the Cistercians and the Carthusians who are learning one way of settling the matter. The trouble about "speak no evil" is that it hails me every time I open my mouth at all. Everything I say seems to have some edge to it, or some suggestion in it, or some veiled reproof or remark. I'm too clever. O Charity, where art Thou?

The Uzzah Syndrome

In the Old Testament there is a peculiar account of a man named Uzzah. In a certain situation, he was apparently the only man who cared enough to try to safeguard God's glory when it seemed to be in jeopardy. God struck him dead for his pains. The Second Book of Samuel, chap. 6, tells how the ark of God was about to tumble off the cart that was carrying it, and how Uzzah reached out to steady it. He did not want to see God's glory in the ditch. But God responded in a curious way to his zeal.

The frame of mind exhibited in this man's act is not a bad one. It is earnest, courageous, well-intentioned, and helpful. And it has a rigorous set of priorities. Its loyalty is attached to God, and it is quick to spring to God's defense.

What, then, is its error? What can have been meant by including this odd story in Scripture? Surely, it is not a story that will encourage people to be zealous for God's glory. But that is exactly the point. There is a proper enthusiasm for the glory of God, and there is a blasphemous one. And, alas, it is the infirmity of the religious mind forever to incline to the latter. Ironically, there is a point at which our eagerness to be on the side of the angels surpasses God's intention, and at that point we become inquisitors. God will be the custodian of the Glory. We preempt that role to our peril.

Originally published in *Eternity* (September 1968): 17–19. Reprinted with permission.

Scripture and history are full of stories of this sort of thing. Bildad, Eliphaz, and Zophar were anxious that Job not escape with any low notions concerning God's justice, but their efforts to shore up that justice were disallowed by God. The rabbis preserved and refined the Law for centuries with exquisite finesse, but Christ dismissed their washings, tithings, and prayers as whitewash. Peter, in a moment of floundering ecstasy, thought it might be nice to commemorate the Transfiguration with a shrine, but he was silenced. Saul of Tarsus saw a threat to the ancient tradition and set about to extirpate the whole thing. But he found himself struck down by the very Glory he sought to defend.

Kings and popes sought to reclaim for the Christian God the holy places defiled by the scimitar, but God showed little interest in their crusades. Torquemada saw the heretics, but his efforts to guarantee the Faith seem hardly consonant with the freedom proclaimed in that Faith. The elders of Geneva, Edinburgh, and Massachusetts Bay preached a sturdy doctrine under which many a good Christian soul wilted.

Is this to imply that religious loyalty is a thing to be lightly regarded and that rigor and austerity in holy matters are inappropriate? On the contrary. A man cannot possibly love God too much, nor can he be too careful to see that he is following in the Way. This is, eventually, the only important question that faces him. The difficulty arises when he reaches out and assumes to himself the custody of God's glory.

The forms this inclination takes in our day are almost innumerable. I speak from the evangelical tradition, but I suspect that the orthodox mind, whether religious or political, almost universally inclines to certain tactics.

For one thing, the orthodox mind is nearly always eager to simplify. If you can get things lined up with the good *here* and the bad *there*, you can manage them. Unmanageability is a thing eminently hostile to orthodoxies. But since human existence tends to appear unmanageable, we find it threatening. We cast about for schemata by which we can describe existence, and when we get it arranged, we feel that we are perhaps safe.

Our own tradition attempts this simplification, all unwittingly, by resorting to various forms of gnosticism, a heresy that is, of course, disavowed by all of us. But what is in the books and what filters down to the popular imagination are frequently two different things. The books are all right in our tradition, but the popular imagination is often a gnostic one: It sees a dichotomy in the universe between matter and spirit with matter defined as evil and spirit good. This is, in effect, a denial of the Creation, the Incarnation, and the Resurrection, but we do not make the connection.

The popular evangelical vision has seen escape from earth into a "spiritual" realm as our goal. True religion has consisted in devotion and "fellowship", and not especially in visiting the fatherless and widows, doing justice and loving mercy. The cup of cold water has not been our specialty, unless accompanied by a tract. The locale of true religion for us has been the assembly, and the focus has been on the state of the soul. The effort has been often to safeguard the purity of our religion by a flight from the bewildering actualities of existence.

This unwitting gnosticism has been exhibited most dazzlingly in our approach to morals. In the effort to safeguard the high standard set at Sinai and reaffirmed by Christ, we have out-godded God. We have built hedges that He refuses to build. And we have tried to bind into a perpetual childhood the sons of God, who should grow up from their schoolmaster to Christ.

Someone is probably murmuring "antinomianism" at this point. Not so. The quarrel is not between rigor and laxity, nor even between a law and liberty. The Christian is committed to the notion of law, but it is the law of being. He does not seek a supposed freedom that lies outside the strictures of law. Rather, his freedom consists in the discovery of the truth of our being and in the entry into the given rhythms of existence. Freedom is coming to terms with what, in current argot, is called "the way things are". The Christian understands the way things are from the Scriptures and the life of Jesus the Christ. Thus the Christian seeks his own best being, not in the bacchanal, as popular mythology would have him do (*Playboy*, et al.), but by participating in the *donnée*, the given, God's world. All the phenomena of existence are a sign of ultimacy to him, so that he enters into work, responsibility, marriage, and fidelity as foreshadows of Paradise.

The purity and truth of any life lies in the heart of the man. The pioneer missionary on his knees in Outer Mongolia, the grand duchess in her salon, and the university don over his ale and pipe may all be leading valid Christian lives.

Our tradition has also attempted to answer questions that might have been left unasked, and to answer them for the whole group. We have simplified the struggle between good and evil by finding an identity between evil and *things*. We placed certain things under interdict and thought we had guaranteed goodness. It was a well-intentioned attempt. Its motive was the glory of God. But, like the effort of Uzzah, Bildad, Peter, Saul, and Torquemada, it miscarried. It loaded people with burdens too heavy to bear. It made possible a fatuous vision of holiness that was entirely repugnant to Christian categories. It cultivated in its zealots a noxious sense of well-being that had nothing to do with true goodness.

It is, to be sure, natural for us all to want to make things safe, clear, and positive by getting them into specific terms. It is much easier to say, "Gems are evil" than to say "Vanity is an evil." For if you refuse to say the first, then your women don't have exact guidelines for adornment, and the first thing you know, you end up with a group of Jezebels and Nefertitis. The earnestly religious mind fears this sort of thing. But God insists that what makes the Jezebel is not the jewelry but the vanity. The vanity spoils the gems, not vice versa.

We have only to test our own lists of evils against those in Scripture to see how wide of the mark we have been. Both Christ and Paul spent half of their time knocking in the head the religious effort to keep things manageable, but neither of them could be accused of antinomianism. On the contrary, they both fulminated against evil, but the evils that they listed were evils proceeding out of the heart. It was, to be sure, an infinitely more difficult scheme to urge than that which the rabbis or the Galatian church urged, but it was, alas, the divine scheme. God will have man free to be good, and therefore free to be bad, and He will not have that freedom crowded.

We must, I think, confess to our gnostic timorousness on this point.

The descendants of Uzzah often find the world threatening. That is, God's glory is a shaky thing, assaulted on all sides by actuality. If we are not careful, it will be sullied and probably ruined altogether. Thus Uzzah's reaction. But the fact that God obliterated Uzzah did not mean either that the Ark was in fact going to land in the ditch or that God did not care. It simply meant that He would see to it that His glory survived.

In our terms, this means that the forms in which we understand God to be especially present—the Word, the Faith, the sacraments, the Church—are *never* threatened by truth. There is no new data discoverable that could suddenly overthrow the whole thing. Copernican cosmology did not destroy anything but the geocentric view of the world: Any theology that posited that idea had, of course, to be quickly repaired. But the Christian vision of the world had never really implied such a notion.

Yet the religious mind in our epoch often adopts an attitude of dismay toward the increase of information. "Where will it all lead?" is the question—with the reply assumed to be, "Anywhere but God." But it is not the increase of information that is at fault. The fault lies in the evil myth that attends the rush of research in our epoch—the idea that our special methodology (which is a late arrival in history) has an axiomatic validity that cancels all realms not subject to its scrutiny. Hence logical positivism. *This* is the enemy, not science.

But, as with morals, the anxious religious mind often makes the mistake of locating the threat in the wrong place. One hears well-meant lamentations over cybernation, life in a test tube, and space travel. But perhaps this kind of activity is obedient to the divine command that humanity subdue the world and have dominion over it. If, in this high task, men decide to build Babel, they err. But ignorance and credulity are no servants of the truth, and no Christian has anything to fear from research itself. The only thing he has to fear is what men must fear with mortal dread, and that is the pride and arrogance that follow upon man's awareness of his own capabilities.

The fully Christian response to human existence is one of zest. It is not an anxious, brittle, or hostile one, for it confesses the Lord of Creation for its God, and it understands that this God will not be taken by surprise. Nor will His Ark fall into the ditch.

Vuppies

About fifty years ago, we began to come across neologisms that had been cobbled up to designate sociological categories. The beatniks came first, I think. Then hippies. Then yuppies. Then dinks (Double Income No Kids). After that, I lost track. But I have one that needs to be added to the list—vuppies. Very Unimportant Persons. This one forced itself on me, since it is the only category into which I can insinuate myself: an English teacher, retired, having spent his entire professional life at very small institutions of which no one has ever heard. I suppose nobbies would do as well (nobodies), but that has a certain ring to it that falsifies the matter. The nobs: That's British provincial for posh people, and I can't even scrape up any ancestors who would get me in that door. (I think there was one who saved Robert the Bruce from a bull, hence my middle name, Trumbull, from Turnbull. But that is as close as I can come to the nobs.)

But what do you do when you wake up one fine morning to the bald truth that vuppy is the slot for you? This is the stuff that sends people to their therapists with identity crises. All the little hooks and handles and toeholds and rungs to which you aspired in your youth and middle age as somehow securing you a "place" have come unscrewed, or collapsed altogether. No Rhodes Scholarships.

Originally published in *Crisis* (July 1, 2005). Reprinted with permission.

No reverend professorships. No CEO or board chairmanships to fill in on the CV. No fellowships at All Souls. No address to make everyone genuflect. (This is very big in the Northeast, where I live: Jupiter Island, Lyford Cay, Point O' Woods, the Upper East Side, North Haven, Cold Spring Harbor. Actually, I live—literally—on the wrong side of the tracks in my town.)

So, in my dotage I visit my doctor. Perhaps there is a euphoria pill that will furnish me with some sense of worth? A spa, possibly, where I can be Rolfed (there is such a thing, but I don't know what it means) and made to feel fit and ready to fight 'em? Maybe a membership in a club that only those who know know about? (My trouble here is that I have a way of dropping out of clubs, feeling like the house oaf.) Whatever.

There is, Deo gratias, another aspect to the thing, however. My father was an ornithologist (no—this itself does not crown me with the dignity). But I grew up among Lapland longspurs, olive-sided flycatchers, prothonotary warblers, godwits, and saw-whet owls. Very interesting birds, these. If you were a member of the Delaware Valley Ornithological Club and could check one or more of these off from your bird-hike, you were, if not a Very Important Person, at least a Very Interesting Person (or had seen a Very Interesting Bird).

At the bottom of the bird list, however, we find the proletarian of proletarians (pops?): the English sparrow. Here's a nothing bird if there ever was one. Scrapping and cheeping and quarreling away in every bush in every jerkwater town on the map. But this lowly bird has a Very Special Identity. It happens to be the bird singled out by the Most High in the course of His making a major point about Himself. No sparrow falls without your Heavenly Father noting it. Then I don't have to be a semipalmated plover or a fairy wren in order to catch His glance? Apparently not.

The saints—those anonymous seventh-century Yorkshire monks, forsooth would insist that there is one cachet next to which all other cachets evaporate: to be known by God. There is our dignity.

What about the Day of Wrath?

My thoughts today may have particular import during Lent, but they touch on a subject that is much more far-reaching. Indeed, it is a topic that ought to be inscribed along the horizon of one's imagination in some permanent form, if one is at all serious about his mortal (and, let's face it, his eternal) existence.

I am speaking of the Last Judgment. What brought this inconvenient topic to my mind—other than the fact that, being seventy-two years old, I think about it a great deal of the time—was a performance of Mozart's *Requiem* at Boston's Symphony Hall my wife and I attended a couple of days ago.

Strictly speaking, a "performance" of the Requiem is an anomaly, since it plucks the thing from its context (the words form the Sequence in the Mass for the Dead). At the same time, in the hands of a Tomas Luis de Victoria or a Mozart, the authenticity of the thing is not altogether lost.

The words are no longer ordinarily in use in the Church's liturgy, so if they are ever heard at all, it will be only in a musical setting. To what extent listeners' attention might be flagged down by the terror of these words is a question.

Nonreligious concertgoers will, of course, have the luxury of placing the text in a category with the texts of *Dido*

Reprinted with permission by CatholiCity, March 10, 2008.

and Aeneas and the *Nibelungenlied*—affecting, no doubt, but scarcely threatening. Protestants who inherit from Calvin the notion of the "perseverance of the saints" may happily dismiss the thing as typical of late medieval fright about one's destiny (the text is thirteenth century). Thoroughly modern Catholics will find it all somewhat embarrassing and hope no one will tar them with any such primitive brush. So who will ponder this awful Sequence?

Day of Wrath—that Day of which both David and the Sibyl speak, when the earth will be reduced to ashes—that Day of fear when the Judge appears and everything comes under scrutiny—with a horn sending out an enormous sound over the region of the sepulchres—with both Death and Nature stupefied at the sight of men rising up in response to the summons to Judgment—[Who will hear any of this as seriously apocalyptic?]

Then a Book will be proffered, in which everything is contained and from which the world will be judged.

When the Judge sits down, everything that has been concealed will be revealed. Nothing will remain unavenged.

What will I, miserable wretch, say then? To what patron will I appeal, when the just are scarcely safe?

The above lines are a very wooden, sketchy, and schoolboyish approximation of the opening Latin lines of the Sequence. (The poetic renderings that one finds in old manuals of devotion are, as a rule, insupportably saccharine and, in order to keep up English rhyme, must stray far afield from the original.)

The Sequence goes on to appeal to the *Rex tremendae majestatis* for pity and invokes Jesus, reminding Him of His mercy in suffering on the Cross for my redemption (the voice speaking is first-person singular by this time). The language of repentance is extreme, as is the supplication that one be rescued from damnation. "Among the sheep and separate from the goats, place me on the right hand, when the wicked are confounded and consigned to bitter flames: call me with the blessed."

But then the intercessions for all of the dead return: Merciful Jesus, grant to them rest.

And then the great Offertory:

> Lord Jesus Christ, King of Glory, deliver all the souls of the faithful dead from the punishments of hell and from the deep lake; free them from the mouth of the lion, nor let Tartarus swallow them, nor let them fall into oblivion; but may Thy standard-bearer Michael lead them into Thy holy light, as Thou didst promise to Abraham and his seed.
>
> Sacrifices and prayers, with praise, we offer to Thee, O Lord; do Thou receive these in behalf of the souls for whom we make this memorial today; cause them to rise from death to life, as Thou didst promise to Abraham and his seed.

This whole line of thought is, to say the very least, remote from the lines along which our own thoughts like to run nowadays. Indeed, the stark violence of the language is too rough, we will object: Surely this is not the gospel of love and light and hope? We never hear this sort of thing even from the pulpit; it all went out at the end of the Middle Ages.

Perhaps it did. The question might be put, however: Should it have? Was there a new Revelation somewhere in there that changed the whole picture, so that sin was no longer sin, and God's judgment on sin was waived, and the human soul's need for His pardon was found to be superfluous, and the sacrifice of Calvary not something to be urged quite so stridently, and hell certainly not to be spoken of among modern and courteous souls?

It might also be politely urged here, "Oh, but it's a question of *emphasis*, surely?" One doesn't want too much wailing and gnashing of teeth. It's not healthy. We need to be upbeat. But what is authentic, godly upbeatness? Whatever it is, it can't be built on fastidiousness and Hallmark cards. It had better be grounded on the apostolic gospel of my sin and God's grace in supplying a remedy for that sin (and hence my real danger of everlasting loss) in sending the Savior.

Death is never treated with euphemisms in Sacred Scripture. If the event of someone's funeral is not the occasion for a pensive facing of all that is at stake in our mortality and in what God has done for us in His Mercy, then what, pray, might that event be?

Redrawing the Moral Map

I have found myself in a brisk correspondence in recent weeks with a Calvinist friend from my school days sixty years ago. The topic touched on in our correspondence entails the redrawing of the moral map of the universe, which has been undertaken in the West since the 1960s. That redrawing arrived on the crest of the seismic wave that flooded the West at that time, sweeping away ten thousand years' worth of universal suppositions concerning authority, manners, the public order, ethics, dress, the nature of the Good, and indeed the nature of human existence itself. One aspect of this Revolution, as it came to be known, touched on the nature of man and woman and of the relationship that might obtain between these two modalities under which we mortals appear.

This latter question sailed not infrequently under an ensign on which was blazoned, "The Sexual Revolution!" It had a ring about it that seemed exhilarating to youth, the media, academia, the literary establishment, liberal Protestantism, and, presently, almost everyone.

Here was the great chance, at last, to declare our independence from the trammels that had held the human race in such insulting bondage for so many eons. The ancient religious and ethical codes were clearly long since otiose. "Man come of age" (a slogan proposed by a famous Protestant theologian) could no longer credit, much less bow

Reprinted with permission by CatholiCity, January 4, 2010.

to, such codes. We now declare, so goes the credo, that we have stepped, late in time, into our authentic adulthood as a race. We are our own masters. We need consult nothing other than lately hatched notions on all matters that concern human existence.

Common social codes vanished, superficially, in the matter of dress and manners. The waif look, even that of the slattern, became the thing when it came to garb. The whole ponderous business of the man opening the door for the woman, or walking on the side next to the curb as they went along the sidewalk, or holding the woman's chair at the table, or of young people standing up when an adult came into the room, seemed now to have been merely a scheme on the part of men to keep "the ladies" safely subordinate. The sheer fury often aroused over such matters tended to dismay those who had somber misgivings about the Revolution.

But, of course, more fundamental issues arose. What is gender? Is it, after all, the theatre of war? With the vanishing of customary codes, no one knew where he (or she?) was. Apparently nothing now stood between a boy and a girl but the freedom to follow impulse. The taboos guarding such matters—at work in every religion, culture, tribe, or society since the day after the expulsion from Eden—had been revealed to be, it seemed now, insulting to our native autonomy. It was all found to be merely "society's stereotypes".

It was this question of gender that occupied my correspondence with my friend. He sees himself as most certainly "on the side of the angels" on all moral issues. But don't we need to review the whole matter in the name of Christian charity? Surely "compassion" will oblige us to redraw the map for the sake of many who suffer from its stark lines. The holy Sacrament of Marriage, for example:

Who proposed that it occur only between a man and a woman? Was it Queen Victoria? The Puritans? The Catholic Church? The Republican Party? Moses? Who?

My only recourse so far has been to try to revisit the vision of things spelled out not only in the Mosaic code, or in historic Christianity, but testified to by every culture from the beginning. *Is* it, really, "society's stereotypes"? Is it cruel? If, in fact, this twofold modality of man and woman (under which all of us appear) belongs not to some power struggle, or to stereotypes, but rather to our origins in the Creation itself (I could suggest this, since my friend is a Christian), then might we think of it once again as belonging to our true dignity and freedom? Here are the man and the woman, made (apparently) even physically, *for* each other.

For any Sacramentalist (my friend, I think, would not quite wish to be thus tagged), the physical, in all creation, is the avatar of the Ultimate. (I avoid the word "spiritual" here since it makes us all think "disembodied", which is the Manichaean and gnostic heresy. C. S. Lewis speaks of Ultimate Reality—i.e., heaven—as "knobbly"; that is, far more solid than our merely terrestrial bodies, or raspberries, or autumn leaves, or leaf smoke, or new-baked bread. These are the diaphanous *hint* of the Reality toward which we travel, so long as we are in this mortal coil.)

If that is so, and if the union of the man and the woman is indeed rooted in the Divine Wisdom Who "was with God at the Creation"—and is hence one of the bright fixities or among T. S. Eliot's "Permanent Things", like the orbits of the stars—then may we redraw the map of that scheme under the pistol of a few decades' efforts at countervailing the mystery?

My own argument is that we can't, much as we would wish to relax the strictures that seem to attend the scheme for the sake of those for whom coming to terms with it seems a Himalayan climb. Is the "pastoral" problem on this point analogous to that of abortion? God knows, the lives of millions of women seem to be eased by the simple "procedure". But this easing overlooks one small matter: It entails murder. We can't, in the name of compassion, help these women *that way*.

So—this moral map. There are all sorts of Himalayan scrabbles for us mortals when we try to stick with the contour lines. Monogamous, heterosexual fidelity would seem to constitute a massif almost insurmountable for many people. But what is the Church to do? Redraw the map? Should there not be at least one voice encouraging us climbers to trust it?

A gigantic pastoral task. But the Church is aware of this and is also aware of the compassion that has to animate all of her pastoral duties, since She is the Body of the One who Himself took our infirmities.

What about the Dragons Now?

A topic arose recently in a group discussion relating to the vexed matter of "intelligent design". My impression is that, in its broadest outlines, the question at stake asks whether science, at the end of the day, is obliged to acknowledge a Designer at the root of things, and that, at least as matters stand now, the answer is widely thought to lie in the negative.

All of this is considered axiomatic in academic discourse. What caught my attention was the profound extent to which the men in the group espoused this line. The point here is that these men are Christian academics (they are Protestant), all of them with doctorates, none of them scientists or philosophers. A relatively recent discovery about the human *eye* seemed to constitute a watershed for their thinking: Apparently, some mechanism in the eye is now thought to have developed without any discernible divine involvement. Well, if this can happen, then this pretty well settles the matter, doesn't it? Actually, all of these men already assume a broadly Darwinian position on things. It may be remarked that they are also ex-fundamentalists and live in unremitting mortal terror of being taken for biblical literalist, six-day creationists.

I find the greatest satisfaction in wringing the noses of these briskly modern friends of mine, so I began droning a litany: "He made great lights ... the sun and moon....

Reprinted with permission by CatholiCity, October 15, 2007.

He calleth the stars by name ... Who laid out the earth ... Who giveth fodder to the cattle.... He giveth snow like wool ... and maketh the grass to grow upon the mountains, and herb for the use of men.... Praise the Lord upon earth: ye dragons, and all deeps.... *Benedicite, omnia opera Domini Domino!*"

What? We were having a serious discussion about science, and you regale us with fanciful Hebrew *poetry*, forsooth. May we now return to the topic?

But this *is* the topic. Weren't we speaking of the elegance of things? Their structure? The architecture and complexity and delicacy that we see? Weren't we then raising the question of attribution here? Whence does it all arise?

My friends are all theists and would say they are Christian—that is, they wish to keep God in the picture somewhere. But when I asked them how, exactly, they might wish to distinguish their outlook from that of the deists of the eighteenth century, they had some difficulty. In what sense, that is, has God *not* gone off and left things to run by themselves, as the deists would have it? (This is a grotesque oversimplification in one sense—but not altogether so.) It is said of our Lord in Saint Paul's Epistle to the Colossians that "by Him all things hold together". Ah well—only poetry, of course. Only pious vaporings. First-century cosmology. Irrelevant to the discussion of intelligent design.

It brings up a point. Was I being quixotic to start hailing them with psalms in the middle of such a discussion? Not really. Remember, that is still the language of Christian worship. Is it a hermetically sealed language, unattached to reality? No. It is language that is flatly true *in principio, et nunc, et semper.* When all the rum facts uncovered by astrophysics, genetics, and microbiology show up in the final unfurling of the sempiternal architecture of things, the whole edifice will resound with *Laudate et superexaltate Eum in saecula!*

My friends were very earnest. They feel that a grave time has arrived. Science is taxing faith's hitherto blithe and perhaps callow assumptions. The literalist creationists are naïve, poor lambs; we must construct a new sort of outlook. (What that outlook might be, I could not get them to say.)

It may be held as an article of faith, it seems to me, that the rhapsodic language of psalmody and liturgy touches on fixities that do not shiver when Magellan, Galileo, Copernicus, Newton, or Einstein get busy.

The Omen

Two years ago, Hollywood convinced us we wanted to see *The Exorcist*. This was a whole new direction, it said. The ads were understated: You saw the silhouette of a solitary man in a homburg, casting an ominous shadow. You did not know who he was. He looked very much like an approaching strangler or medium, and the darker side of your imagination stirred in anticipation. As it happened, he was a priest, and a saintly one at that. He was the exorcist. Now, most cinemagoers had never, Hollywood knew, come across exorcism. So it all had to be explained. The film did an excellent job of corralling everyone into this dark and straitened defile, and by the time the action got round to the exorcism itself, you knew what was going on. You knew that this was something more thrilling than counseling or surgery or psychoanalysis. When you were up against the wall, and the situation defied all the craft of science, you turned to the Church and her ancient wisdom and powers.

The shrewd thing about *The Exorcist* was that it didn't turn to witchcraft or necromancy or any other form of the occult for its thrills. It used rare stuffs that lie, not in the dens of the warlocks, but in the sacristies of the Church. It was not heterodoxy you saw but orthodoxy, all splayed out across the bloody screen.

Originally published in *Christianity Today* (August 1976). Reprinted with permission.

The confusing and horrifying thing about the film to the orthodox imagination was, of course, that it was *Hollywood* that was doing this. The entertainment industry had reached its long hairy arm into the sacristy and had pulled out the most recondite things it could find. It had no more idea about the taboos that surround the use of these things than it had about the splendors of the City of God. It was like a baboon that had found communion wafers in the pyx, squeaking and gibbering and playing tiddly-winks and shove-ha'penny with the little discs. Even for Protestant Christians, who, if they believe in exorcism at all, would tend to try to accomplish it by prayer alone, the spectacle was obscene.

Hollywood is very astute. Its barometers still show The Violent and The Bizarre to be drifting about in the atmosphere. But another buildup of cloud has clearly showed up on the gauge. It is The Prophetic.

As far as the filmmakers are concerned, this reading is just another subdivision of the bigger category Box Office. They have picked up exciting low-pressure indications like Planet Earth and Armageddon and Anti-Christ. "Now what's all this?" they ask themselves. "What's this that people are buying now? What? Prophecy? The Bible? Now wait—tell us more. Where's a Bible? What page? Revelation? Where's that? At the end? Oh. Right. Let's see now [flip, flip, flip] ... oh ... is this it—this about the Beast, and battle, and signs in heaven and on earth? Hey, that's pretty good. Now are you *sure* that this stuff is selling? I mean, is anyone besides Billy Graham talking about it?" And so forth.

So they have made us a film about that now. Oh, no—you won't see Saint Michael in armor flying on Pegasus through the air over Palestine, or the hosts of Gog and Magog and the Chief Prince of Meshech and Tubal surging toward Esdraelon. You will see Gregory Peck as the American ambassador to the Court of Saint James, Lee Remick as his wife, and their five-year-old "son" (there was a hugger-mugger birth-exchange, actually), who turns out to be the agent through whom the Devil proposes to begin his End-time moves. (The producers have made a pretty muddle of prophecy, so do not imagine that you will need the theologians to help you sort it out: It is pre-Sunday-school stuff.) With this scenario, they can do almost anything, and they do. There is a black dog, for example, with glittering eyes and red mouth, who growls menacingly when anything awful is about to happen, the way Peter Lorre whistled "In the Hall of the Mountain King" in the movie *M* just before he murdered his child-victims.

I had an odd experience with this nefarious dog as I sat in the nearly empty theatre at the shopping mall in Manchester, New Hampshire, at a 3 P.M. showing. A menacing panting and snuffing began to sound just under a seat nearby. No one was near me; there were only about six people in the whole theatre. I thought at first it was the stereophonic sound, arranged under our seats to frighten us. But it wasn't. Then I thought perhaps it was someone who had fainted during the 1 P.M. showing and was now coming to life. But I could find no body. I thought of a stray dog skulking about, but there was none. Finally I tried out my own breathing: Perhaps I was puffing asthmatically and the acoustics of the theatre were bringing it back to me from a few feet away. But I could not get it to synchronize with the noises. So I did what you do when you find yourself alone with the unmanageable: I sought company. I moved back to where two boys and an old man were sitting. I thought that if some miserable and blackguardly ghost were going to use this tawdry scene for an entry (and for any Christian this is never completely ruled out), he'd have to cope with more than one person.

In any event, there is a black dog, and there are prophecies (all higgledy-piggledy), and strange people who know things, and then a sequence of increasingly sinister events that takes you from London to Rome to the excavations at Megiddo, and that finally leads to the violent death of every single character in the film.

I do not think I am spoiling a good story for you by letting the cat (the dog?) out of the bag like this. The first thing to be said about the film is that it is not worth anyone's two hours or two dollars. For a start, Hollywood and its actors have no resources, emotional, dramatic, or intellectual, to draw on for this sort of subject matter and hence have to draw on their usual bag of melodrama, sentimentalism, and sham-horror, evoked for the audience by stuttering, brimming eyes, jutting jaws, gritted teeth, and mad dashes up and down stairs. Gregory Peck may have talent, but he is miscast here.

Besides this, the "special effects" are not nearly so stunning as they were in *The Exorcist*. (If it is objected that I am spending too much time in comparison with that film, the rejoinder is that the makers of this film have invited, nay forced, such comparisons, by patently trying to cash in on the *Exorcist* market. They will have to live with the comparisons they have purchased.) In *The Omen*, you have people dangling from ropes and crashing through high windows to the street below, and one man's head being sheared neatly off by a huge pane of glass that slips from a truck, and a priest impaled with a toppling lightning rod at the door of a church, and so forth. The unnerving thing about all this is that the producers are apparently correct in supposing that you can mix biblical prophecy and this sort of jejune carrying-on, and get the public to buy it. It is like trying to dramatize the Ascension by using the Pink Panther: It is bad enough to find it done at all, but infinitely more dismaying to discover that it is selling.

But there is more than film criticism to be done here. Two points need to be made. First, a film like this *is*, alas, a yardstick. You *can* tell something about a civilization from its artifacts. If they are made of enameled gold, that indicates something. If they are made of polystyrene foam, that suggests something else. If you find copies of Sophocles buried in the rubble, you can make some guesses about what the people liked. If you find cans full of celluloid strips with spectacles like *The Omen* recorded on them, you can guess what *they* liked.

When a civilization has jettisoned the platitudes of plain, ancient, moral truth that are the very guardians and guarantors of its people's real freedom and joy, then it sets itself on the feverish quest for excitements to replace that moral truth. This quest leads with depressing predictability straight through from the diverting to the odd to the bizarre to the grotesque to the bestial to the de-monic. With increasing stimulus, boredom sets in, and at the same time the threshold of people's capacity for being aroused goes up and up. This is why pornography, orgies, violence, gladiatorial combats, and jiggery-pokery crop up in rotting civilizations: People are bored with ordinariness and don't know what to do, and it takes more and more to rouse them from their ennui. I was amazed, for example, at the sheer force of the sounds and colors used for the screen announcements that told us we could smoke only in the restrooms, could rent the theatre auditorium, and so on. These items were accompanied by crashing Sousa-type fanfares over the PA system and whirling kaleidoscopic and stroboscopic effects on the screen. Clearly we are a people who need to be assaulted if we are to be budged at all. *The Omen* was made for the likes of us.

Secondly, the film is a disquieting reflection of the vocabulary and preoccupations of contemporary pop Christianity, and the evangelical church is not without guilt here. Biblical hucksters in the last seventy-five years have made Daniel, the Gospels, and Revelation their toys, giving us wild and vivid pictures and graphs as to what it was all about. Evangelicalism bought a great deal of this trinketry and helped to bruit it abroad, and Hollywood has heard the sound thereof. In so doing, this wing of the Church departed from the ancient stream of Catholic orthodoxy that has always affirmed, "We believe that Thou shalt come to be our Judge", but has at the same time been reluctant to nail a given prophetic text down to a given historic event of either the past or the future. Dragons and phials and bowls and horsemen and falling stars and splitting mountains—what do they all mean? They mean something, surely, but it is something infinitely more dread and real than what our charts depict for us. And it will all be recognizable when the time comes. The recognition will not come from alchemists and grizzled hermits with their retorts and their cabala, or even from shouting stump-preachers with their flapping Bibles. It will come, rather, from holy souls who have lived faithfully in obedience to those ancient platitudes of moral truth found, not by picking the Scriptures to bits and Scotch-taping them back together into a scrapbook, but by submitting their entire imagination to the whole counsel of God.

Foreword to *More Christianity* by Fr. Dwight Longenecker

One of the conundrums of modern Church history attaches to the ecclesiology of the most widely read Christian apologist of our epoch: Why did C. S. Lewis never become a Roman Catholic?

The question is asked over and over. The question itself is intriguing, since one might reply, "But why ask the question to begin with? You don't ask that about Billy Graham." But there is something at work in the whole fabric of Lewis' vision of reality that seems to push things in the direction of Catholicism. For one thing, of course, he not only takes the sacraments seriously (he speaks of "the Blessed Sacrament" and made a practice of auricular confession), but his work, most notably his fiction, is unmistakably "sacramentalist". It is doubtful whether *The Chronicles of Narnia* could ever have been written by a full-blown Protestant, since Protestantism is quintessentially a verbalist, propositionalist, discursive handling of the faith, whereas Catholicism is profoundly narrative, dramatic, and participatory (for example, the fifteen mysteries of the Rosary, and the Mass itself). The sacraments are the physical points at which eternity touches time—the Incarnation itself, of course, being the Sacrament of all sacraments.

Readers may justifiably object here, "But Lewis was a Protestant: What do you mean, it is doubtful whether

Originally published in *More Christianity* by Ignatius Press, 2010.

a Protestant could have written the Narnia tales?" A fair question. Lewis stoutly and stolidly insisted that he was a Protestant, and an Ulsterman into the bargain. Nothing Romish about him. But attentive readers, with the greatest trepidation, may find themselves in the awkward position of wishing to quarrel, ever so meekly, with Lewis. "You are not as Protestant as you think, sir." The point, of course, is that he was an Anglican, for a start, and that church has never quite made up its mind whether it is Protestant or Catholic (we are in a minefield here and must tiptoe along with fearful caution). The Anglican church is episcopal, hierarchic, sacramentalist, and claims to be apostolic. These categories are very far from being the common currency of Protestantism. Furthermore, one gets the impression that Lewis wore his Protestantism like a cockade in his hat, or, perhaps closer to the mark, like a helmet and body armor, ready for battle.

The most important remark here remains to be put forward: Lewis loathed ecclesiology because ecclesiology is the topic par excellence that divides Christians, and Lewis wanted most earnestly to speak as a "mere Christian". He stuck rigorously to the creedal matters upon which all serious Christian believers are agreed, and he eschewed like the black pestilence any topic at all that would excite Christians to bickering with each other. He avoided all discussion as to the mode of baptism, for example, and anything that concerned itself with the details of the eschaton (from the Greek for "the end" or "the end of the world"). Hence (and I speak as a partisan of Lewis who will champion him to the death—or at least to the mat, shall we say), Lewis' work cannot be said to encompass the whole substance of the Catholic Faith. His Christianity (or more exactly, his published Christianity) while robust, wise, and ardent, is incomplete.

It would be a very rare breed of browser among books who will not recognize instantly Dwight Longenecker's explicit and calculated debt to Lewis in the title of the present work: More Christianity. "Forsooth!" we might cry. "Are we to understand that you have set yourself the task of improving on Lewis' best-known theological work? Come. It won't do." Mr. Longenecker is wise enough to steer clear of any such claim. What he does bring to our attention in this work is the titanic matter of the Catholic Church, which topic Lewis sedulously avoided. Lewis was a loyal churchman but did not wish to be drawn into any discussion of the matter. He was Anglican because that happens to have been the sector of the Church into which he was baptized. He simply "went to church", as any Christian ought to do, he would have urged. But holding to such a minimalist position, he would have had some heavy sledding if he had found himself in a conversation with Peter, Clement, Ignatius, Polycarp, Cyprian, Irenaeus, Justin, or any of a score of others.

These gentlemen would have wanted to know how it came about that Lewis claimed to be a "mere Christian" and yet had attached himself to a body that had cleaved itself from the only authentically apostolic Church known to them. They would have wondered why Lewis avoided certain "extras" that they considered essential parts of the Christian Faith. These "extras" are the topics that inevitably arise in Catholic-Protestant discussion century after century: the Marian dogmas, the papacy, the Mass, Purgatory, the communion of the saints, and such practices as penance, the Rosary, and so forth.

To touch on only one of these (since Mr. Longenecker treats the topic magnificently in the body of the book), the ancient Church increasingly became aware that Mary had been granted a dignity, by God's grace, unparalleled by any other creature in the universe, including the seraphim. There were patriarchs, prophets, kings, apostles, the Fathers, the martyrs, and all the angelic orders. All of these bear witness to the Word: Mary bore the Word. No seraph has ever been drawn into the mystery of Redemption in even a remotely analogous manner. In the early Church, the right doctrine and the right devotion concerning the Mother of our Lord was inextricably linked with the right doctrine and devotion toward Jesus himself. As such, for the early Christian, devotion to the Blessed Virgin Mary was not an extra but an essential.

The title of Longenecker's book reveals the theme, and it would be a highly interesting business to ask whether Lewis himself might not be given pause, and then possibly even applaud, were he given the chance to read the chapters that follow. He was aware that he was sticking rigorously to the "mere" aspects of the Faith (and gigantically mere they were, to be sure). He was certainly aware that the Church herself, from the beginning, most notably in the Fathers, discovered and took into her worship, confession, and doctrine all of the matters that constitute this "more" of which Mr. Longenecker speaks. The "more" does not stand over against the "mere", much less does it cast the "mere" into question. It is, quite simply, the "more" that developed organically as the ancient Church reflected on the Scriptures and the tradition handed down from the apostles. Instead of the "more" being something different from the "mere", the "more" turns out to be of one fabric with the "mere" of which Lewis so eloquently spoke. It is to be most sedulously urged that all believers (Catholics who have not much reflected on their own *Catechism of the Catholic Church*, and Protestants who have approached all these matters only as points to be refuted) ponder with open minds and open hearts what follows here.

Dwight Longenecker has not written a Catholic diatribe. This is not a Catholic attack on Protestants. Rather, with immense tact, clarity, sagacity, and learning, he takes us the rest of the way along the road charted in *Mere Christianity*. Again, it must be stressed that Longenecker is not presuming to piggyback, or cash in on, Lewis' work or to set himself up as Lewis' successor. There is no hint of this in the book. We find here all of the questions that arise vis-à-vis the doctrine of the Church and the fullness of doctrine that she teaches. It is a beautiful book, and one that any believer serious about the ancient faith ought to find vastly rewarding.

A Better 'Jesus' Movie

On the surface, the idea of another film of the life of Jesus would seem to be a bit much. Besides the recent and very-much-touted *Jesus of Nazareth*, which Zeffirelli made for television, and *The Gospel according to Saint Matthew*, which attracted a good deal of interest some years ago by its rather spare, fierce, unsentimental picture of Jesus, one seems to recall a more or less steady stream of these things. (Didn't they make one called *The Greatest Story Ever Told*? And wasn't there a gigantic production of near Cecil B. DeMille dimensions called *The Bible* that one remembers from one's youth? And all those lesser productions in which one's principal impression was of striped bathrobes and terry cloth towels and sandals?) How can anyone muster the sheer *chutzpa* to embark on yet another production? Perhaps there is an inexhaustible market for the commodity, like the market for books on jogging and losing weight and miracles.

Yet this film, *Jesus* (distributed by Warner Bros.), is better than its publicity, which fervently claims that it is "totally authentic". Now that is an astonishing claim to make for a film whose setting is the ancient world. Very few historians, and fewer archaeologists, would claim, surely, that we can approach "total authenticity" in recreating *any* epoch, the ancient world least of all. But my point is that

Originally published in *Christianity Today* (December 21, 1979): 28–29. Reprinted with permission.

the film is better than the publicity, which would seem to leave itself open to the charge of sensationalism. The film itself steers as true a course as one might ever hope to see in a film on Jesus in avoiding the soft sands of sensationalism and sentimentalism.

The wisest decision the producers made was to stick quite rigorously to the text of the Gospel of Luke; you cannot get a better script than that. The screenplay, by Barnet Fishbein, is to be commended for its fidelity to this text. Although one or two minor departures seem gratuitous—instead of mere scribes and Pharisees in one place, for example, we find "the hypocritical section of the scribes and Pharisees"—for the most part, a multitude of errors has been avoided.

The action of the film is quick and spare, since it must follow Luke's narrative. This is exactly as it should be. This Gospel—indeed, any of the Gospels—makes no attempt to give us a biography of Jesus, much less a drama. We are given as many of the bits of Jesus' life as the Gospel writer chose for the particular pattern he wished, and no more. Here again, the producer, John Heyman, and the codirectors, Peter Sykes and John Kirsh, are to be commended for not being afraid of the sparse, selective nature of the Gospel materials. They move us along to the next incident, and the next, in obedience to Luke, calling the film a "docu-drama", which, while we may deplore this hybrid word, does catch something of the angle and flavor of the film.

Apparently nine years of research went into the production. No effort was spared to get authentic costumes, and even authentic faces for the five thousand extras. An "extras manager" ransacked the countryside of Israel for the sort of face they wanted for the crowd scenes and came up with a throng, mostly of Moroccan and Yemenite people, none of whom were actors by profession, trying, they tell us, to avoid the picture postcard world of Renaissance painting.

A young English actor, Brian Deacon, was given the title role. The image he projects reminds one of those very rugged and handsome pictures of Jesus drawn in recent years by Richard Hook. Here again, artists and, a fortiori, film directors and actors work with a terrible problem: How shall we show Jesus? The particular look of first-century Jews might not serve the special iconography of sanctity, purity, tenderness, and whatnot that Western piety has ordinarily sought. Suppose Jesus had a head full of coal-black ringlets, all tousled and matted with salt and wind and dust? It would not do, we suppose. But on the other hand, when we try to catch those qualities of sanctity and tenderness, and so forth, we end up with Sallman and are in worse trouble. Brian Deacon's face is probably a very good one, in that it is strong and handsome without being glamorous and tender without being saccharine. They have fixed him up with what we have come to expect in Jesus, namely, long straight brown hair parted more or less in the middle, and a short, uncurly brown beard. To depart from this imagery would be to make a laboriously conscious effort at iconoclasm and would probably defeat its purpose by siphoning our attention off, making us whisper to each other, "Dear me—I don't think I had thought of Jesus as looking like that."

Mr. Deacon does well with the supernally difficult job of depicting Jesus. The problems must be insurmountable. There are no dramatic conventions available to an actor that are quite adequate to the task, surely. One would have to have achieved perfect charity himself in order to have any idea how Charity incarnate might have spoken or acted. How do you *say*, "You have heard it said ... but I say unto you", or "This poor widow hath cast in more than they all"? And how do you arrange your face in the meantime, if you are the actor? When do you glower, if ever, and when do you decide to look foxy, or arch, or pained, or affectionate? Since the original script was not written by a dramatist, surmise plays a big part here. And you (the actor and the director and whoever else is in on it) are having to surmise about the most extraordinary character ever to appear on the stage of history. Can it be done at all? Or, more solemnly, *ought* it to be done? Who can say? After a hundred years of trying to get the gospel onto celluloid, we may all in the end conclude that we may as well have tried to reproduce Chartres in papier-mâché or Mozart on an ocarina. It can be done, after its fashion, but something has ebbed away in the process.

Which is not to liken Brian Deacon's performance to papier-mâché or an ocarina. The critic's task is as elusive as the director's and the actor's: How do I *know* whether it was a good job or not? All of us are uneasy about even the best efforts to portray Jesus; there are simply too many imponderables entailed, not the least of which is whether it should be attempted to begin with. On the whole, Deacon has avoided the traps of sentimentality and eccentricity. He smiles, and even chuckles, and this seems not a bad note to strike. He is very good in the scene with the moneychangers, where he could have been pardoned for giving way to mere bombast and ham, but where he manages to convey the sort of ire and outrage Jesus both felt and wished to teach on that occasion. When we come to the Crucifixion, surely we are all in water altogether over our heads. To have Jesus yell in pain is certainly in the interest of dramatic verisimilitude: But does dramatic verisimilitude turn out to be grotesquely inadequate to the mystery of the Passion? It is not delicacy that objects here, it seems to me, so much as a certain paralytic hesitation in the precincts of mysteries as titanic as this. Outside of the biblical narrative, perhaps only liturgy and music are made of hard enough material to hold the burden.

The filmmakers are to be commended for avoiding several snares where less-disciplined imaginations might have blundered into all sorts of disconcerting banalities. The "special effects" used at the Annunciation and the Transfiguration and at the rending of the Temple veil and the Ascension are very good—good because they come close to not existing at all. Extreme understatement has saved the day in all these cases. One blot on an otherwise clean sheet here, though, is the snake they used for the devil in the wilderness. Surely ...

The film deserves a great deal of praise, and has done, we may venture to guess, as good a job as anyone has ever done with the attempt. Perhaps when filmmakers and actors approach the gospel story, their task is like a sculptor's: All you have to do is take *away* what you don't want. The sculptor chips away the excess marble; the director and actors must get rid of melodrama and schmaltz and ham and all the other things that try to cling to the drama. But when you have laid down strictures like this, you realize that nobody but a saint or a sage could do very much with it all. How a commercial enterprise, with the box office pistol held to its head, is to compete with Fra Angelico and Michelangelo and Saint Ignatius Loyola and Rembrandt and Milton in reworking the gospel materials, is a taxing question. We may keep it open, and at the same time give tentative laurels to this film.

An Hour and a Lifetime with C. S. Lewis

Dr. Thomas Howard was raised in a prominent Evangelical home (his sister is well-known author and former missionary Elisabeth Elliot), became Episcopalian in his mid-twenties, then entered the Catholic Church in 1985, at the age of fifty.

Dave Armstrong writes of Howard: "He cites the influence of great Catholic writers such as Newman, Knox, Chesterton, Guardini, Ratzinger, Karl Adam, Louis Bouyer, and Saint Augustine on his final decision. Howard's always stylistically excellent prose is especially noteworthy for its emphasis on the sacramental, incarnational, and 'transcendent' aspects of Christianity."

Howard is a highly acclaimed writer and scholar, noted for his studies of Inklings C. S. Lewis (*C. S. Lewis: Man of Letters* [1987]) and Charles Williams (*The Novels of Charles Williams* [1991]), as well as books including *Christ the Tiger* (1967), *Chance or the Dance?* (1969), *Hallowed Be This House* (1976), *Evangelical Is Not Enough* (1984), *If Your Mind Wanders at Mass* (1995), *On Being Catholic* (1997), and *The Secret of New York Revealed.* Howard's story of his how and why he became Catholic, *Lead, Kindly Light: My Journey to Rome*, was published last year by Ignatius Press. His book

An IgnatiusInsight.com interview with Dr. Thomas Howard, November 16, 2005.

on T. S. Eliot's "The Four Quartets" will be published by Ignatius Press in 2006.

Carl E. Olson, editor of IgnatiusInsight.com, recently interviewed Dr. Howard about apologist and author C. S. Lewis and the approaching release of the cinematic adaptation of Lewis' famed Chronicles of Narnia.

IgnatiusInsight.com: When did you first discover the work of C. S. Lewis and what attracted you to it?

Dr. Thomas Howard: I first heard of, and then began to read, Lewis in the mid-1940s when an older sister of mine came home from college with *Mere Christianity*. I was only ten or twelve, but I seem to recall knowing that here was a writer whose work I would like to pursue. Later, when I was an undergraduate, the *Narnia Chronicles* were coming out, and since they became a sort of fad immediately, I, rather perversely, put off reading them. I read them while I was in the Army in the late 1950s and was utterly overwhelmed, shedding copious tears.

IgnatiusInsight.com: You had a correspondence with C. S. Lewis many years ago. How did that come about? Did you ever meet Lewis in person?

Howard: While I was in the Army, a friend sent me the Tolkien trilogy. I was so swept away that on an impulse I fired off a letter to Lewis, whom I knew to be a fellow of Magdalen (I didn't know how to find Tolkien). I just addressed it to "C. S. Lewis, Magdalen College, Oxford, England". He wrote back a most gracious letter all about Tolkien, and then thanking me for liking "my own little efforts". An intermittent correspondence ensued, and some years ago I gave all the letters to the Wade Collection at

Wheaton College, Illinois, where there is the best collection of Tolkien, Lewis, Charles Williams, Dorothy Sayers, Owen Barfield, and other writers, outside of Oxford.

While I was living in England in the early 1960s, I arranged to pop out to The Kilns [Lewis' residence] one time when I was in Oxford visiting a friend at Queen's College. Lewis received me most jovially, and we sat and chatted for just under an hour, as I recall it. I asked him about hell: "There might be such a place", he said. We talked of Purgatory, too. I can't remember the whole conversation since I could not bring myself to sit jotting notes, and I don't think we had tape recorders in those days (which I wouldn't have used anyway). Lewis looked just as you would hope he'd look: stout; rubicund face; twinkly eyes; baggy tweeds; and a magnificent bell-like voice.

IgnatiusInsight.com: Lewis was one of the most popular Christian writers of the twentieth century, perhaps the most read Christian author of the past fifty years. Why has he been so popular among a diverse readership that includes non-Christians, Protestants, Catholics, and Eastern Orthodox? What sets him apart as an author and communicator?

Howard: Lewis' popularity derived, I am sure, from the remorseless clarity of everything he wrote, plus his glorious imagination, plus his splendid mastery of the English language. Of course his gigantic intellect and his rigorous training in argument from his mentor, the "Great Knock" [W. T. Kirkpatrick], set his work altogether apart from most other writers, especially popular writers, whose "intellects are not so hard at work as they suppose" (Lewis' remark about some schoolboys). His vast readership, drawn from nonreligious types, and from every ventricle of Christendom (Roman Catholic, Orthodox, Anglican,

Calvinist, fundamentalist, and everything else) testifies to the qualities I have mentioned above. He refused to be partisan in any cheap sense, although of course his robust Christian orthodoxy no one could escape.

IgnatiusInsight.com: You recently wrote, in your regular "Ashes to Ashes" column in *Crisis* magazine (Nov. 2005), that you "have read every syllable Lewis ever wrote, including all the books no one else has read. What are some of the lesser-known books of Lewis? Which of Lewis' books do you think deserves a wider readership? Why?

Howard: Of Lewis' lesser-known books, I would mention: *The Discarded Image*, a glorious book about the medieval outlook on the universe; *A Preface to Paradise Lost*, which I would say is infinitely worth reading even if you never get around to Milton; his *Poems*, which incline me to say that they are his best work; *The Allegory of Love*, about the whole nettlesome topic of "courtly love" in the late Middle Ages—and beautifully readable even for non-scholars; and then his huge *English Literature in the Sixteenth Century: Excluding Drama*, which I open at random just for the sheer delight of it. I often find myself laughing at Lewis' obvious hilarious delight in the works he is treating. I would say any of these books would reward readers who have read only his most famous works.

IgnatiusInsight.com: *The Chronicles of Narnia*, of course, are very well known and have sold over eighty-five million copies since first appearing in the 1950s. Why do you think that series has been so popular? What distinguishes it from other works of children's literature?

Howard: The *Narnia Chronicles* owe their worldwide popularity, surely, both to Lewis' love for the genre fairy tale and to his unpatronizing delight in children, knowing, as he did, what would draw them into his world. They differ from most other children's literature in that they draw us all into the precincts of sheer Goodness (without sentimentalism), and Joy, and, finally, Holiness. That is an achievement when you are writing for children. I would put his work in a class with Pooh and Alice and Beatrix Potter's books, and *The Wind in the Willows*.

IgnatiusInsight.com: Do you plan on seeing the movie adaptation of *The Chronicles of Narnia?* If so, what do you expect or hope to see?

Howard: Yes, I most certainly plan to see the movie. I have already seen excerpts (I think they are called "trailers" now). The film is good beyond one's wildest hopes. It will take its place with *The Lord of the Rings*, I predict. After the somewhat abortive, not to say pathetic, efforts to get up a film of Narnia over the past twenty or more years, this one is a prize.

IgnatiusInsight.com: You mentioned some of the strengths of Lewis and his writing. Did he have any notable weaknesses as a thinker or writer? Are there any topics that he avoided or didn't address that you wish he had?

Howard: Any weaknesses in Lewis? Who would wish to find himself saying Yes to that! The only case in point I can think of is, perhaps, the "defeat" (if it was a defeat—I think Lewis thought it was) at the hands of Elizabeth Anscombe in a debate about, I think, *Miracles*, in which she seems to have found some wobbly spots in his argument.

But are there topics he avoided? Most emphatically Yes! He avoided, like the black pestilence, the whole topic of The Church. He hated ecclesiology. It divided Christians, he said (certainly accurately). He wanted to be known as a "mere Christian", so he simply fled all talk of The Church as such. He would not participate in anything that remotely resembled a discussion of matters ecclesiological. He was firm in his non- (or anti- ?) Catholicism. People ask me if he would by now have been received into the Ancient Church, and I usually say yes. I don't see how, as an orthodox Christian apologist, he could have stayed in the Anglican Church during these last decades of its hasty self-destruction.

IgnatiusInsight.com: Do you have a favorite book or series of books by Lewis? For those who haven't yet read Lewis, where do you suggest they begin? What Lewis books should be read?

Howard: My favorite Lewis books? I would say his Space Trilogy (*Out of the Silent Planet*; *Perelandra*; and *That Hideous Strength*) and the Narnia books. In these books we find, clothed in drama, all of the ideas that he treated in his more strictly discursive works. The remorseless clarity with which he saw Good and Evil is prophetic. What he wrote in the 1940s could have been written tomorrow. I would invite any newcomer to his work to start here.

The Triumphant Vindication of the Body: The End of Gnosticism in *That Hideous Strength*

That Hideous Strength is unique in Lewis' fiction, in that there is no "secondary world" into which we are boosted for the landscape of the narrative. Narnia is such a world: It bears no relation to either time or space in our own "primary world". You can't get there with charts, compasses, or any conceivable hardware.

The Malacandra of *Out of the Silent Planet* is, of course, our Mars: But it is very far from being the dusty, dead planet that shows up in Voyager and Hubble photographs. Perelandra whisks us to our Venus, but again, it turns out to be a world wholly inaccessible to our most advanced technology, ruled as it is by eldila (or, shall we say, more accurately, stewarded by the eldila, since it is a world made for human beings).

The bus trip in *The Great Divorce* takes us from Purgatory/ Hell to Heaven—quite outside of our earthly scheme of distance and chronology. The same is true of *The Pilgrim's Regress* and *Till We Have Faces*.

A note on this matter of primary and secondary worlds. In his great essay "On Fairy Stories", J.R.R. Tolkien

Originally published in *Mission and Ministry* (Volume XI, No. 4 and Volume XII, No. 1. Ambridge, PA: Trinity Episcopal School for Ministry, c. 1997–98): 29–33. Reprinted with permission.

suggested that the power of myth and faerie lies in the fact that they set up a secondary world, with its own laws and qualities, but that these laws, at least, differ by not one whit from the laws governing our own planet.[1]

We are speaking of the moral law, of course, not questions of speed limits and stoplights. In a world uncluttered by diminutive mignons with gauze wings or brownies who curdle the cream, we find ourselves in "the perilous realm". It is perilous since we mortals are there hailed with Reality in such stark shapes and colors that our sensibilities (not to say our souls) are jolted awake.

In the dim murk of our world, Eustace Clarence Scrubb can pass for merely a tiresome and desperately spoiled egoist.[2] In Narnia, he turns into a dragon, not because some great Power has said "What punishment shall we visit upon this wretched child, eenie-meeni-miny-moe", but rather because he is a dragon, in any world. It only becomes visible in the sharp clarity of the atmosphere of Narnia.

In our world, Sarah Smith of Golder's Green is a charwoman, but in Heaven she is honored by a great procession of chariots and beasts and music.[3] Here her beauty and virtue were hidden under mops and pails and cheap work clothes and a cockney accent, but now we see who she really was all along. Her simplicity and integrity and faithfulness—this is what those things really look like, but we must be yanked into the secondary world to see them.

[1] "On Fairy Stories", *The Tolkien Reader* (Ballantine Books, 1966), pp. 27–84. Tolkien preferred the spelling "faerie" for the region, since it dismisses summarily and immediately any notion of frivolous creatures flitting about toadstools or the mischievous sprites that even Shakespeare evokes in "A Midsummer's Night's Dream" and "The Tempest".

[2] *The Voyage of the Dawn Treader* (Macmillan/Collier Books, 1970), chapters 6 and 7.

[3] *The Great Divorce* (Macmillan/Collier Books, 1975), chapter 12.

The secondary world, for Tolkien, exists in an *analogous* relation to our primary world and thus throws new light on things here. And, as Lewis made so clear in *The Abolition of Man*, no story in Heaven, earth, or Hell, can introduce a new moral scheme. Good and evil are like primary colors: You can deny them by shutting your eyes or turning out the lights, but you cannot replace them.

You can't make up a fiction that lauds venality, or extols pusillanimity, or celebrates duplicity. Perhaps you can, but your story will fail since it will carry no conceivable reader with it. The coward wants to read about heroes, not cowards. Even the venal and pusillanimous and duplicitous want to see themselves in some semi-heroic light. We don't *like* duplicity—neither we, nor fauns, nor eldils—because it is essentially and forever odious.

That is, despite the sundry marvels we never encounter in our world—wardrobes that back up onto the land of Faerie, centaurs, Seroni, Pfifltriggi—we all find ourselves overwhelmed soon enough with the very strong hunch that what we are reading is a "true" story, true as a tuning fork or plumbline, and that the reality of centaurs and Pfifltriggi is entirely irrelevant when it comes to the very narrow question of the tales' credibility.

On the most profound level, the tales are more true than any factual journalism or scholarly history our world thinks true. This is so because ours is indeed the "Silent Planet", which voluntarily demurred at the choreography and the harmony that mark "real reality" (as Francis Schaeffer put it) and plunged itself into darkness, discord, suffering, and death. In the secondary worlds of these tales, we hear something of that harmony we were meant to hear. The secondary worlds are, in a sense, the real primary world.

Now what is *That Hideous Strength*? Judged by the canons that preside over the discussion of fiction, especially of the novel, *That Hideous Strength* is, in some senses, a great ragbag—or, shall we say, treasure-chest—of virtually all of Lewis' moral theology. Nearly every topic that Lewis touches on in his essays and discursive books finds itself unfurled in solid colors and solid forms here.

Written in the 1940s, it finds itself at the very cusp between good and evil as they are manifesting themselves in the 1990s. In many ways, a reader who had only this one of Lewis' many books would have as excellent a condensing of his thought as could be asked for.

In *That Hideous Strength*, we are never outside of England. However, the Reality that breaks through the scrim that divides Thulcandra (Earth) from the blissful choreography apparently visible and audible in the rest of Creation, turns out to be the Reality that we have all along been penetrating in *Out of the Silent Planet* and *Perelandra*.

In this book, the secondary world muscles its way through the Scrim that hangs between our ordinariness—a sort of blindness, you might say—and the titanic truth of things. We stay in England: But all Heaven and all Hell have broken loose.

Nothing we see at first is unexpected: Two young intellectuals with a troubled marriage, he trying to advance his career, she left at home feeling unfulfilled; the quiet, cynical plotting of academic politics; a few old-fashioned dons trying to maintain the old ways; some new research institute with vaguely utopian goals—just fundraising, that, we think; an atheistical, left-wing priest of a type not (alas) uncommon. Even the "counter-cultural community" of Saint Anne's seems a familiar sight.

The story turns out to be the story of salvation for the two main characters, Jane and Mark Studdock. Their marriage is altogether threadbare.

Jane conceives of herself as an intellectual and resents all the hints that her society cherishes connecting women with hats and tears and domesticity. "Matrimony" is the first word of the book. We meet Jane reflecting, to the disadvantage of her husband, on words from the marriage rite in the *Book of Common Prayer*. "Matrimony was ordained, thirdly, for the mutual society, help, and comfort that one ought to have of the other."

Of the first purpose of marriage, "It was ordained for the procreation of children", we hear, significantly, nothing. For Jane wants to be a "mind". She is busy with her dissertation, which, with exquisite irony, concerns Donne's "triumphant vindication of the body". The irony here is that Jane is a Manichaean or a gnostic, having fallen into the common trap of supposing that the physical realm is inferior to the spiritual realm and is therefore to be eschewed.

Jane's taste for clothes that are "severe" and "really good on serious aesthetic grounds", her dislike of hats and anything else stereotypically feminine, her desire to be seen as "an intelligent adult and not a woman", all this seems harmless enough. It is certainly understandable. But: The drama in this story discloses to us the diabolical horrors that stand at the far end of any division of mind and body. At the end of this gnosticism lies Belbury, and Babel, and chaos, and suicide.

Her husband, Mark, is busy selling his soul for a mess of pottage. It is quite the worst sort of pottage, since it entails one's going to any craven, even groveling, lengths to get "In"—in this case, in to the innermost circle of the faculty at Bracton College. He is an oaf and a cad when it comes to being a spouse, and we all sympathize heartily with Jane's dereliction, even though we cannot but admit that she is a very proud young woman.

There is a hint, later, that Mark is also a sort of gnostic, with the irony that his field, sociology, is one that is supposed to deal with realities. "His education has had the curious effect of making things that he read and wrote more real to him than things he saw. Statistics about agricultural labourers were the substance; any real ditcher, ploughman, or farmer's boy was the shadow."

Hovering over the beginning of the story, then, is the possibility of a tearing apart of something that was meant to be whole. Our young couple, who look upon each other with a "laboratory outlook upon love", are moving, almost inevitably, it seems, to divorce, to the gnostic act of tearing "one flesh" into two. (We note, from hints in the book, that these gnostic intellectuals were not so dismissive of the body as not to enjoy its pleasures, even before marriage, and that this misuse—exploitation, really—of the body is a cause of their division.)

The locale of salvation for these two separates itself out into two small communities, Belbury for Mark, and Saint Anne's for Jane. Things start innocently enough with some routine business at Bracton College about selling some property. The faculty is discussing the matter. All is carried on in the thin and exalted atmosphere of academia. A faculty meeting: What could be more civilized?

The reader has not gone far, however, before he suspects that something is rotten in the state of Denmark. There is a harshness and a serpentine wiliness about the men who are eager to sell the property. All is tergiversation. Language, that is, is being pressed into the service of deceit. Language, made to be a vehicle of truth, is being unmade. All is thickly coated with euphemism and circuitousness.

But euphemism is not the only tool. Brute force will do when needed: When old Canon Jewell, the very archetype of your traditionalist and gentlemanly don, tries to expostulate, he is shouted down.

It is the pro-sale crowd that is clearly the "in" crowd at Bracton, and Mark will do anything—anything—to get in. The reader encounters difficulties here because all the members of this chic group are colossal bores.

Why any mortal would want to weasel his way into such a drab coterie defies credibility—until we realize, to our own vexation, that what Mark is doing we have done over and over. (The hapless third-grader who sees his fellows in great floppy trousers with the crotch-seam worn at knee level and who manages to get hold of such a garment in the forlorn hope that this will constitute an entré is heading down the track on which Mark has been accelerating for some time now.)

It presently comes to light that Mark's crowd (he seems, early enough on, to be making a success of his efforts) have, as a sort of quasi-headquarters, a great mansion outside of town, whither they resort to pursue plans that dwarf the mere sale of Bracton land. A huge program is afoot. The college, the town of Edgestow, and, it gradually dawns upon us, the whole world, is to be remade according to post-theist, gnostic, virtually Bolshevik "efficiency".

All ancient oaks and elms are to be cut down. Ancient buildings are to be leveled. All winding streams are to be bulldozed into straight canals. "Tradition" is to be annihilated in the interest of the new man, who will be, like all such new men, free of bourgeois prejudices, tradition-born timidity, outdated moral codes, and reverence for anything that hales from antiquity.

The reader may stifle a yawn here: How many anti-utopian books must I read? They're all the same. H.G. Wells' fantasies, Aldous Huxley's *Brave New World*, George Orwell's *1984* and *Animal Farm*—they have all pictured such a world, the latter two, of course, by way of casting sardonic aspersions on such fatuity. The poor boys in William Golding's *Lord of the Flies* thought you could organize things so that strife and cupidity could be eliminated. Alas.

And the reader's yawn is interrupted peremptorily. This isn't just another failed utopia. "This is Hell", he finds himself saying about Belbury, the mansion run by the

Progressives. Cynicism and perfidiousness are its principal marks, and its denizens embody these qualities.

There is Curry, whom Mark thought might be his entré. But presently he meets Lord Feverstone, who, in beguilingly intimate conversation with Mark persuades him that Curry is nothing but window-dressing and that the real people one must get to know are so-and-so, and so-and-so, ad infinitum. Naturally, as one moves amongst the company with Mark, each one is jeeringly dismissed by the newest acquaintance as silly and wholly expendable.

Near the center (but where, we, and Mark, begin to wonder, is the center?) we find one Fairy Hardcastle, a burly woman with bobbed hair, police uniform (including jackboots), and a cigar. And there is Straik, an apostate Anglican priest, all-too-recognizable, whose worst fear is that anyone will for a moment suppose that he might possibly mean anything other than the Belburian utopia by such quaint religious language as "the Kingdom of Heaven".

Filostrato turns up, and we find ourselves meeting a man who has carried gnosticism to hysterical lengths. He will have all vegetation shaved right off the planet: Metal trees are more efficient; they don't rot and die and so forth. He can't bear the earth being "furred over" this way. And all loam and nests and eggs and all the riotous fruitfulness that makes such a mess of the world—all will be scoured and sterilized. Spiritual man will come into his own.

There is also a man with a trim white goatee and eyeglasses that make it exceedingly difficult to see into his eyes. He seems to be, in some sense, the head man: But one is never quite sure. His name is Frost (Freud?).

The most baleful figure by far is one Wither. He is the "Deputy Director", and in many ways seems to control things with very little reference to Frost. We very quickly run aground on his syntax. He is able to utter whole paragraphs of elegant prose that, upon reflection, turn out to have meant nothing. Again, at Belbury language is unmade, is pressed into the service of non-meaning and thus of confusion and alienation.

Wither keeps insisting that "We are a family, Mr. Studdock", and one realizes, with revulsion, that Belbury is the very travesty of family. (And we recall Mark's "unfamilial" marriage to Jane: sterile; drab; joyless. His failures there have, perhaps, suited him for Belbury, or left him especially vulnerable to its seductions.)

At the center of Belbury there is The Head. It is literally a bodiless head. The denizens of Belbury are out to prove that man is, or should be, a pure intellect, untrammeled by all the embarrassing viscera, plumbing, and lymph that ruin our dignity. One recognizes, of course, the shopworn agenda of gnosticism, which is ever the same and ever new and always titillating. Spiritual man!

The Head is kept "alive" with various hoses and spigots and tubes, and it drools imbecilities from its ghastly mouth. It is worshipped by Belbury, and most especially by Wither. Its imbecilities are taken as sibylline wisdom. (Hell again? One recalls the ancient notion that evil is imbecilic, finally.)

One finds one's theology of Hell cruising near: Is not Hell the final result of the agenda of evil, which is to unmake the good solidity that marked the original Creation and that is the very mode characteristic of the City of God, with its adamantine foundations? We find "shades" in Hell. Spectres. Damned souls, which are the mere detritus left when evil has leeched and leeched away the good solidity that God made when He made the universe and man.

Thus Belbury, the travesty of travesties. Is this Hell yet once more? Evil can create nothing. It can only ape, with hideous clumsiness, the good solidity that attends the good. We may recall here the ape Shift, in *The Last Battle*. And then we recall, with a start, that some people prefer the shadow, the imitation: Some people choose Hell, as indeed we see Mark doing, although not without qualms, as he sinks deeper into the society of Belbury.

On the other hand, we have Saint Anne's. It is a peculiar house, populated by a random assemblage of unimpressive people. There is Ivy Maggs, the Cockney charwoman; and there is McPhee, the Scottish skeptic; and Dr. and Mrs. Dimble, a nice, egregiously ordinary couple—he is a don, and she is a plump, motherly, barren housewife.

Arthur and Camilla Dennison are an appealingly civilized youngish couple who love "weather" (instead of grumbling about rain—Belbury's Feverstone, we find out later, "had always hated weather"), and who like nothing better than an outing with sandwiches, coffee, and cigarettes. There is also a bear named Mr. Bultitude (Lewis borrowed the name from the nineteenth-century schoolboy tale, *Vice Versa*), a jackdaw named Baron Corvo, and a cat named Pinch.

At the center, and the undoubted head of the household, is Ransom, the hero of *Perelandra*. It turns out that he is the Pendragon of Logres, Logres being King Arthur's kingdom conceived of as a place of justice, purity, charity, and even holiness. Saint Anne's is the only fragment left, now, fifteen centuries after Arthur, of Logres.

It is named after the mother of the Mother of God, and, since it becomes the mother of salvation to Jane, who in turn becomes the mother of salvation for Mark, it seems appropriately named. Jane becomes the theotokos, the "God-bearer", to Mark, since it is (as we will see) by the means of her flesh that salvation is mediated to him.

Jane, as a result of some terrifying and apparently clairvoyant dreams that she is having, finds herself at Saint Anne's on the recommendation of Mrs. (or, "Mother")

Dimble, from whom she has received, in spite of her uneasiness with Mother Dimble's big-breasted motherliness, great comfort and help. She is admitted to Saint Anne's through a small door in the wall at the bottom of the garden and led up a narrow path by one Grace Ironwood.

Lewis teases us here with evanescent suppositions. "Strait is the gate and narrow is the way"—do we hear a fugitive echo of that somewhere? And Ironwood: "sweetest wood and sweetest iron", say the devotions for the Adoration of the Holy Cross on Good Friday. Not to mention Grace. It IS sometimes the case that grace seems a bit severe upon our first encounter with it. (Remember how daunting the advent of Aslan is in the *Narnia Chronicles*.) Miss Ironwood is a severe spinster dressed all in black. One may pursue such foxfires, or not, according to one's wish.

It eventually becomes clear that Jane is a wanted person because of these dreams of hers. Both Belbury and Saint Anne's know about them. Hence we discover Belbury's motive in wooing Mark. He is to bring his wife to Belbury, because she will prove to be the key to their finding Merlin, who, returning to England from Logres, still exercises the sort of authority over the creation that we imagine the unfallen Adam to have had.

Saint Anne's is equally anxious to get Jane, for the same reason. The sticky bit is that Merlin, being innocent, won't be able to tell the difference between evil and good at first glance and may therefore be dragooned by Belbury into furthering their schemes with his power. Saint Anne's must find him first. This is the thriller part of the story—the race to secure Merlin. Meaning and unmeaning.

Of course, as is unflaggingly the case with Lewis' fiction, the narrative is suffused with echoes and resonances. Theology spells the matter out according to its particular mode—discursive, propositionalist, abstract. Narrative spells it out according to its particular mode of indirection and image-making. The matter here is the ancient fight between Hell and Heaven.

Whereas Belbury is busy about unmaking meaning (cf. Wither's syntax, or Belbury's travesty of the notion of "family"), Saint Anne's is built and sustained by meaning. Nothing but the bald truth is tolerated there. Language, *pace* Wither, is brought to its great herculean glory in its total consonance with meaning. At one point, words come out of Dr. Dimble's mouth "like castles".

Jane finds salvation from her prim and nettled egoism at Saint Anne's. Mark is well en route to Hell at Belbury. But some rag of sanity—actually, it is the mere memory of Jane, most especially Jane's body, the body Jane herself has tried, in effect, to escape—rescues him and sends him fleeing from Belbury. No argument, no exercise of "mind", saves them. They are saved, both of them, from their gnosticism by their acceptance of the body.

But not, we must be clear, merely of the body, if that means (as it tends to, these days) mainly sexuality. That would be to exchange gnosticism for materialism. For Mark and Jane, and indeed for all of us, the body must take its part in the great dance of charity, of which marriage is the great model and image.

Mark must come to see himself as he is: a "little vulgarian", a "coarse, male boor blundering, sauntering, stumping in". He must discover that in taking her body "he had plucked the rose, and not only plucked it but torn it all to pieces and crumpled it with hot, thumb-like, greedy fingers."

He must learn to love her, to treat her with reverence: "The word Lady had made no part of his vocabulary save as a pure form or else in mockery. He had laughed too soon."

Mark escapes the apocalypse that comes upon Belbury as the natural and inevitable product of their agenda. They have sought unmeaning: They get it, in the bloodiest terms. Babel is visited upon them. They tried to destroy nature; and nature destroys them. Or rather: They have destroyed themselves, as Frost proceeds to do.

As Belbury collapses in babelian chaos around him, Frost knows that all his plans have failed, but the knowledge does not move him, "because he had long ceased to believe in knowledge itself.... He had willed with his whole heart that there should be no reality and no truth, and now even the imminence of his own ruin could not wake him."

He proceeds to burn himself to death, and after he lights the fire, "He became able to know (and simultaneously refused the knowledge) that he had been wrong from the beginning, that souls and personal responsibility existed. He half saw: he wholly hated.... With one supreme effort he flung himself back into his illusion." Such, Lewis seems to be saying, is the end of gnosticism.

The fruition of things at Saint Anne's, by comparison, is embarrassingly domestic and ordinary. Mark has arrived and has fallen asleep in a little hut at the bottom of the garden, having scattered his clothes hither and thither. Venus descends. Birds coo and chirp in amorous melody. The greenery thrives in its beds of compost.

The director has sent Jane out of the main house to meet her husband, with the instruction to have children. There is the hint here, perhaps, that by fulfilling the first purpose of marriage, she shall receive the third as well.

Jane "descends", through the garden, past the piggeries, to the hut. Through the window she sees Mark's clothes strewn about. He needs a wife. "How exactly like Mark! Obviously it was high time she went in." Jane has been saved and is about to become the bearer of salvation to her poor, proud, craven husband.

And a Weaver of Magical Tales

Who can say exactly what the writings of such and such an author have meant to him? Tell us, in five hundred words, what you owe to Dante or Chaucer or Shakespeare or Donne. What would you say about your debt to T. S. Eliot or, let us say, to Newman or Romano Guardini? Alas: We reach for the old bromide, "Words fail ..."

There would be enormous numbers of us who would have an especially difficult time paying our debt to C. S. Lewis, since his work is so manifold. His apologetics have clarified and undergirded the Faith for us: His essays have sharpened and defined hundreds of issues; his literary criticism has delighted and tutored us; his meditative writings (e.g., on prayer, on the Psalms, on grief) have widened and deepened our capacities; and his fiction—ah, his fiction: Now what shall we say there?

In my own case, if I were cast on the proverbial desert island and told that I could have just a few of Lewis' books, I think I would ask for the *Narnia Chronicles* and *Till We Have Faces* (and, if I had the chutzpa of an Abraham haggling with God, I might hold out for the so-called Space Trilogy, which should be called the Deep-heaven Trilogy).

The point about these tales is that we find in them the principle of analogy at work, which, under its own modality, bespeaks the sacramental principle, which in turn points us to the Incarnation. Lewis' narratives present to us

Originally published in *30 Days* (November 1988): 81–82.

a "secondary world" that is stranger but incontrovertibly recognizable to us. Something that is not our world (Narnia, Perelandra) returns our world to us—that world from which we disinherited ourselves at the Fall, just as bread from our own bakeries (not heavenly bakeries) feeds us with the eternal Bread of Life. Fairy tales turn out to be true. Miracles happen in parish churches.

For example, in Narnia we come upon something that was long ago utterly lost in the consciousness of our world, but that nevertheless strikes a chord that finds an answer in our deepest yearning, namely, that "equality" is a notion so far below the solemn joy in which every creature moves in his own given dignity and splendor that to introduce this dreary idea would be to bring the whole Dance to a dismayed halt. There is no question of the dryads getting their fists in the air and demanding equal time with the beavers; or of the centaurs muscling in next to Giant Rumblebuffin; or of a mouse with a red plume issuing a non-negotiable demand for equal time on the Thrones of Cair Paravel, which must be occupied by Sons of Adam and Daughters of Eve.

Apparently the excellence and nobility attached to each creature are something that no other creature can preempt. Hence there is no restless and kaleidoscopic shuffling of "roles", as though what a creature *is* has nothing to do with what he *does*.

Corollary to this is the way in which freedom presents itself. All creatures in any given world (Narnia, Perelandra, Gloma) are free precisely to the extent that the burden of dispensing wise and perfect justice is borne on the shoulders and on the crowned brow of one who has been appointed to bear this burden. A Cockney cabbie becomes the first High King of Narnia because he has long since learned to be, to his wife and to his customers and to his horse, all that a good and kind and trusty man should be: And what else is an emperor but one who must be just this for all of his domains? Raised to the nth degree, of course, we find that each creature is most exquisitely and ravishingly itself when it is attending upon Aslan, the great Son of the Emperor-Beyond-The-Sea. There is no question of repressiveness or obsequiousness or servitude or thralldom in these precincts.

But how to introduce this unimaginable vision of things into our harsh world, all braying and dinning and squalling for its piece of the (power) pie? Even the word "rights", so unhappily necessary amongst us cruel and domineering men, is never heard in those meadows, cities, and palaces of felicity, since rights are only the rhinestones that dully remind us of the diamond Love.

Indeed—words fail. But my own hunch is that no truer tales have ever been written than the tales of Narnia, Perelandra, and Glome.

About Narnia …

The Narnia Phenomenon, if we may speak thus, first hove in sight in the 1950s. We were all regaled by the sheer sublimity that we found in these tales, not to mention the high drama. Here were children's stories that all of us could read, not only to our children (although I was a bachelor undergraduate at the time), but for our own delectation. We gabbled to each other with sheer delight. And our delight increased as it became clear that the readership of the books was spreading beyond the precincts where card-carrying C. S. Lewis fans gathered and was presently found to be worldwide and numbering in the millions.

And now, perhaps not suddenly but nevertheless impressively, we find that the thing has become gigantic. Narnia seems to be taking its place with Tolkien's saga at the forefront of public excitement.

Public excitement is an untrustworthy gauge, of course. You can get the public excited about anything, viz. the cover stories on all the glossy magazines at the grocery store. Most of it is ephemera, and noisome at that. And it is more difficult than ever now to sort through things, since we all have avalanches of items, insisting that we drop everything and take up the hue and cry, coming at us at light speed via email, the Internet, cinema, television, CD's, and a hundred

Originally published in *StAR* (January/February 2006): 16–18. Reprinted with permission.

other mechanisms, most of which escape me altogether (what is an iPod? What is a Palm Pilot?).

But, difficult as it may be to do so, if you step back and try to assess things in the light of history rather than the mere moment, you might be able to descry some eminences looming above the kitsch that litters the decades. *Alice in Wonderland*, for example; or *The Wind in the Willows*; or the *Pooh* books (including the poems, certainly); or Beatrix Potter's little people—Squirrel Nutkin and Mr. Jeremy Fisher and Mrs. Tiggywinkle. These seem not only to stand out, but to excel in some absolute sense.

How so? How so, indeed. The answer to that question is as hard to come at as the question about Mozart or Vermeer. How are you going to tell someone exactly how that sequence of notes and intervals in the *Requiem*, or that pattern of line and color in the picture of the girl with the milk pitcher, are "greater" than this ditty I've written, or this very pretty painting that I have found at Woolworth's? The fact that the answer eludes us leaves untouched the bald fact: Some things are better than others, *pace* all the egalitarianism and affirmation you want to bring to bear on the matter.

Narnia, then. Perhaps these tales, like those of Alice and Ratty and Piglet and Nutkin, strike a note that echoes in the uttermost recesses of our being. Somehow the story of little Poopsie who has two [lesbian] mothers (this is popular now), while it may tingle with contemporaneity, falls short of the mark achieved by Ratty. Likewise, the adventures of the four Pevensie children and their friends in that land that appears in no geography text seem to summon us like the horns of elfland.

We may find some help in this matter as to *how* one story or sonata or painting excels another by consulting the record of how we mortals have done it over the aeons.

We will find, I think, that whatever the story (let us stick to stories, since that is where we find the Narnia Chronicles) may be, the narrative seems to appear under the light of some point of *judgment*. I do not, of course, mean judgment in the sense of condemnation, as that word is very often used. I mean some absolute point from which what goes on in the tale may be observed and assessed. This point may find its locale in comedy and satire: What fools these mortals be. Or tragedy: All our yesterdays have lighted fools the way to dusty death. Inevitably we find the question as to what is salutary and what destructive (i.e., good and evil) at work. The mere notion that "this is what is happening now: My story presents actuality to you" will not endure the test of time, which is only a way of saying that it will not satisfy the scrutiny that our deepest yearnings will, willy-nilly, bring to bear on it. The maxim "This is what's happening" is the maxim appealed to by the glossy magazines and, alas, by the educational committees who so omnipotently determine what your child's teacher must tell your child.

Real narrative comes from an infinitely more exalted region. It is the region, of course, in which we find the wellsprings of the mystery of our humanity. And there is an interesting paradox here: As often as not, the narrative does its works by carrying us *away* from plodding, workaday actuality. Even if the protagonist is the son of some little woodcutter who shared with most of us the humdrum necessity of eking out a living by hard work, nevertheless that woodcutter and his son lived in the Black Forest once upon a time, and not in the Edgeware Road. It may be noted here, of course, that things ordinarily do start in the Edgeware Road in nineteenth- and twentieth-century fiction, but if those things are ever to rise from that road to a realm that interests us in some worthwhile sense, the narrative must discover in the Edgeware Road some theme that rings bells for us who live in Primrose Hill, Runcorn, or Ultima Thule.

But again I say, Narnia. These chronicles do for us, under the genre Fairy Tale, something of what, say, Sophocles did for us in the story of Oedipus, or Virgil in the *Aeneid*. None of us is a king of Thebes or a Trojan hero. So far, the stories would seem to be remote and therefore irrelevant to our quotidian actuality. But herein lies the paradox mentioned above: By taking us away from our plodding actuality, narrative that endures illumines that actuality for us in a particularly stark manner. We can see in that king of old Thebes the conundrum that looms whenever we try to juxtapose our own "free" choices with the grim fate that would seem to preside over everything, nullifying our best efforts to establish some validity to our own story. The distance and perspective gained by Sophocles when he asks us to ponder Oedipus throws our immediate situation into huge relief. Likewise none of us is a fugitive hero from Troy driven by the gods to found Rome. But we do not read far in the story of Aeneas before we find ourselves saying, "Ah: I know what that's all about." And so it goes, with your Parzifals and your Don Quixotes: The remote figure becomes the very mediator to us of what is forever true, not to say intimately recognizable.

Lucy bumbles through the Wardrobe and finds herself in a snowy landscape. The story hails us with all of the elements we want to find in fairy stories, which, by the way, along with ancient myth and medieval romance and all worthy tales of quest and peregrination and ordeal, strangely accomplish this mediation for us. Here are a spell and a faun and a witch and innocent little creatures and heroism and majesty. And eventually it becomes clear that what is at stake is, quite simply, the Good and its opposite, Evil. What else has circumscribed our mortal life since the beginning? Surely this is The Story of all Stories?

Here, perhaps, we find a suggestion as to how Lewis' Narnia tales have risen above the mob. He speaks unabashedly of Goodness. That is not easy in our own epoch, softened and undermined as it has been for well over a hundred years, first by skepticism, then cynicism, then bitter denial, then the Babylonian rumpus that always follows in the wake of those unhappy currents. How is a storyteller like Lewis ever to flag us down with Goodness, which by all modern notions is at best a matter of whistling in the dark and, at worst, a horrible delusion? Well, one way you can attempt the business would be simply to lure us away from the scene, like some Pied Piper. That lays us (or Lewis, shall we say) open to the charge of hoodwinking everyone. How can you extol Goodness when we all know that all such illusions have been jettisoned by intelligent modern men?

We don't know that, Lewis would answer. It is possible to fool all of the people some of the time. This is one of those unfortunate times. The note I strike in my tales is a note that has sounded *in principio, et nunc, et semper, et in saecula saeculorum*. Goodness is bigger than Evil: Joy is deeper than Sorrow. Dante knew this: He took everything to the bottom of hell, but drew us to the Love that moves the sun and other stars. The Lady Julian, far from being a simpleton, looked at everything and saw that "All shall be well, and all manner of things shall be well."

Lewis, like all good artists, drew upon the timeless mystery of Incarnation for his stories. That is, in Narnia we do not find any heavy disquisitions about Goodness and Evil. You can get that in *Mere Christianity* and all of his works on ethics and apologetics. God bless those works. But here is a different genre. Here we find that the abstractions take on flesh. It is a fairy tale, and in fairy tales you have to have people doing things, not abstractions being discussed. And Lewis' stories do not draw on symbolism, by the way. With symbolism and allegory, what we find are paper figures who have no existence apart from the abstractions they represent. So Bunyan's Hopeful or Giant Despair are allegories of Hope and Despair; they are scarcely three-dimensional characters, although we all praise Bunyan for having brought allegory to virtual perfection as a genre.

In Lewis' tales, we find Lucy for a start. She is an ordinary little girl with all of the curiosity and good will and apparent naïveté and hopefulness that belong to little girls. (The difficulty of bringing into play the term *good* little girls here is itself an index of where we are now: That term would only invite catcalls from our epoch.) But, like it or not, we have Lucy, who is manifestly on the side of the angels. And Mr. Tumnus. The poor faun has got himself into the toils of the White Witch; but he is no good as a spy and abductor. His native goodness prevails, and he returns to his true self as a good faun—at great cost, we might add. Presently we find Mr. and Mrs. Beaver. Here, in my opinion, along with the figures of Reepicheep, Puddleglum, Frank the cabbie and his wife Helen, and Jewel the Unicorn, we have pure Goodness incarnate for us. Goodness, of course, may take on heroic or majestic coloring—in an Aslan, say. On the other hand, we find it in cottages and shops and nursing homes. Lewis had an obvious love for these humble manifestations of Goodness. We find Mrs. Beaver at her sewing machine and potatoes boiling in the kettle, and when it is time to set forth for Aslan's Table, she is the one who thinks of sandwiches for all. And it turns out that she and Mr. Beaver are on the *qui vive* for Aslan. "Aslan is on the move." We recall Simeon and Anna in our own story who amid the hurly-burly of Jerusalem were quietly waiting for their Aslan to move.

How shall we tally all the roster of good creatures in these tales? We find Reepicheep, a wholly noble, valorous, and courteous mouse, forsooth, with a tiny sword, and, at the end, a red plume on his head. And Puddleglum, surely the most unlikely, melancholy, damp, and ineffective creature imaginable, who heroically saves the day by making a burnt offering of his poor webbed feet in order to set up a stench and thus dispel the Green Lady's lethal fragrances. Frank the Cabbie: not much to be said for him except that he was an honest cabbie and took loving care of his horse, Strawberry. But these virtues have made him wise, and it is he rather than the intellectual idiot Uncle Andrew who both sees and exults in the Creation of Narnia. He and his wife, who shows up at the Creation with soapsuds up her arms, are, altogether appropriately, chosen to be the first King and Queen of Narnia. What do we want in our monarchs save honesty and charity and wisdom? And Jewel the Unicorn: We all know the unicorns come from that country whose air blows sweet and for which we yearn with inconsolable yearnings.

Perhaps we might put the matter this way: In his *Narnia Chronicles* (as, certainly, in *Perelandra*) Lewis has done an odd thing. He has, as it were, bidden us to come to the window opening from the foetid room of Modernity and burst open the shutters so that we can see out onto the blissful landscape that stretches into the distance and sniff the sweet air that blows in upon us. How else shall we say it? He did not draw his images from contemporaneity, we may be sure. Anyone who has read much in Lewis' works will know that he had only the most somber misgivings about almost everything modern. In this landscape we find ourselves hailed, not only by pastoral scenery (what Lewis liked best), but also by great virtues: nobility, valor, courtesy, civility, humility, laughter, simplicity, fidelity, dignity, majesty, and so forth and so forth. Virtues not easy to encounter in our own epoch.

But there is Evil, too. No myth, epic, or fairy story would work at all if this were swept under the rug. All is not sweetness and light—*yet*. (We have to go farther up and farther in to reach that realm.) Evil is there, as it is in our own story. The figures in whom we may see Evil are vivid in the extreme, starting with the White Witch. She, along with the Green Lady and Jadis (all one witch?), is Lilith, who, according to the Kabbala was Adam's first wife. Dissatisfied with being a mere "helpmeet" to Adam, and with conditions in Eden generally, she went off into the wilderness and became the archetype of all wicked fairy godmothers who stick pins into infants in their cradles, and all wicked stepmothers (Lewis loved Disney's Snow White, with that cold and regal stepmother of hers) and all sorceresses who loathe fruitfulness and domesticity and happiness. Hence the White Witch's wand, which can only turn little creatures to stone (cf. contra Aslan's life-giving breath—he certainly is *Dominum et vivificantem* in Narnia).

And there is Shift, the ape, who is fraud incarnate. He will masquerade as, if not quite Aslan himself, at least as Aslan's emissary, crowned with all of Aslan's authority. He is a consummate liar. But of course, as is always the case with Evil's attempts to ape the Good, his efforts turn out to be a squalid travesty of Aslan's majesty. We find ourselves revolted by the sheer imbecility of the whole enterprise, which makes sense since "the loss of the good of intellect" (Dante) is one of the qualities of hell. Weston in *Perelandra* would be a case in point of this: He is a don and a philosopher and scientist, who, lifted up by breathtaking vanity, becomes a squatting, grey, mumbling, obscene idiot before his end.

We find also the sad effects on mere boys, e.g., Edmund and Eustace, of their opting for the blandishments of Evil. Edmund follows in the steps of Judas Iscariot, and Eustace becomes a dragon (because he is already a dragon—egocentric, avaricious, inimical to everything). Lewis follows Dante and all of Catholic tradition in having the "punishments" for evil-doing turn out to be nothing at all but the sin turned inside out. The souls in hell get to see their sins in stark exactness.

We also find Evil in its miserable and petty forms, most notably in the stewards on the islands where the *Dawn Treader* docks briefly, whose cheap cynicism, laziness, infidelity to their charge, and rackety life augur worse things to come if they don't pull themselves together. But all of this is to gild the lily. With what else can we conclude here than with the adjuration to "go see the movie."

Why Did C. S. Lewis Never Become a Roman Catholic?

This is a question that is asked almost universally and certainly very frequently.

On the surface of things, the question might be dismissed as frivolous. Why didn't Tillich become Orthodox? Why didn't Karl Barth become Wesleyan? Why didn't Romano Guardini become Associate Reformed Presbyterian? There seems something odd about such a line of questions—odd, perhaps slightly impertinent, and very likely irrelevant. The rejoinder in each case might well be, "Why should he have?"

In the case of Lewis and the Catholic Church, however, different elements come into play. For one thing, there is the nature of the Catholic Church herself. No other ecclesial entity in the world can lay such a sure claim to immense dominical, apostolic, historical, and theological origins and fabric. Hence, as a corollary to this, we assume that anyone as vastly literate in matters Christian as was Lewis will most assuredly have been obliged to face the claims of Rome at some point or another in his reading and conversation.

Lewis was thoroughly versed in Sacred Scripture. What was he thinking as he read Matthew 16, where our Lord's "upon this rock will I build my Church" is addressed to Saint Peter, or John 6, with its uncompromising and

Originally published in *Lay Witness* (November 1998): 8–9.

insistent teaching that the bread and wine that He gives us is indeed His very Body and Blood?

Furthermore, it is difficult in the extreme to grasp how a man of Lewis' acuity and staggering learning can have seen the Church of England as other than an anomaly. "That can't be the Church!" a Catholic is inclined to exclaim. Good heavens—Henry VIII and all that? Erastianism? The Monarch the head? Parliament appointing bishops? No Magisterium? Its weathercock swings with every new puff of heresy and immorality? Its own bottomless uncertainty as to precisely what sort of church it itself is? These are not the marks of the apostolic Church sought so perseveringly, and with great agony of soul, by John Henry Newman. How can Lewis have sailed so nonchalantly through these roiled ecclesiological waters?

There are several angles to the answer to this question. In the first place, there is a one-line dismissal of the whole question that is not altogether devoid of truth. Why didn't Lewis become Catholic? He didn't want to. Period.

More than once he referred to himself as an Ulsterman in this connection—in the same manner in which Eliot identified himself as an Englishman when asked the same question—the implication being that an Ulsterman or an Englishman can never fit into this Mediterranean, rococo, and Irish Church. It is frivolous, of course, and neither man, surely, can have meant his remark to be taken as any sort of substantial ecclesiological reason.

A number of years ago, Ignatius Press published Christopher Derrick's *C. S. Lewis and the Church of Rome*. It is a greatly engaging book and full of interesting information. Yet I have always felt the hunch lurking along the skirts of the matter that the book need not have been written, since there is not very much to say on the topic. "He didn't want to" is, in some serious sense, pretty much the answer.

On the other hand, all of this does lead us up to a second angle from which the matter of Lewis and the Church may be approached. It also is an embarrassingly simple business: Lewis thought Rome was wrong. He did not believe many of the major claims that Rome puts forward. He felt that Rome had gone beyond all scriptural warrant, most especially in her teaching concerning the Blessed Mother, her view of the papacy, and Transubstantiation. He felt that "modern Romanism" (sic) was—astonishingly enough—a "provincial" or "local" departure from the great, central, and ancient mainstream of Christian teaching. (How Rome may be thought of in connection with words like "provincial" and "local" is matter to tease the imagination of any inquirer, be he never so anti-Roman!)

Scriptural warrant. This is a delicate point for Anglicans, since one does not ordinarily hear the loud and peremptory assertion of *sola scriptura* in Anglican circles, although evangelical and Calvinist Anglicans do, in fact, hold to this *sola*. Article VI of the famous 39 Articles of Religion, which are the only charter Anglicanism has, tiptoes through the Lutheran "*sola*" minefield here: "Holy Scripture containeth all things necessary to salvation: so that whatsoever is not read therein, nor may be proved thereby, is not to be required of any man, that it should be believed as an article of the Faith." This is not quite the same thing as Luther's *sola*. Anglicans ordinarily like to posit three legs on the ecclesiological stool: Scripture, tradition, and reason. Whose tradition? A Catholic will wish to press home.

In connection with this point of Lewis' own disagreement with certain Roman dogmas, it is also worth mentioning various aspects of his vision and piety that, to a stark Protestant, would seem to have a "Catholic" flavor. This may be a major factor in arousing the question as to why Lewis never became Catholic. If he held so many quasi-Roman beliefs (the question might run), why didn't he go the whole way? The answer here is that he simply did not believe Rome's claim to be what she is, namely, the apostolic Church.

But, his "Catholic" notions: He had a high place in his scheme for Mary, referring to her as "the Blessed Virgin", at which many Protestants cringe. Further, he made use of the sacrament of auricular Confession. Also he believed in Purgatory ("but not the Romish doctrine", he said, on which point I think he was simply mistaken in what he believed Rome believes about Purgatory). Further, he took the Eucharist for granted as the central act of worship—again, a highly un-Protestant stance. He referred to "the Blessed Sacrament" in his great sermon, "The Weight of Glory", once again an expression very foreign to the Protestant ethos. He believed in prayers for the dead.

And he certainly was at one with Rome on the question as to who will be saved, holding out most firmly the hope that physical death in this realm here does not bring to an eternal halt a man's story, but that men of good will (Ikhnaton, the monotheistic pharaoh, for example) will be given the chance to encounter Christ in some realm—nay, that all men will be vouchsafed such an encounter (cf. *Catechism*, nos. 1260, 1281). From the Protestant point of view, this sails much too near the universalist wind. And yet he also believed that, because of the dread mystery of free will, we must never jettison the possibility of damnation, since it must be possible for a soul finally to say to God, "My will be done."

There is one last point worth making. Lewis wrote as a "mere Christian". He felt that his apostolate was to speak to the unbelieving world on behalf of the Apostles' and Nicene Creeds, so to speak. He resolutely, even ferociously, refused to enter into correspondence or conversation on matters that divide Christians, although his exchange of letters with Lyman Stebbins shows that he would and did make the rare exception. Hence, he avoided ecclesiology, and hence his thinking never reached that point of no return (cf. Newman, Knox, et al.) at which a man has no choice but to follow the light across the Tiber.